CITIES BEYOND CRISIS

Cities Beyond Crisis

Race, Affect, and Urban Culture in Twenty-First-Century Iberia

CATALINA IANNONE

VANDERBILT UNIVERSITY PRESS
Nashville, Tennessee

This book is freely available in an open-access edition thanks to the generous support of The Ohio State University Libraries.

First printing 2025

Library of Congress Cataloging-in-Publication Data

Names: Iannone, Catalina, 1989- author.
Title: Cities beyond crisis : race, affect, and urban culture in twenty-first-century Iberia / Catalina Iannone.
Description: Nashville, Tennessee : Vanderbilt University Press, [2024] | Includes bibliographical references and index.
Identifiers: LCCN 2024025229 (print) | LCCN 2024025230 (ebook) | ISBN 9780826507327 (paperback) | ISBN 9780826507334 (hardcover) | ISBN 9780826507341 (epub) | ISBN 9780826507358 (pdf)
Subjects: LCSH: Urbanization--Iberian Peninsula--History--21st century. | Sociology, Urban--Iberian Peninsula. | Cities and towns--Iberian Peninsula--History--21st century.
Classification: LCC HT384.I185 I26 2024 (print) | LCC HT384.I185 (ebook) | DDC 307.760946/41--dc23/eng/20240913
LC record available at https://lccn.loc.gov/2024025229
LC ebook record available at https://lccn.loc.gov/2024025230

Front cover photo: Homes in Lavapiés. Photograph by Catalina Iannone

For Mom and Dad, who got me thinking.

CONTENTS

ACKNOWLEDGMENTS

This book is the culmination of years of travel to, exchange with, and learning about the cities and people mentioned within, as well as my own journey as a researcher and writer. While book writing is often a solitary endeavor, I am grateful for the remarkable support of my family, friends, mentors, colleagues, collaborators, and editors along the way.

Two formative stages of mentorship helped me develop the scholarly voice and perspective that would become this manuscript. Jonathan Snyder introduced me to the field of urban cultural studies in a course that I took with him during my Master's program at New York University in Madrid. Equipped with the vocabulary to articulate my thoughts on the relationship between culture and the built environment, and a broader notion of what constitutes a text, I embarked on my first comparative study of Spain and Portugal with the support of María López Díez. I am immensely thankful to both Jon and María for their patience and guidance as I found my footing in the field. The mentorship of both Jill Robbins and Lorraine Leu was also vital as I developed my scholarly perspective and situated my work in the academic landscape. Jill, I am so grateful to you for championing my often-unorthodox approach to Iberian studies when I began my PhD and supporting me from afar beyond those first years. Lorraine, thank you for your years of close mentorship and support. You have taught me that we have far more to learn when we reach across and think through distinct geographic boundaries, and I am so fortunate to have you in my corner.

This book benefitted from the institutional support of The University of Texas at Austin, SUNY-Oswego, and The Ohio State University. My fieldwork was facilitated by generous fellowships from the US Department of Education Foreign Language and Area Studies Program and the Fulbright Commission in Spain. An open access version of this manuscript has also been made available to the public, thanks to a substantial grant from The Ohio State University Libraries, and in collaboration with Vanderbilt University Press.

I am grateful to the local artists, community members, and associations who were generous with their time and knowledge during my research process. Thank you, in particular, to Asociação Renovar a Mouraria, Asociación de Comerciantes de Lavapiés, José Smith Vargas, Juan Valbuena, Gonçalo Gaioso, PorFavor, and DosJotas for allowing me to reproduce several of the images included in the book. In addition, Marluci Menezes provided valuable insight into the social and spatial evolution of Mouraria as I laid groundwork for the project.

Thank you to the members of TRECE (Taller de Raza, Etnicidad y Ciudadanía Española) who gave me dedicated feedback on Chapter 3 in a workshop held during the 2021 ALCESXXI conference. Questions posed by Gema Pérez-Sánchez regarding my discussion of *castizo* iconography were particularly helpful as I worked to refine my argument. Additionally, I thank Rafael Córdoba Hernández and Cristina Fernández from the Universidad Politécnica de Madrid, for directing me to several sources of data cited in the manuscript. Jess Combs and Claudio Eduardo were indispensable in refining many of this book's translations, and I am especially thankful to Jess for her adept literary translation of Aymerich's poem in Chapter 4.

I am also appreciative of the editors at Vanderbilt University Press for their sustained support of this project, and the anonymous reviewers of this manuscript, whose feedback and recommendations were instrumental in the publication process. I would also like to acknowledge the *Arizona Journal of Hispanic Cultural Studies* and *Journal of Lusophone Studies* for publishing earlier versions of two of the case studies in this manuscript: my analysis of PorFavor's map of Lavapiés, and the Mercado de Fusão development in Mouraria.

I am fortunate to be surrounded by a vibrant community of intellectual interlocutors who I am proud to call friends. My online writing group helped keep me on task in even the most challenging moments of the project. Thank you to its members: Dean Allbritton, Joanne Britland, Mary Kate Donovan, Leslie Harkema, Peter Mahoney, Gabrielle Miller, Nicholas Wolters, Amaury Leopoldo Sosa, Martin Repinecz, Sarah Thomas, Wan Tang, and Anita Savo. I'm also grateful to former colleagues Emily Bernate and Xosé Pereira Boán for their sustained encouragement during and beyond our years working together at St. Edward's University and SUNY-Oswego. Jessica Carey-Webb has been a faithful friend, confidant, and champion of my work since our time in Austin. Mary Kate Donovan, likewise, has gone above and beyond as a friend and colleague since we met years ago in Madrid.

My family and friends are fundamental to who I am and the work I produce. I'm fortunate to have a wide social network across the globe whose perspectives enrich my life in countless ways. Mom, Dad, and Alejandra, thank you for teaching me to approach life with curiosity, humor, and an eye for creativity. Ivan, thank you for being by my side, and learning and exploring along with me. I'm excited for what's to come.

INTRODUCTION

Cities in Crisis

This study of the urban opens with a crisis. The 2008 financial collapse, a collective shock fostered by a globalized economy and felt acutely across diverse geographic regions, prompted an international reckoning and groundswell of feelings regarding the prevailing social, cultural, and political systems shaping the everyday on the Iberian Peninsula. After the housing bubble burst, first in the United States and extending in succession to countries entrenched in a similar economic model, Spain and Portugal were confronted with a period of mounting social and economic precarity.[1] In light of soaring unemployment, rising taxes, and plummeting social services, a sense of precarity and indignation mounted across the peninsula. With urban centers like Madrid and Lisbon peppered with ghost construction sites, unfinished housing projects, and shuttered businesses, institutions and individuals were driven to negotiate new ways of continuing on. To keep the system afloat, public funds were channeled toward rescuing financial institutions, and both the Spanish and Portuguese governments became indebted to other European member states, fomenting the perception of region as inferior to its more prosperous northern neighbors.[2] This perspective was also encapsulated in the escalation of such discursive tendencies as the derogatory acronym PIIGS, employed as a catch-all reference to discuss the economic vulnerability of Portugal, Italy, Ireland, Greece, and Spain during the recession. Demographic anxieties, meanwhile, were on the rise, amplified by public discourse that focused on the rising rates of emigration in search of better job prospects beyond Iberia, both Spain's and Portugal's aging populaces, and the uneasy reception of newcomers who continued to arrive to these nations as their first or final destination on the European continent.[3] In turn, the sense that Spain and Portugal were being pulled from the promise of prosperity expected of members of the European community took on an explicitly racial dimension, documented in studies of mounting nativist, racist, and xenophobic sentiments among members of the Spanish and Portuguese populace.[4]

In some respects, the crisis led to both Spain and Portugal becoming further entrenched in neoliberal modes of governance, as leaders doubled down on their confidence in capital accumulation as a mitigating force. From legislation like Spain's Investor Visa and Portugal's Golden Visa, to the deregulation of both nations' labor and energy sectors, and the privatization of public assets across the peninsula, the market-oriented mindset continued to drive the creation and contestation of the Iberian every day.[5] At the same time, the social, political, and economic instabilities of the crisis era were met with a demand for social change and innovation, including a renewed interest in participatory democracy visible in anti-austerity movements such as Spain's Indignadxs (The Outraged) and Portugal's Geração à rasca (The Struggling Generation), and the corresponding rise of municipalist political movements, like the founding of a new Spanish national party, Podemos.[6] To date, a number of interventions positioned at the intersection of the humanities and social sciences have explored the role and radical possibilities of culture and oppositional political action that surged in the wake of the financial collapse, from Manuel Castells's study in *Networks of Outrage and Hope* of the systems of communication that facilitated mass demonstrations following the recession, to Luis Moreno-Caballud's discussion of the post-2008 "cultures of anyone" forged beyond institutional culture and political arenas, where citizen collectives exercised agency through grassroots social movements, collaborative production, and digital technologies.[7] Special attention has also been paid to the role of urban spaces as critical forums for maneuvering beyond the collapse, with Jonathan Snyder's *Poetics of Opposition in Contemporary Spain* and Stephen Vilaseca's contribution on counter-mapping and spatial activism published the 2014 special edition of the *Journal of Spanish Cultural Studies* covering the crisis of special note.[8] The sense of a present in progress certainly informed the concerns and predictions advanced in these interventions. Snyder, for instance, introduces his 2015 manuscript as an attempt to "contribute modestly to this sense-making of the present circumstance," citing Lauren Berlant's description of the "stretched-out 'now'" that, with time, finds its form as an episode, event, or epoch.[9]

With more than a decade having passed since 2008, *Cities Beyond Crisis* offers a different temporal perspective on the protracted moment of unraveling and reorganizing provoked by the financial collapse. Aided by this distance from the catalyzing event, which has allowed some of the oscillations of the present to settle into visible patterns, I delve into the impact of storytelling through such mediums as text, visual culture, and urban spaces themselves on the physical and psychic space of Iberian urban centers grappling with the legacy of the crisis, paying special attention to how both dominant, market-oriented narratives and their contestatory counterparts shaped the lived environment. In an effort to expand the conversation beyond Spain, which has received significant scholarly attention on this topic, I also study the evolution of Portuguese urban spaces, providing a broader perspective and space for comparison regarding the evolving social and psychic landscape of the Iberian region during this period. Moreover, keeping in mind the way that financial precarity stoked xenophobic and nativist sentiments across the peninsula, I focus on how each nation's relationship to race was negotiated in this moment of accelerated urban change, analyzing a wide range of texts including advertisements, tours, photo projects, and illustrations indicative of how the public was grappling with the subject. In addition, I incorporate ethnographic methods, including participant observation and interviews, further engaging with the lived experience of the era, and deepening my examination of both deviations and unexpected commonalities in the narratives disseminated by social actors across the ideological spectrum in the years following the financial collapse.

Theories of affect serve as a productive framework for unpacking the range of perspectives and their corresponding spatial products that emerged this period of undoing and reconstruction in Spain and Portugal. This line of thinking draws from Berlant's definition of affect as a sense beyond concrete emotions or feelings: a state of relations that circulate between people, things, and ideas, manifesting in the form of attachments to ideas or objects.[10] Berlant explores two affective modes in the present. First, there are *situations*, the social, political, and cultural forms that unfold in a manner later crystallized and attributed significance through retrospect.[11] To this point, they build on Raymond Williams's notion of "structures of feeling," a framework for differentiating between the constellation-like qualities of the present-as-lived and later, more reductive accounts of the present-as-past.[12] Both Williams and Berlant recognize that affect is central to how meanings and values are immediately lived and felt as formative, singular processes that are later historicized as collective events or epochs. Accordingly, the second affective mode defined by Berlant is the *event*, a discrete moment in which affect is intensified, highlighted, or brought to the foreground, "that element in the situation that elaborates the potential good in a radical break."[13] These moments of acute attention and transformative possibilities are of particular interest given how they bring into view the perils, aspirations, and unfulfilled promises of the social and political models forging the situation of the everyday. The affective event is, in essence, a narrative provocation, where the resulting "patterns of adjustment," reveal both enduring and evolving belief systems regarding the composition of a good life.[14] Berlant asks, emphasizing how moments of heightened affect destabilize such ideals, "What constitutes continuity amid the pressure of structural inconstancy? What is the good life when the world that was to have been delivered by upward mobility and collective uplift that national/capitalism promised goes awry in front of one?"[15]

With the 2008 crisis as the catalyzing event, *Cities Beyond Crisis* takes a deliberate look at how affective patterns shape urban landscapes. More concretely, I explore the conceptualization and construction of two specific neighborhoods in Spain's and Portugal's capital cities that were subject to an accelerated wave of consumer-oriented development during the post-crisis period, paying particular attention to the identitarian (racial, national, and otherwise) attachments and aspirations revealed in this process of production and contestation. The first of the two, Lavapiés, is a historically working-class district known for its ample immigrant populace located a short walk south of the city's central plaza, the Puerta del Sol, and its corresponding commercial district. The second neighborhood, Mouraria, is likewise known for its place in Lisbon's historic center, situated at the base of the Castelo de São Jorge, and adjacent to the avenues of the Baixa Pombalina, a well-known pedestrian shopping area. While keeping in mind each nation's respective regional and national particularities, the similarities between these sites, from their historic relationships to nationalistic myths of origin, to their contemporary repute as multiracial hubs, and proximity to their city's most touristed attractions, offer productive parallels for a comparative study.

Given the hyper-local nature of the everyday, I argue that the affects and effects of this extended moment are best explored in the context of these discrete environments, faced with, as Don Mitchell summarizes in his explanation of the everyday right to the city, "specific social contests, in specific places, at specific times."[16] My attention to the local attends to another of Berlant's claims: that the often-delocalized neoliberal and transnational structures that impact contemporary life do not play out to the same affects and effects in all contexts, and, in fact, "The differences matter, and so do the continuities."[17] These observations support my comparative analysis of

FIGURE 0.1. Contemporary map of the city of Madrid with approximate boundaries of Lavapiés. Map image is the intellectual property of Esri and is used herein under license. Copyright © 2020 Esri and its licensors. All rights reserved

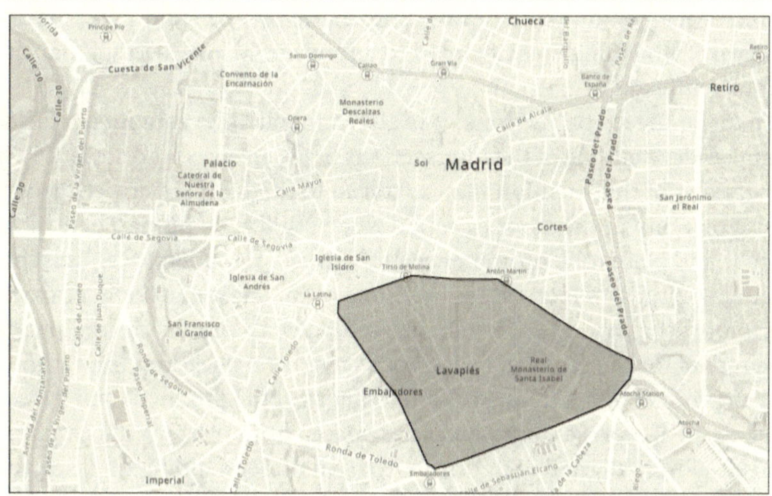

FIGURE 0.2. Contemporary map of the city of Lisbon with approximate boundaries of Mouraria. Map image is the intellectual property of Esri and is used herein under license. Copyright © 2020 Esri and its licensors. All rights reserved

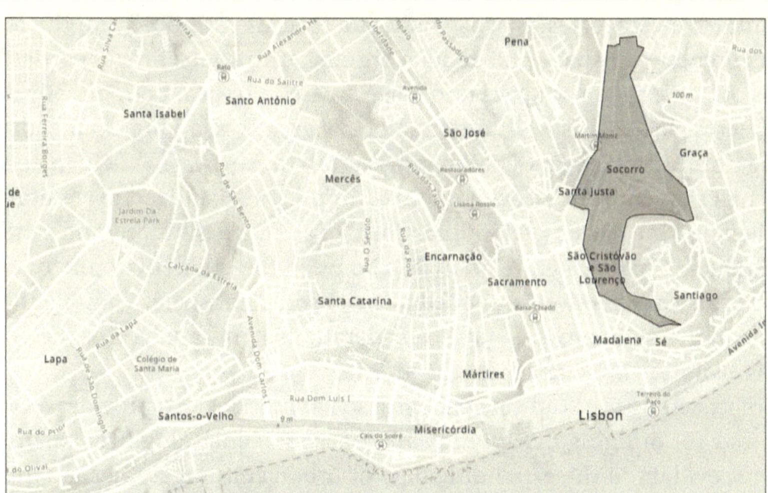

the attachments that circulated and guided Spain and Portugal's post-crisis urban evolution, unpacking the differences and continuities in the affective shaping of these urban spheres. Though guided by the study of Lavapiés and Mouraria, this approach serves as a model for analyzing how affect drives the reciprocal relationship between aesthetic practice and lived space, a framework which may be extended to a range of historical, regional, and cultural contexts.

To make these connections, it is also imperative to establish a fundamental understanding of the intersections between space and society.[18] The foundations of this position may be traced to the boom of critical geography scholarship in the 1970s, a period when studies on human perception of space and place took prominence in the Western academy.[19] Marxist perspectives on these relationships are some of the most enduring, of particular import the writings of Lefebvre, credited with proposing and providing a model for the study of space not as a neutral backdrop but rather as a social product in his frequently cited theory of the production of space.[20] My analysis of representative texts and spaces from two specific neighborhoods is closely aligned with this Lefebvrian understanding of space, and positions articulated by scholars including Doreen Massey and David Harvey who interrogate how lived environments are conceived of, formed, and evolve in tandem with differing social, economic, political, and ecological structures. Massey's assertions in *Space, Place, and Gender*, specifically, set forth a working position from which to understand how the making, remaking, and use of space intersects with the making and remaking of social and identitarian categories. In this study, she focuses specifically on the relationship between space and gender, arguing at the outset that "Particular ways of thinking about space and place are tied up with, both directly and indirectly, particular social constructions of gender relations," and adding, "The implication is that challenging certain of the ways in which space and place are currently conceptualized implies also, indeed necessitates, challenging the currently dominant form of gender definitions and gender relations."[21] This explicit relationship between the built environment and gender may be effectively extended to other social constructs, among them race and the nation, two central considerations in my analysis of the post-crisis evolution of Lavapiés and Mouraria.[22]

Approaching the study of space as a social product also provides a clear pathway for bridging disciplinary approaches to analyzing lived environments, evident in the expanding field of urban cultural studies, an interdisciplinary approach that draws from both humanistic and social science theories and practices to address the role of cultural production in shaping urban centers. In *Toward an Urban Cultural Studies*, Benjamin Fraser creates an explicit outline for this method, advocating for scholars across disciplines to undertake textual criticism in close dialogue with the social sciences and vice versa, "forcing literary and cultural studies to think the city geographically and forcing geography to think the city artistically (in textual terms, defined from the perspective of the humanities)."[23] *Cities Beyond Crisis* works at this intersection between disciplines, delving into the relationships between aesthetic practices and the social, political, and economic production of the built environment. This is most evident in my methodological approach, which combines close reading, participant observation, and interviews as a means by which to capture the range of ways in which different urban cultural actors shape the psychic and physical contours of city spaces. While not an exhaustive list, this approach is indebted to pioneering contributions in Iberian studies by scholars including Fraser, Malcolm Compitello, Susan Larson, Araceli Masterson-Algar, Ellen Sapega, and Fernando Arenas, whose work, explicitly or in spirit with Lefebvre's model of spatial production, weaves together diverse theoretical and methodological strands to study such topics as culture, capital, and urban planning (Compitello, Fraser, Larson), the urban fabric of transnational migrations (Masterson), and spatial manifestations of nationalism and colonial legacies (Sapega, Arenas).

Matthew Feinberg's *From the Theater to the Plaza* is especially germane to this volume given his focus on the interplay between spectacle and the urban environment in Madrid's Lavapiés neighborhood. Feinberg's monograph focuses specifically on theater as a medium for representing and reconfiguring the neighborhood, a method for studying both the "stages in the city and the city as a stage" shaped by such "actors" as urban planners, dramatists, activists and residents.[24] *Cities Beyond Crisis* takes a different approach to the study of Lavapiés, engaging with a range of text types and diverse spaces that render visible the centrality of affect to the making and mediation of both this and another neighborhood (Mouraria) situated in a distinct, though related, national context. Through close analysis of objects of study ranging from digital spaces, visual culture, and the built environment itself, I cast light on the attachments articulated by institutions, social collectives, and individuals—from advocates of neoliberal policy to oppositional actors—as they maneuvered toward an urban future beyond the financial collapse. Moreover, I focus on the centrality of race to this extended period of urban development and demographic change, with the path beyond the crisis increasingly situating these neighborhoods as culturally themed destinations and sites of investment, prompting the question: For whom do we shape these cities?

Contemporary Iberian Racial Formations

Before delving into the particularities of racial discourse as it relates to the post-crisis evolution of Lavapiés and Mouraria, it is imperative to establish a basic analytical framework for both the study of race as a social category and its applications in contemporary Iberia. First and foremost, my conceptualization of how race is presently conceived in Spain and Portugal is in line with the consensus among humanist scholars that racial categories are not indicative of enduring (or inherent) emotional, intellectual, or social qualities of a given collective. Rather, these shifting, and often contradictory designations are informed by an evolving network of historical, economic, political, and cultural forces. Michael Omi and Howard Winant articulate this understanding of the category in their landmark theory of racial formation, speaking from the context of the United States to define race as a malleable category that is delineated according to paradigms of ethnicity, class, and nation, and central to social relations due to the political and ideological weight that it is attributed.[25] This line of thinking about race has been further edified by scholars who debate the theoretical and practical implications of racial categories in a range of geographic, temporal, and national contexts, with some well-known examples including Achille Mbembe's study of necropolitics, Kimberlé Crenshaw's critical race theory, and Gloria Anzaldúa's theory of the borderlands.[26] Indeed, the breadth of existing inquiries into race in different contexts compels stating that studies of the construct, while undeniably intertwined and ripe with parallels, must not be reduced to direct equivalencies between distinct regions. While common factors are evident, scholars increasingly push beyond dominant frameworks, such as the United States, for studying the category.[27] David Theo Goldberg, to this end, employs the term *racial regionalizations* to capture place-oriented distinctions in the study of the production and circulation of race.[28] With this in mind, my sustained comparison between Spain and Portugal throughout this intervention is meant to illuminate points of convergence between sites in a shared geographic context—the Iberian Peninsula—while recognizing regionally informed variances in the articulation of racial categories in each nation.

In this regard, many scholars turn to the logic and legacy of Western colonialism as a point of entry for unpacking contemporary notions of race, arguing that this protracted period expanded and even codified the use of human attributes like blood and phenotype as a means by which to delineate the superiority and defend the corresponding subjugation of different world populations.[29] Aníbal Quijano, for example, asserts that the colonization of the Americas set in motion an "idea of race, in its modern meaning," arguing, "Social relations founded on the category of race produced new historical social identities in America—Indians, blacks, and mestizos—and redefined others. Terms such as *Spanish and Portuguese*, and much later *European* . . . acquired from then on a racial connotation in reference to the new identities."[30] Regarding this position, scholars like Julia H. Chang, Joshua Goode, and Max S. Hering Torres have discussed the complications posed by conceiving of race and racism as a linear process from colonialism to the contemporary era, signaling shifting narratives in the articulation of difference, while reaffirming their recognition of and interest in unpacking forms of racialization in different temporal periods that do not necessarily map neatly on to twentieth- and twenty-first-century categories.[31] I, like Chang, invoke Ann Stoler's apt summary of race as a concept produced in a rhizomatic fashion, to take the position that the "racial truths" that circulate in the present are undoubtedly related to, though not necessarily an uninterrupted linear extension of, historic systems of oppression.[32]

In terms of Iberia, this is particularly evident in the genesis and evolution of discursive tropes with recourse to the colonial era that have had an enduring impact on the way Otherness is articulated within and beyond the peninsula. For Spain, one such example is *Hispanidad*, a discursive trope that gained momentum at the end of the nineteenth century as the nation faced its loss of empire and public intellectuals ruminated on Spain's historical and spiritual footprint on their former colonial holdings. In general, proponents of this discourse cast the memory of Spain's conquest of the Americas as the start of a "special relationship" between Spain and Latin America, conceived as a fraternal bond to be celebrated, and a loss to be lamented, as a means by which to grapple with the anxieties of their present.[33] *Hispanidad* would later be employed as an ideological pillar during the dictatorship of Francisco Franco (1939–1975), its strategic invocation serving to legitimize authoritarian rule by linking Spain's imperial past to its present, and casting Franco's politics as a return to the purported splendor and conservative values of centuries prior.[34]

In Portugal, too, narrative tropes that reframe the legacy of colonialism are informed by the ideological debates, anxieties, and aspirations of their historic moment. One such example is *Portugalidade*, a propagandistic discourse of national identity centered on Catholicism, language, and the nation's history of maritime expansion, mobilized during António de Oliveira Salazar's Estado Novo (1933–1974) as a strategy for promoting a vision of Portuguese identity in line with the authoritarian regime's conservative ideals.[35] It would find significant overlap with *Lusotropicalism*, in that both tropes were employed to defend Portugal's continued colonial presence in Africa and Asia during the twentieth-century period of decolonization. The latter narrative, with its source in the work of Brazilian sociologist Gilberto Freyre, was invoked to legitimize Portugal's empire by emphasizing the supposedly cordial control of Portuguese colonialism, and presenting decolonization as a painful rupture of the bonds that purportedly existed between the colonized and their colonizers.[36] In the twenty-first century, imperial nostalgia through the continued emphasis on fraternity finds its expression in *Lusofonia*, a narrative wielded as a celebration of shared linguistic, cultural, and historical connections between Portugal and its former colonies, and institutionalized through such organizations as the Comunidade de Países de Língua Portuguesa (Community of Portuguese-Speaking Countries).[37] This more recent approach to positioning Portugal as a unifying force among nations and cultures can certainly be interpreted as push-back against the country's often peripheral place in the broader international community, and an effort to be situated more firmly in networks of global capital.

In terms of racial formation, each of the above-mentioned ideological narratives find common ground in that they situate cultural miscegenation and hybridity as central to both Spain's and Portugal's identitarian, and by extension, racial, exceptionalism. In doing so, they obscure the prevalence and continued influence of expressions of race and corresponding racial hierarchies in Iberia. Joshua Goode unpacks this in *Purity of Blood*, arguing that discussions of racial ideals in Spain "have been dismissed because they seemed to have had a different basis—a celebration of racial hybridity that could not then be considered 'racial thought' because it did not conform to the idea of racial purity espoused by the Nazi German model."[38] In Portugal, Miguel Vale de Almeida contends, "Discourses on miscegenation and *mestiçagem* tended to be used as ideological masks for relations of power and domination."[39] Daniel Silva also speaks to this point, signaling the "anti-Black, anti-Arab, anti-Jewish, and anti-Roma foundations of a Portuguese ethos" that instilled hierarchies that endure in spite of the exceptionalism attributed to miscegenation.[40] In short, recourse to hybridity in both Iberian nations is not evidence of the absence of racial notions and their consequences, but rather a different expression of them. Accordingly, Whiteness—the racial category associated with the colonial metropole—is cultivated as an orienting pole for understanding divergences from the purported norm, and maintained as superior through discursive and systemic means.[41] Quijano, in this regard, identifies how such distinctions shape contemporary distributions of power and capital, noting, "if we observe the main lines of exploitation and social domination on a global scale, the main lines of world power today, and the distribution of resources and work among the world population, it is very clear that the large majority of the exploited, the dominated, the discriminated against, are precisely the members of the 'races,' 'ethnies,' or 'nations' into which the colonized populations were categorized in the formative process of that world power, from the conquest of America and onward."[42] As these observations affirm, the racial notions embedded in the social, political, and economic inequalities of the present disproportionately affect those deemed Other (that is, diverging from the category of Whiteness) by the colonial logic underpinning modern systems of exploitation and domination.

Further complicating this dynamic is another dimension of the distribution of power rooted in the colonial era: Spain's and Portugal's semi peripheral relationship to the European continent. The saying "Africa begins in the Pyrenees," employed as an affirmation of the purported backwardness of Spain and Portugal, encapsulates both the racist construction of the African continent as inferior due to the skin color of much of its populace, and the enduring notion that Iberian difference from the rest of Europe is attributed to the peninsula's proximity to Africa, and by extension, Blackness.[43] Nation-building projects pushing against this idea, in turn, were primed to appeal to the category of Whiteness as a means by which to situate Spain and Portugal among their European neighbors.

These enduring tensions are well documented in scholarly interventions interrogating representational practices in contemporary Iberia that both perpetuate and challenge racial formations. In particular, scholars have focused on immigration as a destabilizing factor in Spanish and Portuguese constructions of race, with attention to how the Iberian public has wrestled with the region's migrant boom from the end of the twentieth and into the twenty-first century, the repercussions of which were anticipated and discussed across visual, sonoric, and textual cultural mediums.[44] Others unpack racial anxieties prior to the era of mass migration, focusing on how race was articulated and negotiated under the rule of Franco and Salazar, a period that would foster enduring beliefs and anxieties regarding the Iberian nation's alignment with European Whiteness. Here, many point to the differential treatment of internal "Others," including the Romaní minority, and racial formations related to politically motivated resettlement from regions of each nation's former (or, in the case of Portugal, dwindling) empire.[45] Spain, for example, received migrants and political exiles from Equatorial Guinea and Argentina during the 1970s, while Portugal's landscape of newcomers was largely connected to both economic migrants from overseas colonies and the *retornado* phenomena, when the nation's citizens returned to the metropole following the Wars of Independence in Angola, Guinea-Bissau, and Mozambique.[46]

Racially informed policy and discourse would take off following each country's transition to democratic rule, fomented by the Iberian region's gradual ascent to the fiscal power associated with the rest of the continent and corresponding position as receiving nations of immigrants in search of economic opportunity. Jeffrey Coleman argues that the push toward "Europeanization" during this period, employing Spain's entrance into the European Economic Community, the precursor to the European Union, in 1986 as an example, was not just a political and economic maneuver but also a form of "integration into whiteness."[47] This reaffirmation of distribution of authority along racial lines would most clearly reverberate in the immigration legislation passed in each country in the 1980s, which codified access to the Iberian Peninsula based on point of origin. These legal avenues both created a more difficult path to citizenship for migrants and their children while simultaneously expanding the legacy of the hybridity narrative in Spain and Portugal.

Consider, for instance, Portugal's 1981 nationality laws, which limited claims to Portuguese citizenship by nationals residing on the peninsula while ensuring a right to Portuguese citizenship over three generations for descendants in the diaspora. The law marked a shift from prior decrees that anyone born in Portugal (not one of its overseas territories) was a Portuguese citizen.[48] As Kesha Fikes explains in her detailed study of the citizen-migrant distinction in Portugal during this time, this emphasis on a legal record threatened the path to citizenship for the children of migrants, while the legislation certified that even the grandchildren of Portuguese nationals residing outside of the territory would be guaranteed this right.[49] In 1982 the Spanish, too, adjusted their laws governing nationality by modifying the nation's civil code.[50] The new legislation stipulated similar requirements for a path to citizenship for migrants, including the rule that children born in Spain to foreign parents would only be granted nationality if a minimum of one parent held legal residence in the country.[51] Meanwhile, all children born outside of Spanish territory to Spanish parents would be considered Spanish nationals. In both contexts, citizenship was wielded as a tool for reinforcing hierarchies dating to the not-so-distant colonial era, ensuring preferential treatment for descendants of nationals beyond the peninsula while complicating access to the region for those from former colonies or immigrant backgrounds. These legal frameworks would both shape the demographic landscape of the Iberian Peninsula and perpetuate a legacy of exclusion and belonging rooted in the racial hierarchies of Spain and Portugal's colonial periods.

In another provocative illustration of the racial and identitarian implications of the Iberian nations' maneuvers toward the prosperity associated with Northern Europe, one may consider the spatial and demographic trends of migratory waves during the late twentieth century. Records from Spain, for example, indicate how growing numbers of African, Latin American, and Asian workers headed for urban hubs while large numbers of well-off Northern European populations (the sun-seekers of decades-past) concentrated in the country's coastal regions.[52] These socio-spatial tendencies were also apparent in Portugal during these decades, with wage-seekers hailing from Lusophone Africa, Brazil, Eastern Europe, and Asia congregating in urban hubs and Northern Europeans migrating to the coast for leisure.[53] While these tendencies pointed to the nations' newfound positions on a more privileged quotient of the enduring colonial axis of power, the visibility of racial Other *within* rather than *controlled by* the former metropoles further fomented both identitarian and resource-based anxieties. In turn, expressions of Spanish and Portuguese identity aligned with European exceptionalism would increasingly be articulated in proximity to Whiteness, and the migrant Other as a destabilizing character, a sign of the logical fallacies in still-enduring cultural hybridity discourses.

Prior to the 2008 financial collapse, the aforementioned tensions were most visible in acute moments of racially motivated violence: the 1992 murder of Lucrecia Pérez in 1992 at the hands of an off-duty Spanish civil guard, Alcindo Monteiro's 1995 killing by nationalist skinheads in Lisbon, and a wave of racist and xenophobic violence in 2000 in El Ejido, Almería, following the killing of Encarnación López Valverde by a Moroccan citizen.[54] More often, however, the production of race and racial difference on the peninsula blended into the rhythms of the everyday. As the heightened affective climate prompted by the financial collapse agitated the enduring political, cultural, and racial schisms between the Iberian nations and other members of the international community, these everyday modes of racial and racist thinking would become increasingly visible.[55]

Namely, three intersecting invasion narratives informed by race-based claims to each of these nations and their corresponding resources gained momentum in the aftermath of the crisis. The first of these narratives was triggered by a still-growing population of low-income and undocumented immigrants whose presence was perceived as a threat to enduring myths of national and racial identity, and as a drain on local resources. The second perceived invasion, complicated by and often conflated with the first, was that wealthy foreigners, emboldened by pay-your-way paths to residency like the Golden Visa and Investor Visa schemes, were colonizing the region through investment.[56] Finally, a third narrative trend responded to growing waves of visitors to the peninsula, encouraged by partnerships between the public and private sectors, who were seen as depleting Iberian cities of whatever so-called authenticity they had left. The complex ways that these three groups were perceived and discussed would come to a head where they converged: historically marginalized yet centrally located precincts of the peninsula's most populous urban areas like Lavapiés and Mouraria. There, different stakeholders struggled to shape their cities' futures.

A Legacy of Storytelling in the Making and Mediation of Lavapiés and Mouraria

A brief review of historic narratives is essential to properly contextualize the affective attachments driving urban change in Lavapiés and Mouraria following the 2008 collapse. In particular, the developmental trends that surfaced in each of these districts, and their relationship to the meanings and values circulating across modes of cultural production, illustrate the relationship between the way the spaces were perceived, shaped, and lived. This dynamic was frequently fueled by ideologies—political, cultural and otherwise—given, as Lefebvre posits, "What is an ideology without a space to which it refers, a space which it describes, whose vocabulary and links in makes use of, and whose code it embodies?"[57] Over time, a range of stories, or "representations of space," as Lefebvre terms them, have shaped both of these neighborhoods, a closer look at which is revelatory of the ideological motivations and aspirations that would continue to circulate as each city evolved in the post-crisis era.

Lavapiés's and Mouraria's reputations have been fostered by a blurring of history and popular mythology. Omissions, exaggerations, falsifications, and contradictions undoubtedly influence the stories circulating regarding their respective evolutions. These narratives (historically grounded or not) have proven themselves a lasting dimension of the life and landscape of these spaces as Madrid and Lisbon change with and around them. To date, both neighborhoods are treated as distinct sectors of their respective cities, though neither is officially recognized through municipal districting.[58] This lack of precise boundaries, coupled with a storied past of marginalization, lends itself to diverse territorial claims on the part of the government, private enterprise, and the area's inhabitants. While the class of socially and economically peripheral populations lending the neighborhoods their stigma has varied over time, a legacy of difference has endured in the public imaginary, been immortalized in cultural production, and lives on in public discourse. Moreover, the stories that circulate about Lavapiés and Mouraria have and continue to reinforce their popular conception as discrete sectors of the city even as, in the present, these distinctions are drawn colloquially, rather than through official attribution.

Take, to start, stories regarding the origins of each of the neighborhoods. Despite confident accounts in travel guides and popular history, Lavapiés's genesis is still debated in historical circles, with questions remaining including why the settlement that would later become Lavapiés had developed on the southern slope of the plateau where Madrid was settled, outside of the enclosures erected when Felipe II relocated his royal court to the city in 1561, and whether these inhabitants had lived by choice or mandate in this area.[59] Numerous theories circulate, with the most common connecting the area to the long legacy of religious persecution on the peninsula. Feinberg explores these narratives at length in his monograph-length study of Lavapiés, with special emphasis on efforts by many to historicize the space through a close analysis of its name and landmarks. For example, he cites Federico Bravo Morata's speculation that the neighborhood was named for the tradition of washing the feet of the poor, Fidel Fita's popular argument that Lavapiés was once the city's Jewish quarter, and Pedro de Répide's connection in *Guía de Madrid* (1921) between the etymology of the district's name and ablutions performed by its Jewish residents, noting that Répide's explanation was an "erroneous conflation of Jewish ritual practices and the Muslim foot washing tradition."[60] Though many of these assertions, Feinberg demonstrates, have either not been corroborated or have been thoroughly debunked, their discursive resilience signals a consensus in conceiving of the neighborhood as distinct from more prosperous sectors of the city because of its relationship to a marginalized populace.

As the etymology of Mouraria's name ("Moorish quarter") indicates, there is much more formal evidence that corroborates how the Portuguese district, which lies at the foot of Lisbon's Castelo de São Jorge, originated as a designated precinct for the city's Muslim population. Marluci Menezes, a contemporary ethnographer of the district, has discussed at length how the sector was established in the twelfth century, following D. Afonso Henriques's conquest of the city, as part of a broader project to segregate Lisbon's remaining Muslim and Jewish populations through spatial measures.[61] Accordingly, the stigma attributed to Mouraria as both a space and community was explicit, intentional, and articulated through urban design and civil channels. In addition to the population's isolation from broader urban and commercial networks, distanced from both the Tejo River and what was then the growing city's commercial center, their marginalized social class was subsequently forged and enforced through measures including additional taxes and occupation restrictions.[62] As the quarter shifted in tandem with the changing social, religious, and economic landscape of the city of Lisbon, its stigma endured.

The connection between each of these neighborhoods and marginality has also been fomented by the material consequences of their sustained relationship to their respective city's poor and working-class populace from the centuries of religious persecution and expulsion in Iberia to the contemporary era. In particular, as migrants flocked from rural to urban regions of the peninsula in search of economic opportunity in different eras of internal migration, the limited infrastructure of these districts became increasingly strained. Following the urban expansion that accompanied the industrial boom of the nineteenth century, Lavapiés was widely considered Madrid's *barrio bajo*, a moniker attributed to both its topographic situation in relation to the city center and its association with the city's *clases bajas* (lower classes) and their corresponding living conditions. The sense that these unhygienic environments were an extension of those who populated them and vice versa was chronicled and reinforced in seminal texts like Ramón de Mesonero Romano's *El antiguo Madrid, 1861*, who describes Lavapiés as "the lower-class neighborhoods." He continues, "The most helpless populations naturally go to these new, remote and humble districts; as the population has grown in size and importance, it has overtaken the old city walls, the hilly streets and limits of town have been covered with buildings."[63] Similarly, Benito Pérez Galdós's *Misericordia* emphasizes the area's reputation as the district-par-excellence for the city's impoverished classes through the character Doña Francisca's fall from wealth, illustrated by her move from the bourgeoise Salamanca neighborhood to Lavapiés's Calle del Olmo.[64] These cultural conversations also solidified Lavapiés's reputation as the city's *manolería*, that is, home to the "*manolos*," a class of urban dwellers Mesonero Romano describes as having a "uniquely Madrilenian character, an extremely original and special type, though made up of Andalusian grace and boasting, Valencian liveliness, and Castilian seriousness and tone."[65] These representations would continue well into the twentieth century, with notable cinematic interventions emphasizing the distinct class and character of the space and its inhabitants including *Domingo de Carnaval* (Edgar Neville, 1945), and José Antonio Nieves Conde's *Surcos* (1951), which drew criticisms from the Franco regime for its politically charged depiction of the suffering of Lavapiés's populace following the Civil War.

Perceptions of Mouraria during these same centuries were similarly conditioned both by the area's precarious infrastructure and the overcrowding of its populace, garnering the space a reputation as a type of "back door" to the city where the reputed underbelly of society converged.[66] By the nineteenth century, Mouraria's landscape was significantly degraded, not from the devastation of Lisbon's 1755 earthquake from which it had emerged relatively unscathed, but rather from haphazard efforts to accommodate the city's growing working class during the previous centuries of urban expansion.[67] The mythology of the neighborhood tied to this period is most famously encapsulated in the figure of Maria Severa Onofriana, a *fado* singer who lived part of her life and died in a single-story building on the district's Rua do Capelão. The lore of *A Severa* was widely circulated in publications such as Júlio Dantas's 1901 novel of the same name, a fictionalized account of Severa's life as a sex worker with Romaní roots, and her musical journey through Mouraria and other lower-class sectors of Lisbon. This understanding of *fado* as the product of society's criminals and social outcasts, developed in a distinctly urban manner in clandestine taverns and bars, and its connections to the Romaní populace, a racial Other, both reinforced and romanticized the role of Mouraria as unsavory in both landscape and populace, and facilitated a more cohesive construction of *fado* as Portugal's preeminent musical genre via these emblematic figures. The mythos of the neighborhood as the *berço do fado* (the cradle of fado), entangled with the Maria Severa folk history, and the essence of marginality implicit to this classification, was likewise fortified in film, theater, and *fado* itself.[68] Take, as an example, an excerpt from the song "O meu bairro" (My neighborhood), written by Conde Sobral for Fernando Maurício, a former resident of the district.

> Eu nasci na Mouraria
> Na Rua do Capelão
> Onde a Severa vivia
> Onde o fado é tradição.

I was born in Mouraria
at Rua do Capelão
where Severa lived
and *fado* is tradition.[69]

This entanglement between musical tradition and the area's stigmatized history continues to influence the way Mouraria's identitarian and cultural significance is cast in the public eye well into the present day.

The interchange between narrative and the physical and psychic terrain of these districts was also significantly impacted by Spain's and Portugal's respective periods of authoritarian rule, decades during which both neighborhoods suffered the tangible consequences of each regime's hostility toward the lower classes. In Spain, the class-based antagonism of the Spanish Civil War continued in its aftermath through political actions like the Franco regime's post-war reconstruction plan, the *Plan Bigador*. This urban initiative neglected Lavapiés and other portions of the city's historic center associated with working-class sympathizers of the former Republic, focusing instead on building a new class of homeowners in districts and housing blocks on Madrid's expanding periphery. The hostile view of the renters who had traditionally lived neighborhoods like Lavapiés is famously encapsulated in architect and politician José Luis de Arrese's declaration, "We want a Spain of homeowners, not the proletariat," when honored with the title Agente de Honor de la Propiedad Inmobilaria (Real Estate Agent of Honor) in 1959.[70] This institutional vision had a critical impact on Lavapiés's already insufficient infrastructure, with sidewalks, streets, and buildings falling into disrepair as money was divested from public works and social services. Moreover, laws like the *1946 Ley de Arrendamiento Urbano* (1946 Law for Urban Renting), which on the surface had seemed to benefit renters in a time of post-war rebuilding by freezing the amount of monthly rents and putting an indefinite duration on rental contracts, instead accelerated antagonistic practices by proprietors like intentional neglect in order to dislodge renters whose occupancy did not generate income.[71]

Mouraria, too, faced a similar wave of institutionalized hostility toward its working-class population during the Salazar regime, propelled by a modernization discourse that zeroed in on the "unhygienic" qualities of the historic quarter and, by extension, its inhabitants. This included such plans as Duarte Pacheco's *Plano de Urbanização e Expansão da Cidade* (Plan for the Urbanization and Expansion of the City) and Faria da Costa's *Salvação Barreto*, which supported the demolition of large sectors of the district.[72] Mouraria, in conversations regarding such plans, was described as a "neighborhood of clumsy and ugly old buildings that now had no place in the city center," and thus obstacle to the progress envisioned by the regime.[73] This approach to urban planning as a civilizing mechanism followed the trend of interventionist design that spread across Europe during the nineteenth century, with Georges-Eugène Haussmann's demolition and redesign of large swaths of Paris a foundational model for such interventions. The Salazar government, in the Haussmann spirit, demonstrated an overt disregard for historical patrimony and the displacement of populations when they razed and rebuilt substantial portions of the neighborhood during the regime, producing an uneven social and architectural landscape with which the city would continue to contend in future decades.[74]

As later chapters will explore, the recontextualization and recasting of the gloomier dimensions of each of these district's histories is often at the heart of narrative trends that drive cultural representations of both Lavapiés and Mouraria. Michael Colvin, in this regard, points to the *fados novos* of the 1940s and 60s which idealized the pre-Estado Novo Mouraria, reading them as an oppositional response to the regime's vision of progress and corresponding urban interventions. During this period, performers of *fados novos* covertly lambasted the regime by invoking Mouraria in terms of *saudade*, a term employed to describe a complex type of longing tinged by feelings including nostalgia, loss, and happiness. Songs like "Ai Mouraria," (Oh Mouraria) and "Já não vou à Mouraria," (I don't go to Mouraria anymore) Colvin argues, depended on *saudade*'s "capacity to denounce the present in light of a glorious past."[75] In this case, the revisionary rhetorical strategy was employed as a form of opposition, denouncing the Estado Novo's manner of governance and its impact on the district. This return to and reworking of Mouraria's past as a response to the debates of the present would continue well beyond the regime, adapting to evolving anxieties and desires regarding the neighborhood and its inhabitants.

Selective engagement with historical precedent is also evident in contemporary emphasis on Lavapiés as one of the city's most *castizo* districts, a term rooted in lifestyle practices attributed to Madrid's urban slums in the seventeenth and eighteenth centuries.[76] Along with *manolería* and *manolos*, terms specific to Lavapiés, *castizo* has evolved as an aesthetic category that captures a particular Madrilenian character often distanced from its more stigmatized origins. During events like the Lavapiés's San Lorenzo festival, which grew in popularity during the latter half of the twentieth century after the reconstruction of the church of the same name, revelers would don the clothing typical of these working-class archetypes in a nostalgic invocation of myths of origin, and tribute to a specific notion of urban authenticity.[77]

By the time that Spain and Portugal transitioned to democratic rule, both neighborhoods were firmly situated in the public imaginary as problematic sites in the broader urban history of their respective cities. It was at this point that the stories told about Lavapiés and Mouraria would develop an explicitly racial dimension, in light of the shifting demographic composition of the Iberian Peninsula entangled with its expanding position as a receiving region of immigrants. The districts, though degraded, were affordable and well-situated and thus attracted many of the less-prosperous newcomers to the peninsula from regions of Africa, Asia, and Latin America seeking access to work, commerce, and social services. It was in this climate that each neighborhood's respective insalubrious reputations became increasingly conflated with their multiracial populaces, a discursive trend especially palpable in media coverage. Headlines like "Man stabbed and robbed, allegedly by a Moroccan national," covering an attack in Lavapiés, and "Immigration worries the Mouraria neighborhood," forged the archetype of the racially Other immigrant as a mounting threat and invading force in these spaces, connotations and corresponding concerns that would only become further entrenched as waves of migration continued steadily through the turn of the twenty-first century.[78]

It was also at this point that the Spanish and Portuguese governing bodies were pushing modernizing narratives about their newly democratic nations, a discursive shift with spatial consequences that sought to situate the countries as members of the broader European community in the decades following extended periods of relative economic stagnation under authoritarian rule.[79] Amid this effort in the '80s and '90s, each state sought to make ambitious changes to urban infrastructure, with particular attention to public works projects, historical patrimony, and cultural installations. In some more well-known cases, these undertakings were guided by preparations for a mega event that would draw international acclaim, including the Barcelona Olympics and Seville World's Fair, both of which were held in 1992, and the Expo '98 World's Fair in Lisbon. As Jean-Paul Carrière and Christophe Demazière point out in their study of the Portuguese fair, many of these plans adopted the flagship approach, wherein civil leaders invested in high profile and high-end retail, residential, entertainment, and tourist spaces in so-called underused or derelict areas.[80] In general, the flagship model of urban development emphasizes renovations in the service of the comfort and needs of those with capital—the middle class, tourists, and investors.[81]

Madrid, while not the host of a specific event during this period, was still the site of an increasing number of flagship interventions, including the debut of the Reina Sofia contemporary art museum in 1992, earning the city the title of "Cultural Capital of Europe."

Notably, these efforts to integrate the newly democratic nations into the broader European community were accentuated by an explicit emphasis on their imperial pasts, given that both the Spanish and Portuguese World's Fairs were organized in commemoration of the fifth centenary of Christopher Columbus and Vasco da Gama's respective maritime expeditions.[82] To this end, their triumphant debut on the world stage was couched within the rearticulation of their historic place on the colonial axis of power, each nation in a position of authority that, as discussed in the prior section, drew from a logic of racial stratification. Indeed, this narrative return to the colonial era reinforced each nations' proximity to Whiteness via the invocation of their history as a European imperial power, and by extension, the political and economic privileges associated with the category.

The modernization discourse of the late twentieth century was thus a driving factor in the mounting trend of both conceiving of and producing sectors of Madrid and Lisbon in terms of their economic potential rather than their practical use. Beginning in the 1980s, both cities' leaders designed and enacted interventions that would increasingly draw criticism from urban activists for disregarding local need for community services and expanded access to affordable housing in the push to situate the capitals as cultural and financial centers. In Madrid, Lavapiés would be impacted by the 1997 Plan General de Ordenación Urbana (General Urban Development Plan), the Partido Popular's (People's Party) revision of the 1985 plan by the Partido Socialista Obrero Español (Spanish Socialist Worker's Party), and its designation as a "preferred rehabilitation area," which culminated in renovations of neighborhood infrastructures (like sewers and gas lines), architectural modifications, and the construction of several new facilities like the Casa Encendida, a former Caja Madrid (Madrid Savings Bank) restored as a cultural center.[83] Fernando Díaz Orueta notes that these operations did not address "long standing neighbourhood demands such as the construction of a new health centre or improvement of the local state schools, overwhelmed by new pupils."[84] Lavapiés's reputation as a site of resistance would likewise grow during this period, due in large part to its prominence in the Okupa movement, urban activists who used squatting as a form of opposition to the prevailing urban agenda, their ideology encapsulated in their slogan "Kontra la Especulación Okupación" (Occupy to fight against speculation).

Mouraria, too, was the site of increased interventions during this period in terms of its potential for development, and according to the catalyzing spirit of city-wide preparations to host the Expo '98. The 1996 *Plano de Urbanização do Núcleo Histórico da Mouraria* (Urbanization Plan of the Historic Center of Mouraria), for example, laid out a series of tasks including rehabilitating sites identified as historic patrimony, the degradation of which dated to the Salazar period of institutional neglect and demolition. Prior to the World's Fair, the municipal government also debuted the newly renovated Praça do Martim Moniz (Martim Moniz Plaza), which included forty-four kiosks offering regional souvenirs, antiques, and artisanal goods. While these interventions aimed to enhance the cities' global profile and economic appeal, they, like in Lavapiés, neglected more local demands, intensifying the tension between the push for development and community welfare.

This approach to urban planning, wherein the state takes on a servile role in matters of the market, would continue in the years to follow as neoliberal models of governance expanded in both Spain and Portugal, seen as an avenue toward economic prosperity. In turn, narratives regarding the unexploited potential of Lavapiés and Mouraria would increasingly circulate in through the early 2000s, with the districts discussed in terms of their latent supply—social, spatial, and otherwise—for market demand. Subsequent plans like the 2005 Lavapiés Rehabilitation Plan and 2009 QREN-Mouraria Action plan, laid out efforts to address security and social welfare in the same breath as designs to foment commerce and tourism, with public resources serving as an avenue to attract and expand investment.[85] For example, while the QREN-Mouraria plan, also known as AiMouraria, outlined changes to public health and infrastructure, a significant portion of the proposed projects focused on recasting the district's public spaces in terms of their creative or commercial value, with urban image, patrimonial value, and the creation of appealing leisure spaces of special prominence.

Manuel Delgado Ruíz, a prominent critic of late twentieth- and early twenty-first-century urban development in Iberia, describes these consumer-driven initiatives as central to the rise of the "ciudad-negocio" (business-city). In his view, as these cities underwent "massive renovations to serve the interests of multinational corporations," they became "parodies or caricatures of themselves, large exclusionary machines that expel any resident or foreigner deemed financially insolvent."[86] The tensions Delgado Ruíz identifies—particularly the issues of inclusion and exclusion—were especially acute in neighborhoods like Lavapiés and Mouraria, where histories of marginalization and resistance came into sharp conflict with the priorities of profit oriented urban transformation. These contradictions would become even more palpable following the financial crisis, as both districts faced renewed pressures from networks of global capital.

Chapter Outline

The structure of this book may be understood in two parts. In the first three chapters, I focus on the narratives and cultural forms produced in the post-2008 era that, in a continuation of the trends set in motion during years prior, cultivated both Lavapíes and Mouraria as productive consumer territory and arenas in which to mitigate the impact of the crisis. With the relationship between affect and the production of urban space at the forefront, I pay special attention to how each neighborhoods' associations with the racial Other were increasingly aestheticized in the service of their promotion.[87] Likewise, I note how these invocations of plurality were yielded in tension with the nostalgic invocation of myths of origin that, too, were shaping the physical and psychic space of the districts, pointing to enduring and evolving belief systems, informed by racial thinking, that molded notions of the proper use and form of each space.

Chapter 1, "Branding the City," introduces dominant discursive patterns driving the consumption-oriented branding of Lavapiés and Mouraria, which I describe as affective expressions with socio-spatial consequences. To illustrate this, I discuss the opportunistic engagement with both Lavapiés's and Mouraria's complex legacies of neglect, marginalization, and racialization in digital and visual spheres where watered down narratives of plurality and difference circulated, highlighting how similar affective patterns recast these historically dispossessed areas of Madrid's and Lisbon's urban centers in terms of their symbolic capital, priming them for further intervention and development. Case studies include Airbnb advertisements for both Lavapiés and Mouraria, a set of walking tours organized by Renovar a Mouraria (Renovate Mouraria), a local nonprofit organization, and a food festival celebrating culinary diversity in Lavapiés organized by the neighborhood's business association. Through these examples, I discuss how expressions of love and celebration were central to invoking disenfranchised figures and histories as a form of cultural currency, and point out how this narrative trend evaded how enduring challenges for these populations, such as a right to housing and social welfare, were aggravated by each neighborhood's repositioning as a consumer hub. My thinking in this chapter draws from Sara Ahmed's theoretical position that emotions like love and happiness may direct or obscure hate and injustice.[88]

In Chapter 2, "Taking Shape," I look more closely into how the urban environment in Lavapiés and Mouraria shifted in tandem with the evolving values, economic prospects, and social relationships of the post-crisis era. Here, I conceive of each neighborhoods' lived spaces—plazas, buildings, streets, and monuments—as cultural objects in and of themselves, the construction and design of which reveal evolving power and social structures. As an example of how the feelings explored in Chapter 1 manifested in the built environment, I study Mouraria's Mercado de Fusão (Fusion market), a development project executed under the auspices of the QREN-Mouraria AiMouraria program. My analysis hinges on my concept of manufactured multiculturalism, a discursive strategy with spatial repercussions where interest groups capitalize on an opportunistic engagement with (and construction of) racial and ethnic diversity. I employ the term *manufactured* to emphasize how the pastiche of peoples and cultures that form the basis of this trope depart from miscegenation narratives grounded in colonial relationships, offering, instead, a more disjointed account of cultural plurality that, in this case, situated the Portuguese within an aspirational vision of globalized modernity.[89]

Chapter 3, "Capturing Community in Lavapiés and Mouraria," turns to the power of documentary-style photography in shaping how both cities' populations were recast in the public imaginary, focusing on ways of viewing each neighborhood's populace that ultimately served the post-crisis surge in branding and development. Specifically, I assess the affective implications of two specific projects that situated race at the forefront of their visual construction of the quotidian in Lavapiés and Mouraria: Juan Valbuena's *Nosotros: Un album colectivo del barrio de Lavapiés* (Us: A collective album of the Lavapiés neighborhood), an exhibit and book published in 2009, and *All Around Us* (2013), a public installation by photographer Gonçalo Gaioso in Mouraria's Praça do Martim Moniz. While keeping in mind how each of these texts embodies different notions of viewing and visual production and was developed in distinct social and geographic contexts, I consider the similarities in their ways of looking at and constructing difference in each neighborhood, and the ways that these ways of looking contributed, directly or indirectly, to the branding of each space. To this point, I demonstrate how in both instances a White mediator uses visual strategies to advance a narrative of celebratory multiculturalism grounded in the notion that proximity to a racial Other equates conviviality, a measured expression of difference articulated as a collective desire.

A third text, Camilla Watson's *Canto do Sol* (Sunny Corner), a 2017 installation that uses photographs of the members of the Mouraria community to explicitly condemn the impact of speculative development on neighborhood life, serves as a transition to the second portion of the manuscript, in which I focus on interventions that ostensibly contest or propose alternatives to the cultural narratives implicated in the production of Lavapiés and Mouraria as consumer terrain. Through this brief interlude, I establish my objective in the latter half of the book: to assess which issues and whose interests came to the fore in these oppositional cultural texts, with particular attention to how different social actors engaged with race and racial difference in the process of contestation.

In Chapter 4, "Markets and the Limits of Opposition" I study the grassroots renovation of Lavapiés's Mercado de San Fernando, spearheaded in 2011 in the wake of the Indignadxs movement, which was positioned as a response to the prevailing model of redeveloping the city's municipal markets through leisure-focused upscaling. In my introduction to this case study, I employ Svetlana Boym's discussion of nostalgia as a window into the affective implications of debates regarding the proper use and function of the city's markets during this period. Through both my reading of this space as a cultural text, and interviews with participants involved the process of redevelopment, I discuss some of the identitarian limits of this endeavor, including representative lacunae and discursive tropes that reinforce hierarchies of belonging, and argue that the pursuit of alternatives to the status quo in the urban development and design of the market did not automatically constitute a radical break with enduring racial hierarchies in the neighborhood.

Finally, in Chapter 5, "Vision and Opposition," I return to the realm of visual culture to highlight two artists who employ digital tools and platforms to both create and disseminate alternate ways of viewing the urban evolution of Lavapiés and Mouraria in the post-crisis era. In my analysis of a map and physical installation by Spanish street artist PorFavor and illustrations by Portuguese artist José Smith Vargas, I contemplate how these artists critique both the invocation of racial heterogeneity as an aestheticized trope, and the strategic dissemination of myths of origin in the promotion and design of these districts. With my findings from Chapter 4 in mind, I assess how these pieces depart from the ideological trappings and exclusionary tropes discernable in conversations surrounding the second life of the Mercado de San Fernando, and in doing so contribute alternative perspectives on demographic heterogeneity and urban change. With visuality at the forefront, I argue that these case studies offer a panorama of the range of contestations probing systems of power both intersecting with and extending beyond the influence of capital, and an example of how cultural producers seek to contest the discursive status quo studied in previous chapters.

Cities Beyond Crisis, as a whole, points out which stories gained traction in the heightened affective climate of the post-crisis era, and how these narratives manifested in the ongoing reorganization of the built environment. While my analysis of both Lavapiés and Mouraria is informed by regional specificities, I build on the understanding that these processes find many parallels beyond Iberia, especially in regions where the notion of a "good life," to borrow from Berlant, is informed by the promises of their colonial past and the economic aspirations of the present. To this point, comparison of these two neighborhoods in the chapters to follow will also inform ongoing discussions regarding the broader networks of power and knowledge generation directing public discourse and shaping spaces beyond the Iberian Peninsula.

A NOTE ON POSITIONALITY

This book is the product of more than a decade of cultural immersion and scholarly inquiry in Spain and Portugal that, notably, began in 2008 when I first traveled to Madrid as an exchange student from the United States. While the formal research, including interviews and participant observation, contained in this manuscript was largely conducted in Spain and Portugal during the summers of 2014 and 2015 and as a Fulbright Scholar in Madrid from 2016–2017, my perspective has been strongly impacted by the years that I lived, studied, and worked in Spain prior to my doctoral studies. At this time, my experience of the immediate aftermath of the financial crisis in Iberia was that of an inside-outsider: surrounded by yet protected from precarity by intersecting forms of socioeconomic, racial, and migratory privilege. I lived and participated in such watershed events as the 15-M protests in the Plaza del Sol as they unfolded, alongside yet distinct from many of the social collectives contemplated in this study. In this sense, my exploration of the constellation of affective patterns that circulated during this era in the chapters to come is informed by both my time living this moment, now memories, and the scholarly training and research that I have conducted in the years since.

CHAPTER 1

Branding the City

Madrid might be the world's most exciting capital right now, and #Embajadores (in the Lavapiés barrio) is its most colourful neighbourhood—the coolest in the world right now.

—*TIME OUT* MAGAZINE, 2018

To step foot in Mouraria for the first time is to experience a subtle but immediate shift; a heightening of perception. This once forgotten district is an oasis of local life, which has become a rarity in Lisbon's centre. Here, the labyrinthine streets are teeming with history, evolving for all to see.

—"LISBON'S HIPPEST NEIGHBOURHOOD: A POCKET GUIDE TO MOURARIA," 2018

This chapter serves as an overview of dominant discursive patterns that drove the consumption-oriented branding of Lavapiés and Mouraria in the post-crisis era, which I interpret as affective expressions with socio-spatial consequences. Namely, I highlight striking comparisons in the opportunistic engagement with and recasting of Lavapiés's and Mouraria's complex legacies of neglect, marginalization, and racialization by local stakeholders that appealed to an evolving spending class. The influence of shifting tourism and leisure tastes is discernable in digital and visual spheres where opportunistic narratives of plurality and difference circulated, influencing public perception of the symbolic value of these districts. Leading rhetorical tropes demonstrate the tendency to recast dispossessed areas of urban centers through similar affective patterns.

My thinking throughout this chapter is informed by Ahmed's argument that one may obscure injustice by pointing to it as the origin of a good feeling.[1] As an example, she takes on the fantasy of the happy housewife, which, she asserts, "conceals the signs of domestic labor under the sign of happiness."[2] In these neighborhoods, I find that power to conceal through good life images extends beyond the domestic sphere to the expression of urban social ideals. As I will explore in each of my selected case studies, the promotion of Lavapiés and Mouraria as viable sites for consumption and leisure depends on a practice of casting points of conflict (like immigration and racial plurality, which destabilize notions of a homogeneous national ideal, or the long historical association between these spaces and the working poor) as positive social values. I argue that this narrative tendency is ultimately a superficial engagement with specific histories, populations, and even spatial forms that looks to such qualities only to the extent that they contribute to a marketable aesthetic. A closer look at tangible expressions of these spaces' symbolic value following the crisis provides further insight into the enduring attachments and aspirations that circulated in these urban spheres in this era of economic precarity and demographic change.

The rapid evolution of neighborhoods like Lavapiés and Mouraria for the benefit of the spending classes is commonly understood as gentrification, a term coined by sociologist Ruth Glass to describe the process wherein the character of an urban environment shifts due to an influx of affluent residents and businesses.[3] While gentrification was certainly at play in Lavapiés and Mouraria in the wake of the crisis, I consider it a symptom, rather than catalyst, of changes to these environments.[4] With this assertion, I follow the logic of Sharon Zukin, who argues that explaining away the upscaling of neighborhoods as gentrification "minimizes and oversimplifies the collective investment that is at stake" in these processes of urban change. While acknowledging gentrification as a stage in many districts' respective urban evolutions, Zukin advocates for a closer look at the organized effort between agents in the production of the city including real estate developers, the public and private sectors, and community organizations that turn once-derelict areas "to gold."[5] This closer look, I contend, reveals a range of affective attachments and aspirations that inform the production of once-neglected or overlooked districts as attractive terrain for individuals with more spending power.

The opportunistic promotion of Lavapiés and Mouraria in the post-crisis era was significantly related to their perceived potential value in the commercial panoramas of Madrid and Lisbon, particularly in terms of tourism and leisure. Subsequent interventions in each of the districts would likewise exemplify Harvey's theory of a spatio-temporal fix, that is, a way that new terrains for capital accumulation are forged by financial and state institutions in an increasingly tight landscape of resources through avenues including long-term capital projects, social expenditures, and the creation of new markets.[6] The leisure market, which was well established in both Spain and Portugal long before 2008 collapse, had proven itself a resilient sector in each nation's economic landscape and thus came to the fore as a priority for fomenting growth and investment as an avenue beyond financial precarity.[7] While much pre-crisis development of tourism to Iberia had centered on promoting leisure travel to Spain's and Portugal's coasts and islands, a renewed emphasis on cultural tourism during the aughts, which encouraged visitors to take a more active role in learning about and "discovering" different regions, shifted attention to the growth potential of previously unexploited areas in centers of cultural capital like Madrid and Lisbon.[8] This urban focus had been facilitated by the development of cultural and leisure spaces in Spanish and Portuguese urban spheres during decades prior, the brunt of which were tied explicitly or in spirit to large-scale events like the Olympics and World Fairs.

Mounting attention to urban centers as leisure destinations in the first decades of the aughts also aligned with a growing awareness of and resistance against the artificial nature of tourism. Increasingly, visitors sought a travel experience that emphasized connections with local populations and quotidian environments as an alternative to traditional accommodations, attractions, and destinations.[9] These evolving practices, which sought a purportedly "authentic" rather than simulated experience, would have a direct impact on visitors' interactions with—and by extension, how tourism shaped—the urban landscape in Iberian cities, which were increasingly positioned for visitor consumption and idealized as conduits of "authentic" experiences through discursive practices. Yet, as Zukin argues, claims of authenticity in such urban settings, have "little to do with origins and a lot to do with style."[10] Rather, she points out, the romanticization of a mythical urban "original," from experiences to people and places, is dictated by cultural stakeholders and complicated by moralist notions of origins, the parameters of which shift according to different social and political contexts.[11] Expressions of authenticity, rooted in the essentialist instinct to organize spaces and society, are expressions of power and influence.

Moreover, despite the fact that evolving tourism practices were positioned as a deliberate unshackling from traditional accommodations, attractions, and destinations, in practice, the brunt of visitors engaging in a search of a so-called authentic experience still sought out the comforts of their day-to-day lives, further impacting the development and branding of burgeoning tourist sites.[12] The traveler who attempts to escape the "tourist experience" may reflect on their role in the tourism industry and, as a result, wander the city in a flâneur-like manner, mimicking the rhythms of everyday life. Yet, in their pursuit of authenticity, which is wielded by stakeholders as a commodity, these practices are absorbed into a new cultural mainstream. Overall, such tourism practices are part and parcel with the spatio-temporal fix as they contribute to the cultivation of formerly disregarded terrains for leisure consumption. As once unremarkable or undesirable corners of the city are rebranded as destinations due to their supposed authenticity, they are increasingly cast as culture on display. This understanding of evolving tourism practices sheds light on how districts like Lavapiés and Mouraria become sites of interest due to their "off the beaten path" characteristics. As the following case studies demonstrate, those who take advantage of these trends for capital gain often cultivate this hyperrealistic display of the quotidian in an appeal to consumers, subsequently impacting the social and spatial landscape of these urban environments.[13] Ultimately, what is framed as authentic for this type of traveler is an expression of cultural power, the ability to say who and what belongs, why, and for what purpose.

The growth of this expanding market therefore prompted the cultivation and corresponding promotion of coherent products for consumption. To this end, I consider what George Yúdice terms the "expediency of culture," a method of sociopolitical and economic amelioration in which culture is a resource that may be marketed and sold.[14] Harvey, similarly, discusses the instrumentalization of culture in the context of "the art of rent," describing how cultural products, events, and even localized ways of life are attributed commodity status, giving way to a "struggle to accumulate marks of distinction and collective symbolic capital in a highly competitive world."[15] These scholars allude to a critical step in the process of exploiting culture as a resource: its *extraction*. I conceive of this extraction, in the context of urban development and design in Lavapiés and Mouraria, as the process through which each neighborhood's cultural—and therefore fiscal—real and imagined attributes were identified and subsequently cultivated by institutional actors and local stakeholders through frequent reference and even themed interventions. Short examples include discussions of Lavapiés as a central site to Madrid's *castizo* tradition, or Mouraria's distinction as the professed birthplace of *fado*. Often, this process of extraction occurs gradually vis-à-vis a collective investment on the part of developers, government officials, and local residents, whose return to these narratives is propelled by the demands of the growing leisure sector. Culture-as-resource, excavated and instrumentalized by these social actors, establishes the framework for recognizable brands that may be repeated ad infinitum in the process of selling space.

Branding, accordingly, is an instrument of affect that involves both explicit expressions intended to change people's perception of a place and, more implicitly, attachments to the potentials and ideals of the subject of such branding initiatives. Urban brands and their affective attachments are forged by social actors explicitly charged with, or opting to take on, the task of researching, changing and promoting local identities, cultivating a sense of pride, and building recognizable symbols for the city. Commonly, branding is enacted as a cohesive project designed by institutions and centers of influence that disseminate their message to local stakeholders and the general public who may, in turn, perpetuate this vision.[16] These tenants of the brand make their way into the public consciousness through repeated reference to representative images, texts, and language created in this process. In effect, branding as a means of influence is often wielded at the national level as a type of soft power, a practice defined by Joseph Nye in relation to world politics as the act of influence through cultural persuasion rather than compelled action.[17]

Take, as a brief example, the "symbol of Portugal" a logo developed by artist José de Guimarães in 1993 for the Instituto do Comércio Externo Português to promote tourism to the country. The image, the use and dissemination of which remains closely regulated by the National Tourism Board, features a figure standing with arms outstretched—its face the sun, its body the Portuguese flag—that stands on a base meant to represent the sea. Guimarães's piece is a personified symbol of local attractions and identities, weaving together the sun, the sea, and the nation itself, that was and continues to be reproduced in a range of visual and embodied ways to trigger the thought of Portugal as a destination, featuring sun-soaked, coastal activities a central pillar of its appeal to visitors. One may also read the image as a celebration of the nation's history of maritime expansion, as the figure stands on the water and extends its arms into the beyond. Overall, the logo is a functional component of a brand that serves an explicit national project enacted by a state-sponsored institution. Through the broad dissemination of this and similar representations of the nation shaped according to this vision, a wider public is influenced to conceive of the country and its cultural (and thus commercial) value along these lines.

This type of top-down branding initiative is also illustrated in Spain's Marca España, literally, "Spain Brand," which launched in 2012 through an executive order by the Partido Popular. Under this order, a commission was created with the task of promoting economic, cultural, social, scientific, and technological interests abroad, an example par excellence of institutional efforts to influence public perception of the nation and its economic potential through marketing and strategic partnerships.[18] To advance this endeavor, the commission launched a since-defunct website for the project, marcaespana.es, a platform meant to disseminate information about Spain to potential visitors under the slogan "Un país para ti" (A country for you). The Marca España website featured such content as a page dedicated to the Spanish flag and crest, one article championing the Spanish language as a "unifying bridge" between nations, and another naming the country as "history's first globalizer," reinforcing narratives that privilege unity over plurality and positioning the nation's imperial legacy as a badge of honor. The branding initiative was ultimately criticized by many for disseminating what they considered to be a monolithic and problematic view of Spanish culture overseas. While the initiative did not have staying power, its creation shed light on the close cooperation between the public and private sphere, including government agencies, nonprofit foundations, the creative industries, and transnational enterprises alike, required for bringing such a brand to life.[19]

As these two examples indicate, it is evident that governmental institutions wield great power and often act as a guiding light in branding processes. The barriers to cultivating a brand in the public consciousness, like the pushback against the conservative ideologies promoted by Spain's Marca España, also demonstrate how branding is not necessarily a straightforward or linear process in which an idea is simply introduced, accepted, and repeated by a single entity in a single medium. In this regard, this chapter delves into the ways a range of stakeholders forged a consensus across digital, visual, and spatial spheres of influence regarding the symbolic value of Lavapiés and Mouraria after the crisis. This accord across text types and between seemingly disparate actors serves as a provocative point of entry for understanding how affective patterns take shape, and in consequence, give shape to urban environments. Moreover, the similar affects and effects of this appeal by different local actors to the tastes of visitors to these two neighborhoods further highlight the parallels between Spanish and Portuguese patterns of adjustment to the post-crisis era.

Selling Place in the Digital Sphere

Since its founding in 2008 (notably, the same year as the global financial crisis), the Airbnb platform has played a visible role in the discursive branding and spatial development of both Lavapiés and Mouraria. The online marketplace was designed at its inception as a broker and intermediary for short-term housing that would receive commissions from bookings without owning the real estate advertised in the listings. According to this model, which was marketed to the public as the "sharing economy," access to short-term accommodations would be expanded now that practically anyone could leverage their private property on the platform. Moreover, in difference to the hotels and holiday apartments that had traditionally been built and marketed based on their proximity to attractions, the Airbnb market would be quickly flooded with an array of rentals beyond more typical hospitality districts. Visitors, many of whom were explicitly disinterested in established tourism precincts and activities, were thus set up to select their new "home" in a world of digitally developed "hosts" and "guests." Of course, it should also be noted that Airbnb did not limit the number of properties that one could rent on the platform, effectively providing the framework for management companies and investors with multiple listings to exploit the minimally regulated renting model for their benefit, often hiding behind individual user profiles.

According to the parameters of the platform, Airbnb "hosts" and "guests," were positioned to attract one another as storytellers through image and text. Users would fill out a profile section including an image, their languages spoken, employment information, and a brief blurb about themselves, ostensibly sharing information to motivate "hosts" to welcome them as a visitor to their home. Similarly, hosts were provided with space in both their advertisements and profiles to sell themselves as local guides and their rental property as a home away from home. While couched in this rhetoric of personal connection, the rise of Airbnb was that of an innovative for-profit rental framework for investors, landlords, and private companies that was able to expand rapidly in cities like Lisbon and Madrid during this period due to liberal housing policies.[20]

As local governments grappled with the extent to which they should attempt to regulate the urban footprint of the platform, Airbnb quickly revolutionized the terrains of tourism. In the past, visitors were commonly limited to staying in areas of cities zoned and developed for their use, yet the initial expansion of Airbnb's user-to-user model had effectively sidestepped zoning requirements, opening new markets in neighborhoods that at the time had either limited or no hospitality infrastructure, like Lavapiés and Mouraria. This expansion seemed to compliment the growth-oriented agenda to increase tourist infrastructure through expanded rental accommodations, a demand recognized by Spanish and Portuguese government officials. Yet, as the expanding housing marketplace propelled speculation and development in Lavapiés and Mouraria, public perception of the platform would begin to sour.[21] Largely, complaints focused on housing shortages, price increases, and displacement of residents in exchange for higher-paying short-term renters. Between 2008 and 2015, for example, the annual number of short-term apartments registered in the city of Lisbon shot up exponentially, from only five to more than 2,000, and by 2018 this number reached an astounding 6,964.[22] In another notable jump, from the first quarter of 2016 to the last quarter of 2019, the median real estate price per square meter in Lisbon increased more than 70 percent, reflecting an increased demand for property.[23] Yet, as both short-term accommodations and property prices rose, access to affordable housing would decline, stoking concern among local residents regarding their staying power.[24]

In this section, I examine Airbnb as a cultural text, viewing it as a productive example of how communication environments shape the construction of meaning around lived and conceived space, with tangible effects visible in the built environment.[25] As a born-digital platform, Airbnb was ostensibly designed to foster more intimate relationships between users and consumers, propelling the rapid and seemingly decentralized spread of narratives about the spaces being marketed for consumption. While the platform's online presence distinguished it from other spheres of influence, I find that a more critical factor in the affective impact of Airbnb's narratives was its "host" and "guest" model, which contrasted with the more impersonal tradition of booking stays in established tourist precincts at hotels and hostels. By emphasizing local expertise, Airbnb catered to emerging tastes shaped by the evolving tourism industry. These displays of intimacy obscured the more impersonal market-driven pressures on property owners to exploit burgeoning markets, like Lavapiés and Mouraria, reframing the transaction as a peer-to-peer exchange, and positioning the expansion of the hospitality industry into less-traversed areas as an appeal to the quest for authenticity. With the affective power of personal connection in mind, let us now delve into some of the stories that circulated across the platform in the service of promoting these neighborhoods as viable destinations.

Take, as an introduction to the genre, a listing titled "Enchanting Loft in Lavapiés" posted by a host named José who, as of early 2020 had more than 120 reviews of his property.[26] In addition to the usual photographs and list of amenities included in postings on the platform, the advertisement features a description in Spanish and English translation (by the host) of the surrounding neighborhood. He writes:

> Located in the heart of Madrid, Lavapiés is one of the capital city's most multicultural neighborhoods, offering a wide variety of overwhelmingly alternative

> entertainment options. In Lavapiés you'll find restaurants serving cuisine from around the world including Indian, Lebanese, Greek, Senegalese, and more, as well as, of course, Spanish food. The neighborhood is also teeming with theaters including the Centro Dramático Nacional Valle-Inclán, Teatro del Barrio, Pavón, and an endless number of bars that adapt to host all kinds of artistic events (live music, poetry readings, microtheater, etc.). On top of that, Lavapiés also is home to San Fernando Market, one of the most charming in Madrid.[27]

Here, the host effectively outlines what he observes as the Lavapiés's most marketable qualities. To open, José describes the neighborhood in terms of its central location and diverse populace, characteristics that situate a stay in the district as convenient for visitors to the capital while simultaneously distinct (in terms of demographic makeup) from Madrid's most well-known tourist precincts. In this same vein, he highlights the district's "leisure offer," which he distinguishes as "alternative." The term "alternative," in particular, does a significant amount of heavy lifting in order to situate Lavapiés as a viable terrain for consumption. This vague reference to and celebration of unconventional ways of life and leisure attributes social and commercial value to unnamed alterities, distinguishing the precinct from other parts of Madrid's broader urban landscape through emphasis on its divergence from a purported mainstream. Further details in this description illuminate what, exactly, constitutes the alterity to which the host refers. In addition to outlining—in a direct appeal to the sensibilities of the anti-tourism tourist—opportunities for cultural engagement that diverge from more well-known stops on visitor itineraries, José explicitly enumerates a list of the area's gastronomic offerings that give shape to the more nebulous multiculturality referenced at the outset of the description. The varied culinary offerings of Indian, Lebanese, Senegalese, and "of course" Spanish origin are the extension of a racially and ethnically diverse populace, a reality of Lavapiés that, as framed by this storyteller, is a positive attribute that should motivate outsiders to observe, explore, and consume in the district.

This discursive pattern is similarly encapsulated in the listing "♥City centre, walking distance to all landmarks!!!" In this advertisement, Silvia, a host on the platform since 2016, writes of Lavapiés, "The area has lots to offer, it is the most multicultural area in Madrid, a bit bohemian as well and traditional spanish at the same time. It is becoming more and more fashionable, full of bars for tapas, restaurants and cafes to enjoy. The area was identified by *Time Out* magazine as the top neighborhood in their '50 Coolest Neighbourhoods in the World' list in 2018."[28] Again, the notion of an "original" against which Lavapiés's (marketable) alterity is measured surfaces through positive expressions. Silvia's story of this space articulates a clear dichotomy between the district's multiculturalism and her notion of "traditional Spanish." The listing does not lament such distinctions, but rather wields this combination of sensibilities and origins as a point of pride that is further reinforced by the author's emphasis on the neighborhood's "cool" designation. Evidently, alterity sells.

These selling points, and their corresponding implications, are similarly apparent in Airbnb advertisements of properties in Mouraria. "Capelão 15 - 2º," a listing from host Nuno named specifically for the apartment's address, describes the district as follows: "Nowadays Mouraria is the most multicultural place in Lisbon, with small buildings where entire families live and a wave of rehabilitation to host immigrants from Europe to Asia, younger people who opt to live in the city center and tourists. Restaurants thrive in this environment with a vast offer with all type [sic] of world cuisines around."[29] Several critical observations may be made regarding this overview of the neighborhood. First, the word "nowadays" emphasizes the relative newness of Mouraria's diverse racial and ethnic makeup, which is attributed here to the "hosting" of immigrants from other parts of Europe and Asia, a term that underlines a sense of temporality in the presence of these unspecified immigrant populations, and benevolence on the part of the Portuguese. The unstable qualities of this group are juxtaposed with Nuno's reference to buildings where "entire families" live, fixed social and material structures that, according to the logic of the sentence, are tied to autochthonous residents. Mouraria's position as a cultural intersection between new and old, fleeting and permanent, is also emphasized by Nuno's mention of (presumed) Portuguese nationals and immigrants comingling with "younger people" and tourists, two populations referenced without racialized subtext. Like in the Lavapiés example, this connection is expressed as a positive attribute through mention of culinary offerings, a consumable product, in its most literal sense, that will entice additional visitors to the area.

The Capelão 15 - 2º listing exhibits how the "multicultural" moniker often appears in these types of advertisements in tension with assertions of authenticity. As mentioned previously, authenticity, in this context, is a narrative a tool wielded to impose claims to the look, feel, and experience of a given urban space. It is a nebulous category given that it may be employed differently depending on the position and aspirations of those who articulate the term, a catch-all denomination attached to the idea of origins that it implies. For example, the idea that Mouraria encapsulates a desired look and feel for those seeking a purportedly "true Portuguese" is emphasized through repetition of terms like "real," "traditional," and "typical," positioning the experience of the neighborhood-as-exhibit in opposition to unnamed inauthentic areas of the city. In another advertisement titled "Charming and traditional Lisbon apartment," as an illustration, visitors are invited to stay in a home that "embodies the concept of the real Lisbon, the amazing old buildings and lovely building facades with their traditional tiles," which, according to the host, offers, "a real sense of living in Lisbon."[30] Small variations in listing descriptions also illustrate a more ambivalent relationship to, rather than wholesale rejection of, the cultural and racial diversity present in this district. "1881 Lisbon - Rose Apartment," in this regard, reports, "Nearby, you can find several grocery stores and local commerce, as well as restaurants and the typical 'tascas,' where the life of the most multiethnic and colorful quarter of Lisbon is experienced."[31] In this case, the racialized populace is highlighted for lending the quarter its "color," viewed from and passing through longstanding institutions like *tascas*. Here, these residents serve as another, albeit different, marker of authenticity for visitors in search of the "real Lisbon."

As the success of Airbnb indicates, cultivating attachments to authenticity is an effective marketing device. To this point, we may return to Zukin's observations of the category. She writes, "We are often seduced by appearances and assumptions. How many times do we think, "the cheaper the beer, the more authentic the bar," or, "the grittier the streets, the more authentic the neighborhood"? How we think about these questions makes an ethical as well as social statement about the way we want to live, and so our stand on urban authenticity is ultimately subjective because it refers to us."[32] This framing, which develops in tandem with consumer tastes, is evident in the promotion of neighborhoods like Lavapiés and Mouraria where each district's distinct qualities, many of which were forged historically through spatial and social acts of marginalization, are recast as desirable objects themselves. This is evident in "Sunny & Spacious room in Central Madrid," where the host advises potential renters, "the ethnical and cultural variety and the constant hustle and bustle or the streets make it very special and appealing for many people but other people might find it a bit gritty, so it is up to you!"[33] "Gritty," a term used to express what is unrefined or dangerous, is wielded here as a matter of taste. With the final invitation to choose, "it is up to you," the host directly addresses how qualms for some visitors might be a selling point for others, demonstrating the moral valuation of consumptive practices. In "Mouraria I, Eco-duplex&french balcony&smart access," host Ulrik uses a different technique to respond to potential resistance to and fear of Mouraria explicitly because of its racialized populace, writing, "It is possibly the place in Europe where you are closest to experiencing an Arab medina (without any hassle whatsoever though!)"[34] In this instance, the author of the listing invokes the aesthetic experience of a medina in their description of the space only to the extent that it serves as a themed environment. The way that this neighborhood's inhabitants diverge from social practices associated with Whiteness thus are framed, and promoted, according to what John Hannigan terms the "safe excitement of riskless risk."[35] Mouraria is acknowledged as different to the extent that it cultivates interest, but not *too* different so as to deter a potential visitor.

Through the narratives disseminated on Airbnb, both Lavapiés and Mouraria were deliberately portrayed as storied spaces that offered accessible and varied opportunities for visitors to engage with local life. These claims to authenticity were supported through explicit reference to features of each district that set them apart from more established tourist areas, appealing to those seeking a more immersive stay while still seeking some of the comforts of the hospitality sector. The spatial experience on offer in neighborhoods like Lavapiés and Mouraria took shape as a murky yet discernable "coolness," forged through a combination of divergence from Whiteness as a perceived norm (multiculturalism), essentialist notions of national tradition ("typical" Spanish and Portuguese customs and landscapes), and evolving leisure conventions that diverged from established practices. These narratives would aid the geographic expansion of the terrains of tourist consumption, demonstrating the power of communicative networks in forging a brand with opportunistic emphasis on authenticity and Otherness. Tropes of home, connection with locals, and carefully curated community narratives would resonate with a new generation of tourists seeking to engage with communities at their destination through quotidian and home-like environments. Moreover, these discursive patterns were not unique to either space, as similar rhetorical tendencies appear in advertisements for apartments in both Lavapiés and Mouraria, indicating a broader trend across different national contexts to reframe and obscure histories of stigma with positive feelings. Through this affective maneuvering, legacies of dispossession were not hidden but rather flaunted as points of honor, a restorative practice that conquered, managed, and repositioned the unruly by making it a pillar of the brand. The commercial viability of Lavapiés and Mouraria was therefore propelled by them being a part of, yet distinct from, other precincts of their respective cities.

Airbnb advertisements for Lavapiés and Mouraria are just one of many text genres that contributed to the discursive construction and promotion of these neighborhood's brands in the decade following the financial crisis. Airbnb, a peer-to-peer platform, demonstrates the power of born-digital narratives explicitly attached to the private sector in molding perceptions of and engagement with specific urban landscapes. Next, we will explore how the localized identities integral to city branding are also achieved through the influence and collaboration of local stakeholders, and delve into the narratives presented by a community group who invited visitors to walk Mouraria.

Walking Mouraria

On a trip to Mouraria in 2015 I visited Mouradia-Casa Comunitária da Mouraria, located in the Beco de Rosendo, a raised alley nestled in the steep slope of the hill leading to the Castelo São Jorge. The site was the headquarters of Renovar a Mouraria (Renovate Mouraria), a nonprofit association founded by residents of the neighborhood in March 2008 who, since its founding, have worked toward a stated goal of revitalizing Mouraria's social and spatial terrain. According to their original website, the group sought "to develop initiatives that promote the urban, social, cultural and touristic revitalization of the Mouraria neighborhood."[36] From the outset, this association of residents, through collective organization, became key agents in the promotion and branding of the district during the post-crisis era. Notably, the group's since-amended emphasis on "touristic revitalization" was indicative of their then-optimistic position that consumer-oriented interventions would be beneficial to this landscape and its inhabitants. Renovar a Mouraria's approach was supported by a range of public and private funders including Lisbon City Hall, the European Union, and Montepio Bank, indicating a consensus between the public and private sector regarding the neighborhood's future. With this funding, the association was able to grow their presence and expand their programming, much of which was hosted at the *Mouradia-Casa Comunitária*, a dedicated space inaugurated by the group in 2012. As the association continued to expand, they pursued a variety of avenues for community engagement including Portuguese courses, publishing *Jornal Rosa Maria*, a newspaper dedicated to neighborhood news and topics, and hosting free concerts and leisure events.

During my visit I had the opportunity to interview Nuno Franco, one of the group's co-founders, who described several of the association's latest endeavors and his impressions regarding their impact. At the time, he was very content with the progress that Renovar a Mouraria had made since its founding, citing visible changes to the district that he attributed to the group's activities. To this end, he shared his memories of the association's first years and presence in the neighborhood:

> In February, 2008 we held a parade through the streets with music that drew a lot of attention from neighborhood residents and introduced . . . it was a way of introducing the association and telling people from the neighborhood that we're here, we're fighting, join us. And after, in March, we made the association official. We legally established the association. After that, in June 2008, we had our first *arraial* street festival. For us the *arraial* wasn't just a party, it was a really important moment for us to tell everyone: we're here and we're here to fight. We're here to defend our right to have a playground, something we have now, the right to have a park where people can go for strolls and bring their children to play and fall in love. The right to a green space, we didn't have that then, and we have it now. The right to decent and nice streets that are taken care of. Now we have pretty streets with benches, trees, fountains. None of this existed, and I believe it was the result of our effort, and also the will of the local government. If the Câmara Municipal hadn't joined us in this effort, none of this would have happened, and the association possibly would have withered away from exhaustion.[37]

Franco's reflection underscores how consensus between stakeholders accelerates urban transformation. From the outset, the brunt of the Renovar a Mouraria association's objectives aligned with those of the municipal government. Most visibly, the AiMouraria project, in which Lisbon's Câmara Municipal outlined rehabilitation and beautification projects in the area, provided sufficient organization and directed funding to reform several of the district's public spaces.[38] For Franco, the aesthetic interventions supported by the municipal government are the expression of his community's right to the city. This is evident in his framing: he does not describe changes to infrastructure in terms of how they appeal to non-residents, but rather emphasizes how leisure spaces like parks and playgrounds facilitate community ties, recognizing the power of comingling in sites of community contact often called "third spaces" by urban scholars.[39] Accordingly, events like the *arraial* that Franco mentions are conceived by the group as opportunities for civic engagement, not necessarily market-oriented promotion.

The work of the Renovar a Mouraria association, as expressed by Franco, indicates a vested interest in social welfare and networks of community support among neighborhood residents. Questions remain, however, regarding the extent to which aesthetic shifts successfully advance and defend community welfare at a deeper level. In this respect, I consider what Compitello describes in the Spanish context as "a good plan gone bad," the unintended consequences of urban plans under the pressures of predatory capital.[40] Specifically, Compitello identifies "the fine line between renovation for the sake of development—what is best for the greatest majority of the population—and renovation that fits the needs of the growing 'heritage industry' bent on rehabilitating city centers with the intent of attracting high end projects and clients or laundering a place's image through the mechanics of what critical geographers call selling place."[41] Indeed, one may see how associations like Renovar a Mouraria, though positioning themselves as advocates of social welfare, intentionally or not, contribute to the process of selling place through discursive practices. The impulse to promote the district to the spending class, evident in the association's original objective to promote tourism in the neighborhood, is likewise directly tied to the pressures of capital. This position is informed by idea that tourism and spending-class consumption translates to the well-being of residents, and encapsulates a recurring optimistic attachment to consumption and investment as a solution to social ills. Yet, the demographic impact of drives for consumer-oriented development in once- or still-marginalized neighborhoods has been proven time and again in urban studies as a motor of displacement and disenfranchisement.[42] Namely, when interventions focus primarily on aesthetics rather than providing robust social and economic protections, such as protected housing or expanded public health and education services, residents with insufficient spending power are often at risk of losing their rights to these "improved" areas of the city to those who do not require such support.[43] This, of course, creates a tension between local groups who intend to serve their district, and the realities of urban interventions that often prioritize economic gain over genuine community welfare.

As I left the association's headquarters, I collected a pamphlet advertising the group's walking tours of the neighborhood. The colorful brochure was emblazoned in large letters *Visita a Mouraria* (Visit Mouraria), with the tagline "History and stories with people inside."[44] It advertised variety of two-hour tours in a range of languages at the nominal price of ten euros for adults, five euros for teens, and free for children, including discounts for large groups and school trips. The pamphlet's contents were organized according to the four visits offered by the association: *Mouraria dos povos e das culturas* (The Culture and People of Mouraria), *Mouraria das tradições* (Traditional Mouraria), *Mouraria do fado* (Fado Mouraria), and *Do castelo à Mouraria* (From the Castle to Mouraria).[45]

The brochure was especially eye-catching due to its illustration, completed by Nuno Saraiva, an artist whose work has been frequently employed in the branding and promotion of attractions in Lisbon. Saraiva's pieces are recognizable given his use of clear lines, bold colors, and expression of movement in figures and scenes that depict Lisbon and its inhabitants. The Portuguese illustrator first established himself through commissioned pieces across the city, in addition to his observational humor and social criticism in "Filosofia de Ponta," a collaboration with Júlio Pinto in the weekly newspaper *O Independente*.[46] In Mouraria, Saraiva's work is especially recognizable due to his contributions to the *Fado vadio* (Idle Fado) mural, a 2012 project by the Movimento os Amigos de São Cristóvão (Friends of São Cristóvão Movement) to adorn a neighborhood building in disrepair adjacent to the Escadinhas de São Cristóvão with famous *fadista* figures associated with the district that soon became a certain stop on tourist itineraries through the neighborhood.[47] The scene, composed by artists including Saraiva, Hugo Makarov, Mário Belém, Pedro Soares Neves, UAT, and Vanessa Teodoro, includes references both to the music genre and common lore related to both the neighborhood and city of Lisbon: singers like Fernando Maurício and Maria Severa, bread and wine placed on a table as an allusion to the songs "Povo que lavas no rio" and "Uma casa portuguesa," a large raven in reference to Lisbon's patron saint St. Vincent, and even the likeness of long-time Mouraria resident and *fadista* Franklin, holding a microphone and embraced by Severa herself. Therefore, Saraiva's style and presence as an artist in Lisbon, and more specifically in Mouraria, lends significant cultural cache to the Renovar a Mouraria pamphlet by way of its form. This is, as mentioned prior, a primary tenant of branding: frequent invocations of representative images, texts, and language build recognizable symbols that, through repetition, influence public opinion.

A closer examination of the pamphlet provides insight into how, through a curated, didactic leisure experience, the neighborhood association contributed to recasting both the space and idea of Mouraria as a desirable attraction. Though distinct from the Airbnb case study in terms of medium and discursive agents, points in common across these modes of communication indicate a narrative consensus among stakeholders who, together, propelled consumptive practices. In this example, specifically, I find that the push and pull between the interests of local stakeholders and the demands of the

FIGURE 1.1. *Visita a Mouraria* pamphlet from Associação Renovar a Mouraria, 2015. Except as noted, photographs are by the author

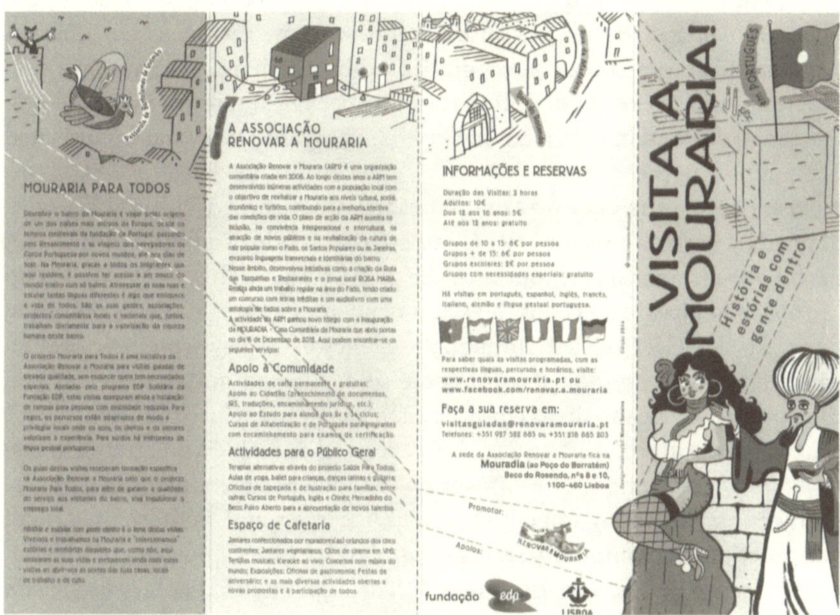

spending class, organized the complex present and past of Mouraria (the "people inside" advertised on the brochure) into a digestible leisure experience. Overall, the *Visita a Mouraria* tours as framed in this text demonstrate how even welfare-focused stakeholders like the Renovar a Mouraria association contributed to the consumption-oriented branding of the district by determining which meanings should be ingrained on and extrapolated from the district's landscape.

The experiences offered to visitors through the organization's walking tours differ from travel to virtual worlds that have been produced as reproductions, such as a museum or world's fair, in that the guide casts the street itself as a living museum, and thus, a themed space. Scholars like Scott Lukas emphasize how consumption is central to the process of theming, defining this practice as "a holistic and integrated spatial organization of a consumer venue."[48] The simple act of consuming a themed perception of a space and reproducing that idea through discourse will therefore propel the further production of this space toward a given thematic tilt. While themed spaces are often self-contained as amusement parks or restaurants, the thematic promotion of pre-existing spaces, like in this case study, may also re-organize such points of interest as venues for consumption. This practice does not necessarily have to be directly linked to capital gain for it to contribute to the commodification of space. Rather, continued recourse to the theme across different publics and cultural producers lends it credibility. Theming a lived space, in difference to a self-contained attraction, is especially impactful in the dissemination of a brand in that it conflates what is organic and what is cultivated in an appeal to the visitor.

Visita a Mouraria likewise exemplifies the production of cultural heritage, defined by Barbara Kirshenblatt-Gimblett as a "mode of cultural production in the present that has recourse to the past."[49] The sector, which opens up the space to give dying economies and dead sites a second life as presentations of themselves, does so through the agency of display: a process through which embodied notions of identity are sold, enacted, and debated.[50] Here, the notion of a "dead" site is closely tied to its commercial productivity, with spaces becoming "lively" as they are perceived as viable and attractive districts for consumption. The cultivation of the heritage industry as a means of injecting "life" into a neighborhood, that is, capital, is therefore an apt reminder of the commodity status of products, events, and ways of life that Harvey describes as "the art of rent."[51] Through in situ displays like *Visita a Mouraria*, these commodities are mediated through their presentation, directing what Urry and Larsen term the tourist "gaze," a socially organized and systematized way to perceive environments as out of the ordinary.[52] Such visits explicitly communicate how the world on display (both lived and imagined) should be interpreted by the visiting public. In turn, narratives that emerge in this process reveal ongoing affective attachments to mythical originals and hierarchies that circulate both within and about these sites of cultural heritage.

With these points in mind, we may turn to the stories of Mouraria's past and present on display in the *Visita a Mouraria* pamphlet. A review of the cover of the brochure serves as an apt introduction to the primary narratives employed in the text to organize engagement with the district's complex past and present. On this first panel, two figures stand in the foreground of a bright green backdrop that features an outline of a castle wall (presumably a reference to the Castelo de São Jorge) and a Portuguese flag. The first figure is a busty rendition of Maria Severa, posing with her thigh partially exposed and her curves accentuated by her posture. She glances to her side at the second figure, a man dressed in a tunic and turban, with a scimitar sword, who is depicted reading aloud from a book. The drawing of Severa is identical to Saraiva's contribution to the *Fado vadio* mural, an aesthetic continuity that, through repetition, is wielded as a recognizable symbol for the neighborhood brand. In the interior of the pamphlet, readers learn that the second figure, the man with the scimitar, is the Alcaide Árabe—the Arab Commander. This character serves as a representation of a vastly different period and historic mythos from Severa, the years between 711 and 1147 when the city was under Arab rule. Together, the four visual symbols depicted on the cover of the brochure—including the wall, the Portuguese flag, Severa, and the Alcaide—synthesize some of the most common referents employed when representing Mouraria as a site of interest for potential visitors.

These visual tokens, and their spatial distribution in Mouraria's urban landscape, are expanded upon further in the interior of the pamphlet. When open, the four panels feature a scene loosely drawn as a map, including landmarks, street names, and representative figures-as-icons. While drawing from the geography of the neighborhood, the map itself is not a literal cartographic representation of the space; rather, it is a collection of allusions to different points of interest sorted according to their thematic tilt, each emphasizing a different cultural asset of potential interest to visitors. These details make explicit the spatial and embodied emblems that will be invoked according to the lens through which the visitor chooses to learn about the neighborhood, with *Mouraria dos povos e das culturas*, *Mouraria das tradições*, *Mouraria do fado*, and *Do castelo à Mouraria* offered as their four options. The illustrations and accompanying text for each of these visits reveal ongoing assumptions, attachments, and distinctions between and within these virtual worlds. Through each of these tours, Mouraria is situated as a material, symbolic, and functional site of cultural heritage through representative, though frequently incongruous, figures, objects, and aesthetic markers that, together, facilitate the branding of the district.

The brunt of these tours employ historical referents to reinforce the neighborhood as a protagonist in Lisbon's broader narrative. *Do castelo à Mouraria*, for example, is organized around the *muralha fernandina*, the Fernandine Wall, a fortification of the city built in 1373 after the Catholic siege of Lisbon that, when standing, descended from the São Jorge castle and crossed the district, ending at what is now the Martim Moniz Plaza. This visit focuses on Mouraria's significance in relation to this wall, which has largely disappeared from the city's topography over the course of centuries. For the tour, visitors are invited to trace the wall's former path, and look upon its remaining vestiges including the ruins of the Torre do Jogo da Pela. The images that accompany this tour description invoke several of Lisbon's foundational myths: in the top right corner of the panel, we see a disembodied Martim Moniz, the knight said to have facilitated the attack on the Arab fortress during the siege of Lisbon. Below this figure, a mummified São Vicente, the city's patron saint, is transported in a boat guarded by two ravens. In a more incongruous reference, the likeness of poet and former resident of Mouraria Afonso Lopes Vieira is sandwiched between the Alcaide Árabe and Martim Moniz, his residence on the Largo da Rosa falling on the trajectory of the visit. These figures are entangled with one another both visually on the pamphlet and through the tour itself, demonstrating how the spatial and conceptual production of Mouraria as a site of cultural heritage is forged through the dissemination of these historically disembodied, strategically recontextualized legends and popular mythologies.

The tours as depicted in the brochure frequently invite sightseers to extrapolate on the observable and extract meaning from the unseen, further demonstrating the role of production and revision in forging cultural heritage. The text promoting *Mouraria das Tradições*, as an example, opens with a discussion of the district's geography "under the majestic view of the castle," going on to describe labyrinthian streets dotted with historic markers and the remains of the medieval city. Visitors who join the tour are prompted to engage in the guided construction of memory; as the blurb states, "this diverse landscape conjures memories of patron saints, professions since-vanished, aristocratic families and ancient routes."[53] Through this route, participants are offered a corporal connection to the stories on display, grounded partially by what they touch, hear, smell, and feel in the act of walking Mouraria's streets, but also largely shaped by what they are instructed to touch, hear, smell, and feel according to the lens of the visit. One might look at a staircase but be asked to imagine a wall, or witness people running errands while being told to listen for the murmur of castle life or the noise of an attack on the fortress. By projecting meaning onto these specters, the guided tour directs the production and dissemination of a given memory of district.

Building on this malleability of the past, the *Mouraria do fado* visit offers a more linear progression from historical events to the present day, articulating the district's weight as a site of cultural heritage through lore of its relationship to the music genre. Saraiva's illustration includes the likeness of singers Maria Severa, Argentina Santos, Fernando Maurício, and Mariza, with the accompanying text detailing each artist's relationship to the district. The visual accompaniment to the text also highlights several material markers of *fado* throughout the area. This includes Saraiva's depiction of a marble statue erected on the corner of Rua do Capelão and Rua

FIGURE 1.2. Interior panels of *Visita a Mouraria* pamphlet from Associação Renovar a Mouraria

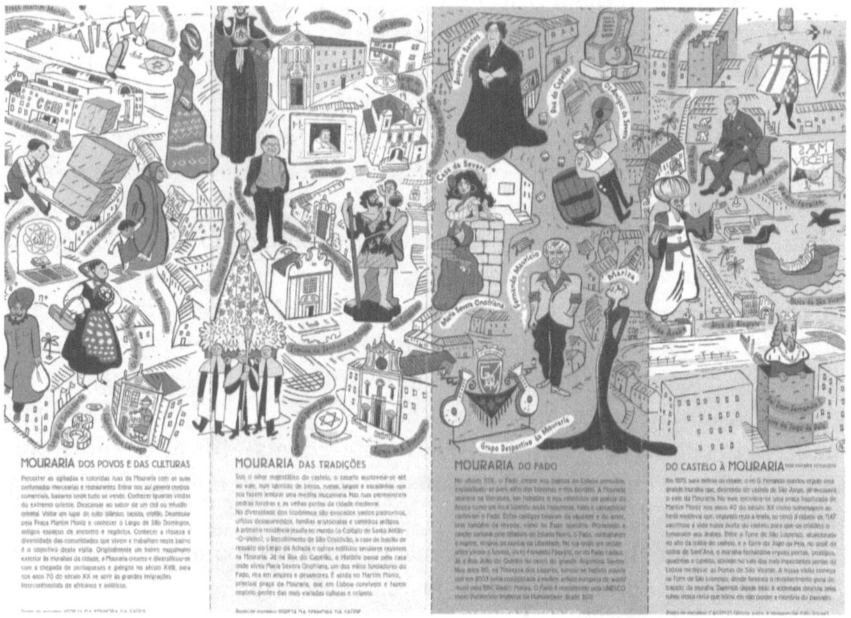

da Mouraria that declares the neighborhood the "cradle" of *fado*, as well as illustrations of landmarks such as the Grupo Desportivo da Mouraria, where many singers began their careers, the Rua do Capelão, where Severa is said to have resided at her death, and Os Amigos da Severa, a bar alongside the same singer's former home. The description on this panel emphasizes the genre's mythicized rise from acts in seedy establishments to national canon, explaining, "in the nineteenth century, *fado* developed in Lisbon's portside neighborhoods, spreading beyond taverns and brothels." As encapsulated in this text, the process of selling *fado* depends on a nostalgic, and often ahistorical reframing of the unsavory spaces and characters credited with bringing the genre to prominence. These referents reinforce the rearticulation of the exchange-value of gritty origins in terms of their aesthetic qualities, an affective process with the effect of recasting what was once negative as celebratory and desirable, and therefore a potential source of profit. This extends to Mouraria, where once-unattractive streets and establishments take on renewed meaning when tied to the mythos of the genre.

Iñigo Sánchez Fuarros, who studies the centrality of *fado* to urban regeneration and tourism efforts in the neighborhood, notes that its utility in Mouraria specifically relies on the genre's preexisting connections to the space both through lyrical references, and the enduring notion that Mouraria embodies the marginality associated with *fado*'s origins.[54] Moreover, Sánchez Fuarros identifies the curious fact that in the years leading up to the financial crisis, there were very few *fado*-related activities in the district.[55] Beginning with the municipal government's 2011 QREN Action Plan, however, the expediency of the genre began to be stridently expressed, with *fado* brought to Mouraria's public and semi-public precincts through singing tours, exhibitions, festivals, and the opening of new performance venues.[56] Renovar a Mouraria's themed walking tour thus follows suit in this push, further cultivating the representation of Mouraria as a character in the story of *fado* by inviting visitors to immerse themselves in its sights, sounds, and stories as they relate to the district. In this other explicit exercise in cultural heritage, Mouraria is cast as commercially viable through recourse to culturally specific historical antecedents—the birth and evolution of a music genre—and a sustained investment in making *fado* visible in the present.

In a departure from the conventional practice of producing cultural heritage through recourse to the past, *Mouraria dos povos e das culturas* demonstrates an effort to render Mouraria as a viable attraction based primarily on its present. For this specific visit, tourists are invited to partake in the bustling daily life of the neighborhood, getting to know the "wealth and diversity of the communities that live and work in this neighborhood" through such activities as purchasing goods and delicacies "from the far east" and visiting Muslim, Taoist, and Christian places of worship.[57] This strategic representation of daily life as a curiosity is, like the other tours, a material and aesthetic endeavor. In this process, the district's qualities are harnessed to the extent that they are useful and interesting to a visiting public. Similarly to the revisionary invocation of the past in the narratives promoted in the Association's other tours, this themed excursion takes on points that are frequently the site of conflict (such as the area's evolving demographic makeup and its racial diversity), and strategically recasts such attributes as positive social values.

Discrete figures and spaces are highlighted on this panel of the brochure in terms of their racial, ethnic, or religious distinction, framing this visit to Mouraria as an excursion to a type of urban world's fair. Such simulated environments, traditionally housed in dedicated precincts and pavilions erected for the occasion, "placed behaviors and entertainments of other cultures in the context of a sideshow" and helped, as Steve Nelson posits, to neutralize "objectionable" aspects of the Other on display.[58] These large-scale events, like Lisbon's own Expo '98, established conventions for the controlled exhibition of culture and commerce, packaging cultures and technologies as entertainment for a mass audience. In the process, the details of a given nation or cultural identity were condensed and connected through devices such as copying (replicating buildings and landmarks), alterations of scale (employing the miniature to give visitors access to a version of large-scale concepts and places), and the display of tokens (both corporal and edified)—simulacra that facilitated the prevailing narrative of the exhibit, which in many cases served to revel in the memory of an imperial past while looking optimistically to the future. While this Renovar a Mouraria walking tour strays from the pavilions and manicured exhibitions of world expositions past, emphasizing instead engagement with in situ displays, it still reproduces many of the conventions established through the genre. In particular, the organization of contemporary neighborhood life into a coherent tour depends on flattening less-attractive dimensions of lived experience, such as the anxieties born of racial, religious, and ethnic plurality, weaving these less-celebratory realities into a parallel, sanitized narrative for the enjoyment of the spectator.

A total of seven representative figures are featured on the *Mouraria dos povos e das culturas* panel, each attributed distinct corporal and spatial referents to illustrate how they embody a given racial, cultural, or religious point of distinction. At the top of the panel, a brown character plays cricket in the Martim Moniz plaza, a clear reference to games between South Asian immigrants and their descendants that once occurred in that space. Below him stands a woman illustrated with black skin, who wears a bright blue patterned dress and headwrap, referencing Ankara, the wax print fabric that is commonly used to make clothing and accessories in Western and Central African nations. This character's portrayal draws on several cliched markers employed in racially charged caricatures of Black women, including framing the figure as a sexual object by drawing her with unrealistically large red lips and an ample backside. This manner of viewing Black women vis-à-vis their sexuality is again reminiscent of the conventions of World's Fairs and similar exhibitions wherein anxieties regarding unfamiliar peoples and phenotypes were metered through their objectification and display. The figure drawn on this panel brings to mind the life and legacy of Sara Baartman, known as the Hottentot Venus, a Black woman cast as a corporal marvel for the white gaze on European stages both during her life and after her death.[59]

Such exaggerated representations, which communicate and control difference through recourse to stereotypes, are evident in the other racial caricatures that decorate the panel. One such figure is a man drawn with slanted eyes, a pointed nose, and a yellow skin tone, who is shown pushing a dolly stacked with boxes that tower over his small frame. Positioned alongside a sketch of the Centro Comercial Martim Moniz—a well-known hub for Asian businesses—this portrayal reinforces the character's role as a representative "Asian" in the display, making use of stereotypes and simplistic visual cues for the benefit of the observer. In another quadrant of the scene, a matronly figure with brown skin and a headscarf is drawn holding a child by the hand as they walk in the direction of a Halal butchery. In the foreground of the panel, a character wearing a turban is situated below the Mesquita Baitul Mukarram, a neighborhood mosque. The deliberate placement of these two characters organizes perceptions of Mouraria's built environment in terms of religious and cultural identities, serving the overall objective of the tour to translate the complexities of daily life in the area into a more digestible experience for visitors. Overall, the scene—which depicts representative figures, their actions, and their surroundings—cultivates essentialist archetypes that distill the district's social and material landscape into a reductive yet ostensibly marketable object.

One of the most provocative inclusions in this panel is the figure dressed in a *traje à vianesa*, a folkloric costume from northern Portugal recognizable for its embroidered red headscarf and dress. This caricature represents the *lavradeira*, a character that personifies the history of the laboring classes in the country's Alto Minho region.[60] In the scene, she appears adjacent to a building labeled Os Amigos do Minho (Friends of Minho), a community organization associated with the region of Portugal in its moniker. This site is a significant reference, as it is where one is most likely to actually encounter such a figure in Mouraria. In fact, the *vianesa* outfit is a costume traditionally donned for special occasions, not quotidian activities. In this respect, the *lavradeira* differs from the other characters on the panel as her iconography exemplifies a more conventional exercise in cultural heritage, where the malleable treatment of emblems of the past—in this case, the history of Northern Portugal and its laboring classes—produces valuable cultural objects in the present. In contrast, the other figures on the panel are depicted engaging in quotidian activities: going to the store, working, attending places of worship, and participating in leisure activities. It is in these incongruencies where enduring attachments to racial and national narratives are most palpable. The *lavradeira* stands alongside figures that are "costumed" in ways that reference physical, material, and even embodied departures from an autochthonous neutral category. Yet the Ankara fabric, racialized features, and references to spaces of leisure, commerce, and worship that distinguish them are not costumes at all. This form of representation is an affective queue, its implications residing in the silences and the spaces between representations. It is especially discernable in visual contrasts: the multicutural display versus the pink-skinned characters that decorate a visit to the neighborhood emphasizing "tradition," or the costumed *lavradeira* who, without her garb, and within the broader visual narrative of the brochure, would be an unmarked object in a scene of curiosities.

In sum, the tours offered by the Renovar a Mouraria association are emblematic of prevailing and sometimes contradictory forms through which the district was cast by local stakeholders as a live display for visitors and other potential consumers. This specific endeavor was explicitly aimed at a visiting public, guided by the optimistic position that cultivating consumption within the bounds of the district would improve the welfare of its inhabitants. The willful production of the neighborhood's exchange-value in terms of its history and populace is further proof of an investment during this period in what Berlant aptly describes as "good life" fantasies.[61] Even more, the narratives told about Mouraria and its populace through this type of text reveal ongoing assumptions regarding the prevailing orders—cultural, racial, and so forth—that shaped notions of tradition and novelty as the neighborhood evolved. In the case of *Visita a Mouraria*, it is also evident that the promotion and branding of the district was not dictated exclusively by a single public or private entity. Instead, local stakeholders—like the neighborhood association—were also leading the charge, their efforts facilitated by the fact that their vision, at the time, aligned with both public and private interests. As a point of comparison, let us next consider how similar dynamics were visible in the promotion of Lavapiés through a different genre of attraction: Tapapiés.

Food and Fun: Tapapiés

The Tapapiés food festival was a two-week long event spearheaded by the Lavapiés business association in 2011 with support from Madrid's city council. Its inaugural tagline, "Having tapas around the world without leaving Lavapiés" sums up its vision: to promote the district as a conduit to metered engagement with racial, national, and ethnic diversity.[62] Under the auspices of Tapapiés, bars and restaurants throughout the Madrilenian neighborhood were encouraged to display different culinary traditions through a special *tapa* offered to attendees. In its first year, thirty-one different establishments participated in the event, their dishes and respective points of origin outlined in a guide for those exploring the route. Accordingly, visitors were invited to sample snacks like the "fusion pincho" from Bar Fantástico, a *tapa* attributed to India and Thailand, and long-standing establishment Portomarín's *zamburiña a la gallega*, a shellfish stuffed with onion, garlic, pepper, and cured ham. Attendees were also encouraged to rate and review the different dishes, with three establishments later recognized through this public vote for having offered the most popular *tapa* during the event.[63] Through display and consumption, the neighborhood's complex demographic landscape was reduced for the purposes of the event to an array of culinary tokens, the grand part of which are explicitly designed as noteworthy in an appeal to prospective consumers' appetites. As a testament to the success of this type of initiative, born of synergy between local businesses, the municipal government, and corporate sponsors, Tapapiés grew steadily since its inaugural year. By 2019, it had evolved into a widely attended immersive festival with one hundred and thirty participating bars and restaurants offering a special *tapa* and *botellín* of Estrella Damm (an official cosponsor since 2012). Additionally, the range of cultural forms on display expanded in tandem with the success of the initiative, with visitors invited to attend one of sixty free concerts held during the two weekends of the 2019 festival period.

The name of the event provides a first look into the assumptions and aspirations revealed in the process of wielding Lavapiés's diverse social and spatial characteristics as components of a consumer-oriented brand. Tapapiés is a punny play on Lavapiés, with the morpheme *piés*, *feet*, preceded by the new focal point of the event, *tapas*, which consequently one usually eats while standing up. *Tapas* also serve as a symbol of national identity—less as a specific dish and more as a widely recognized dining format considered emblematic to Spanish culture, both on the peninsula and abroad. This framing of the festival brings to mind Ahmed's assertion that diversity "becomes happy" based on its proximity to national ideals.[64] According to Ahmed, this process is not necessarily achieved through integration or assimilation, but rather a demonstrated affinity for or connection to markers of national identity. In Tapapiés, establishments across culinary traditions do not simply reproduce or assimilate to Spanish culinary traditions, but rather showcase themselves through the familiar format of a small snack and drink. The *tapa*, due to its symbolic weight, functions as a neutral form from which difference emerges. By showcasing the unfamiliar within a nationally celebrated framework, the festival attributes positive value to what diverges from the perceived norm.

However, the cultivation of these positive attachments relies on the sustained presence of the national archetype, reinforcing the hierarchies inherent in such notions of the nation.

Much like in *Visita a Mouraria*, the Tapapiés festival builds on the neighborhood's tangible and conceptual attributes (space, demographics, reputation, and so forth) in a manner enticing to a visiting public, making difference palatable in its most literal sense. Akin to the Mouraria walking tours, this type of event establishes a discrete framework for engaging with Lavapiés according to a themed lens, a point of entry that serves to organize the district's complex past and present—both real and imagined—into a digestible leisure experience. The representative images, texts, and language that are repeated under the auspices of this lens help shape a recognizable brand that, as argued prior, is charged with affective attachments. The core elements of the brand, and their affective implications, are most legible in material objects produced specifically for the event, like the Tapapiés festival guide, which serves as a compass and directory for attendees, outlining how one should see—and consume—the district.

By 2019 the Tapapiés guide had grown to an expansive sixty-four-page pamphlet including an index of dishes available on the route, a map of the area, and an event calendar. The introduction, set adjacent to a full page spread advertising Estrella Damm, introduces the area as a fantasized precinct replete with unexploited sources of consumption and pleasure. In it, Lavapiés speaks as a sentient character, "Welcome to the magical neighborhood of Lavapiés, I am a melting pot of endless daring tapas, waiting for your big bite," an invitation that situates the district as a site to conquer and consume.[65] This initial framing aligns the visit with colonial paradigms, wherein engagement is a conduit to extraction, an area's resources ingested by newcomers due to their novelty and utility. The text goes on to exalt the "incredible *tapamundi*" available during the festival, with offerings "from Pekin to Quito, Jaén to Bombay, from Rome to Conchabamba [*sic*]" shifting from exploration and extraction to the rhetoric reminiscent of a world's fair, a system of engagement born from and perpetuating colonial power structures, underscoring the continued exoticization of cultural difference. The expressions of power implicit in these statements are amplified by the taxonomic display of the dishes that follow. Each page in the following section of the guide presents images and descriptions of participating restaurant's *tapas* alongside their geographic points of origin, positioning the pamphlet as a type of field guide for the neighborhood. In this regard, the colonial undertones are even clearer: much like a catalogue of curiosities, the pamphlet operates within a framework reminiscent of what Edward Said terms a Western discourse of the Other, a process of production, collection, and classification of knowledge that reinforces hierarchies of power and knowledge rooted in the logic of European imperial expansion.[66]

The map of the district that is included in the guide likewise directs the visitor's approximation to the physical terrain of Lavapiés in terms of its utility as a space to consume Otherness, organizing perceptions of and interactions with the neighborhood according to icons and the cartographic projection itself. For example, Lavapiés's metro station is positioned on the map as the neighborhood's center, truncating the district in terms of its primary commercial arteries. Framing Lavapiés in this manner also incorporates three neighboring metro stations into the map's display, indicating the facility with which one may travel to—and subsequently depart from—this space. This emphasis on transportation to and from Lavapiés is further demonstrated through icons that identify parking and lodging in the district, another convention of tourist maps that are employed to orient outsiders' perceptions of a given attraction. Finally, numbered circles with red arrows point to the location of each *tapa* available on the route, the majority of which line Calle Argumosa, Calle Lavapiés, and Calle Ave María, thoroughfares originating in the Plaza de Lavapiés that extend through the neighborhood. These numbers correspond with the pamphlet's taxonomic presentation of dishes, providing spatial coordinates for each cultural display. In turn, the visitor is prompted to perceive and engage with these discrete spaces in terms of their exhibition in the brochure.

As Said argues, Western narratives about the Other take shape through scholarly (that is, formal) and imaginary (that is, anecdotal) pursuits that are supported by "institutions, vocabulary, scholarship, imagery, doctrines, even colonial bureaucracies and colonial styles."[67] Decolonial scholar Linda Tuhiwai Smith builds on these ideas, critiquing research as a "site of struggle between the interests and ways of knowing of the West and the interests and ways of resisting of the Other," and highlighting how this pursuit of knowledge is intertwined with "informal, imaginative, anecdotal constructions of the Other."[68] Consequently, even purportedly objective accounts such as field guides and other means of documentation like maps are influenced by the authority implicit to the act of organizing the unknown. Tapapiés adds an additional dimension to this exchange: that businesses themselves are those who decide which *tapa* to put on display to the visiting public. The organizing authority that guides the display of Lavapiés in this brochure, therefore, is not an institution or individual, but rather a product of the push and pull of consumer tastes.

FIGURE 1.3. Map of Lavapiés included in Tapapiés guide distributed by the Asociación de Comerciantes de Lavapiés, 2019

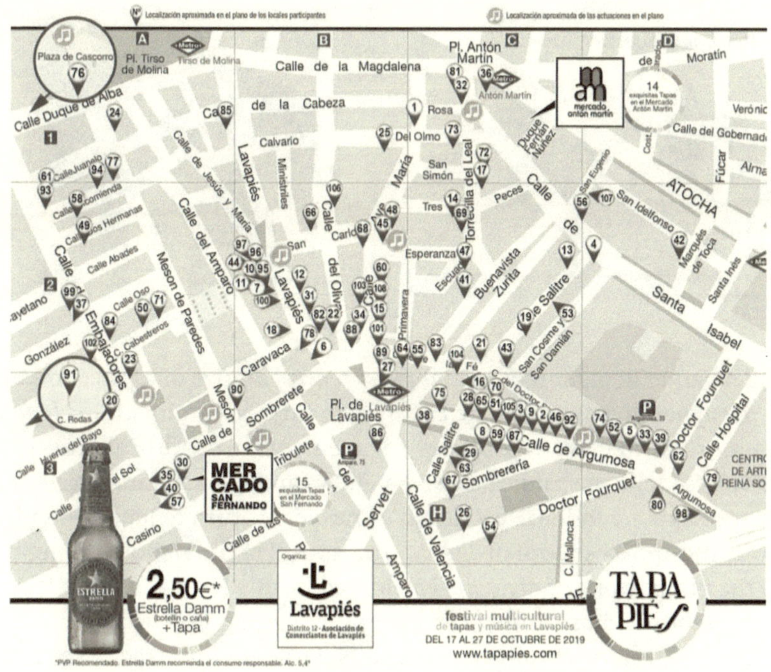

This dynamic is even more evident when one examines how many of the *tapas* are unusual or even illogical dishes designed in an explicit appeal to potential visitors. The *tapas* compiled in the guide, advertised with images furnished by each establishment, are explicitly presented as representations of diverse regions and cultures in miniature, an effort that results in options ranging from the peculiar to the comically contrived. Arapona Indian Restaurant, for example, advertises the *mix roubao*, a snack of phyllo dough and chicken, and attributed to Japan. At the vegan restaurant La Encomienda, one may sample the "Bocado andino," a mix of tofu, quinoa, and chipotle vaguely credited to "South America," rather than a specific country. Each of these *tapas* is a decontextualized nod to both real and imagined culinary traditions that contribute to a broader narrative of multiculturalism to define Lavapiés and its inhabitants. The components of the dishes on display recall Zilkia Janer's assertion that reducing so-called "ethnic" cuisines to sources of ingredients strips them of their historical and political weight.[69]

FIGURE 1.4. Special tapas featured in Tapapiés guide distributed by the Asociación de Comerciantes de Lavapiés, 2019

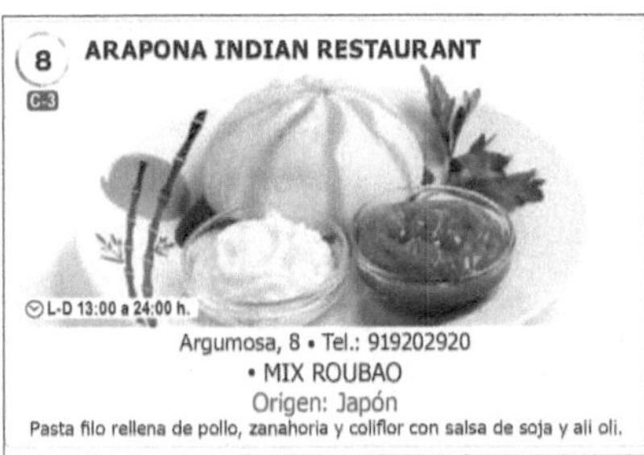

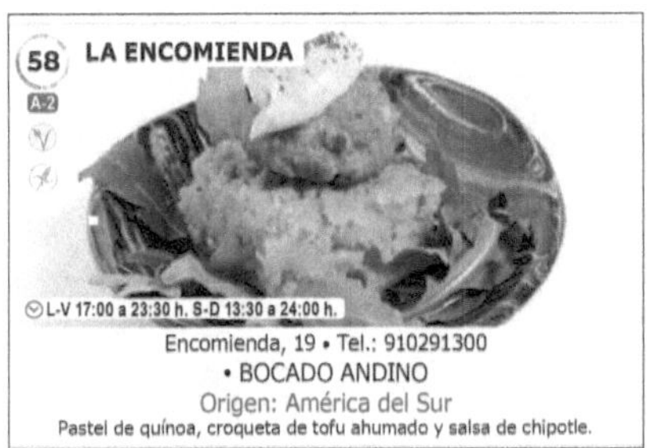

The deliberate depiction of each *tapa* as representative of a place in miniature, designed to entice and be consumed, further demonstrates how the framework of this event prompts engagement with cultural plurality in terms of its exchange-value. La Encomienda's ambiguous "South American" dish and Arapona Indian Restaurant's unexpected turn to Japanese cuisine provide the appearance of diversity in an appeal to the visitor, highlighting how the dimensions of diversity celebrated by this festival are consciously designed for purchase, rather than simply emerging from existing marketable qualities. Here, and in later chapters, I refer to this practice as manufactured multiculturalism, a process in which interest groups capitalize on utopian invocations of cultural plurality that lack historicity and continuity. To this point, I do not deny that existing cultural attributes are wielded as components of the broader multicultural brand, a process evident in each of this chapter's case studies. Rather, I aim to highlight the ways that this management of culture as a resource prompts the dissemination of narratives that frequently depart from social and demographic realities both past and present.[70]

Overall, Tapapíes illustrates how Lavapiés is promoted as a commercially productive space vis-à-vis the extraction of purportedly exotic cultural attributes as resources and their subsequent metered exhibition. This specific manner of promoting the neighborhood, which gained momentum in the years following the financial crisis, recast ongoing anxieties about demographic change as the pillars of a multicultural brand. Undertakings like this festival found success precisely because they appealed to the tastes of consumers in search of seemingly authentic experiences, like the anti-tourists looking to immerse themselves in a given district's purported realities "without all of the hassle," to quote the Airbnb host from the start of this chapter. "Authenticity" is, crucially, a malleable and ideologically charged term, the use of which evokes Zukin's argument that "a city is authentic if it can create the *experience* of origins."[71] These discursive tendencies are not unique to a given genre, medium, authorship, or even national context (though they may shift according to each category). To make matters more complex, they are mobilized in the service of a range of narratives, each of which is charged with different affective implications. This is evident, for example, in the four walking tours offered by Renovar a Mouraria, which offered a variety of lenses with which to view the neighborhood, imbricated with assumptions and aspirations regarding the past and present of the district.

As argued at the start of this chapter, the consumer-oriented branding of Lavapiés and Mouraria that gained traction during this period engaged with specific histories, populations, and even spatial forms to the extent to which they contributed to a marketable aesthetic. While this cultivated attractive opportunities that drew visitors and investors to each of these spaces, more often than not these processes turned their back on the much thornier experience of populations from which these aestheticized reputations were derived. This was an intersectional matter, with residents across multiple and overlapping social categories of race, class, citizenship, gender, and age navigating such challenges as surveillance, racially motivated violence, precarious housing, and insufficient social services.[72] Take, as an acute example of these obstacles, the death of Mame Mbaye Ndiaye on March 15, 2018. The Senegalese immigrant to Spain died in front of his apartment in Lavapiés after fleeing a police raid on unauthorized street vendors. According to official reports, Mbaye Ndiaye was found by police outside of his building on Calle del Oso, having suffered a heart attack stemming from an existing cardiac condition.[73] Other eyewitness accounts contradicted this narrative, claiming that he had been chased by the police from the nearby Plaza del Sol, repeating "No puedo más" (I can't take anymore) until he collapsed in front of his home. Public outcry surrounding Mbaye Ndiaye's death was swift, giving way to a prolonged period of public protest throughout the neighborhood. Activists involved in the debates surrounding this event claimed that the more appropriate culprit was institutional racism, denouncing the structures and systems that had facilitated his passing like Spain's *Ley de Extranjería*, which obstructs access to regular medical care for undocumented individuals.[74]

This chapter's case studies connect to this anecdote in the sense that disenfranchised figures like Mbaye Ndiaye, a Black man from Sub-Saharan Africa, did not entirely disappear from the narratives promoting districts like Lavapiés and Mouraria. Rather, their Otherness—racial, cultural, and so on—was extracted and repurposed in the branding of these spaces through the dissemination of flattened forms: a quippy line in an advertisement, a colorfully dressed figure decorating a tourism pamphlet, or even a small snack accompanied by an inexpensive beer. As Mbaye Ndiaye's story indicates, those lending the neighborhoods the flair integral to their marking, conversely, lacked equal protections as residents. These populations are the casualties of the brand, more productive as an idea and image than as flesh and blood. In this next chapter, I consider how these brands take shape in the built environment itself, a further indication of the relationship between affective practices and the production of space in Lavapiés and Mouraria in the post-crisis era.

CHAPTER 2

Taking Shape

In 2019, just months after Tapapíes, a polemic arose regarding the evictions of a group of families residing on Lavapiés's Calle Argumosa, 11. While a resident subject to removal stated that her rent had risen in the course of a year from four hundred to fifteen hundred euros, the proprietors of the building categorically denied her claim and additional assertions on the part of the building's renters that the evictions were being carried out in order to turn the units into tourist apartments.[1] These fears were not unprecedented. Between 2010 and 2017, average rental prices in Madrid's central district had risen almost twenty percent, making access to affordable housing increasingly complicated, while the number of short-term vacation units on the market skyrocketed.[2] Meanwhile, residents watched as their demand for accessible housing was frequently undercut by the rapidly expanding leisure sector. In one instance, an empty municipal lot-turned-community space known as Solarpiés was shuttered, acquired by the private company Nadego S.L., and redeveloped as a low-cost Ibis hotel.[3] During this same period, similar conflicts were also mounting in Mouraria. One study published by the parish boards of Misericórdia, Santa Maria Maior, and São Vicente noted that housing prices had increased by 36 percent in the course of a single year, between 2014 and 2015, connecting this jump to the growing number of short-term rentals impacting property values.[4] Just a year later, in 2016, residents of Rua dos Lagares number twenty-five became embroiled in a years-long struggle with the municipal government to stay in their rental contracts after learning that their building had been purchased by the developer IberAquisições for conversion to tourist rentals.[5]

These episodes point to the mounting effects in each neighborhood's social and spatial landscape of the push to brand and promote Lavapiés and Mouraria as sites of investment and leisure. Namely, the urban environment was perceivably shifting in tandem with the evolving values, economic prospects, and social relationships of this post-crisis era. The tangible consequences of these social actions is an express illustration of both the Lefebvrian notion of space as a social product and Harvey's emphasis on the economic and political systems that shape cites.[6] In Chapter 1 of this book, I focused on the discursive trends and their affective implications that gave way to these spatial effects as they emerged across digital, visual, and embodied cultural mediums. This collection of diverse text-types served to emphasize how the built environment grew and was grown through deliberate theming and branding, driven by the interrelated socio-spatial practices of private enterprise, local stakeholders, and public investment. Given that these initiatives prioritized consumer desires, the spaces evolved to their benefit which was often—as these anecdotes indicate—to the detriment of long-term residents.

Now, we return to the branding practices studied prior to discuss how the dominant narratives introduced in Chapter 1 materialized in the built environment. In order to do so, I conceive of each neighborhoods' material spaces—plazas, buildings, streets, and monuments—as cultural texts themselves, the construction and design of which reveal evolving power and societal structures. Unlike the narrative tropes reviewed in examples like *Vista a Mouraria* and Tapapiés, each a type of lens for viewing the neighborhood that required a bit of imagination on part of the visitor, the shaping of urban terrain that the present chapter deliberates is quite literal. As a case study, I focus on the rise and fall of Mouraria's Mercado de Fusão (Fusion Market), a public plaza reimagined in 2012 as an amalgamation of food stalls purported to represent the district's ethnic diversity. The market, I argue, was the spatial manifestation of the multicultural narrative first introduced in Chapter 1, one of the prevailing themes in the branding and promotion of the neighborhood. First, I discuss the historical trajectory and cultural significance of this plaza as a site of intervention prior to its redevelopment as a fusion market. Keeping this context in consideration, I then turn to the space-once-reimagined as the Mercado de Fusão, and the ways that this curated intervention gave form, narrative, and place to a utopist multicultural discourse.

My study of this market-display hinges on the concept of manufactured multiculturalism, a discursive strategy with spatial repercussions where interest groups capitalize on an opportunistic engagement with (and construction of) racial and ethnic diversity that departs from established narratives of national exceptionalism like, in this case, *Lusotropicalism* and its contemporary reinvention *Lusofonia*, a postcolonial narrative of cultural bonds forged through linguistic connections.[7] Although the feelings regarding past and ongoing relationships between the colonized and the colonizer in discourses of *Lusotropicalism* and *Lusofonia* may be read as cultivated, obscuring, as Silva argues "how whiteness is built and claimed through imperial extraction, exploitation, expropriation, and genocide," the historic ties are not fabricated.[8] While these narratives are problematic in the way that they reposition Portugal's ongoing entanglements with its former overseas colonies as a type of benign relationship rather than the product of imperial violence, they are concretely situated in the nation's history of maritime expansion through conquest. In difference, I argue in this chapter, is that the manufactured multiculturalism on display in the Mercado de Fusão was a hyperrealistic "real without origin," in the sense that it that did not just reconstruct memories of the Portuguese colonial project but also drew from new, ahistorical relationships born of by market interests that situate the Portuguese within an aspirational vision of globalized modernity.[9]

My analysis of the Mercado de Fusão finds a counterpoint in Lavapiés's Mercado de San Fernando, the subject of Chapter 4. There, I will explore the structural and ideological limits of a project purported as an alternative to dominant trends in urban rehabilitation. Before arriving to this case, however, we must first establish a working understanding of the prevailing modes of development prompting such contestatory spatial practices, beginning with the example from Lisbon. Moreover, I juxtapose these cases from the two neighborhoods to further underline both the continuities and differences in the affective negotiation of these cities' futures during the post-crisis era. This approach is inspired by Berlant's argument regarding the "situation of contemporary life." They write,

> At times I use terms like "neoliberal" or "transnational" as heuristics for pointing to a set of delocalized processes that have played a huge role in transforming postwar political and economic norms of reciprocity and meritocracy since the 1960s. But I am not claiming that they constitute a world-homogenizing system whose forces are played out to the same effect, or affect, everywhere. The differences matter, as do the continuities. My method is to read patterns of adjustment in specific aesthetic and social contexts to derive what's collective about specific modes of sensual activity toward and beyond survival.[10]

While the development of both Lisbon's Mercado de Fusão and Madrid's Mercado de San Fernando are certainly informed by local and national particularities, their points in common illustrate remarkable trends in how the built environment in historically marginalized, racially diverse districts evolved and was shaped by similar affective expressions during this period. Having established these parallels, we may shift focus to the intentional theming and design of the Praça do Martim Moniz in Mouraria.

Setting the Scene

Lisbon's Tourist Board advertises the Eléctrico 28, a trolley that passes by many of Lisbon's famous landmarks, as one of the city's must-do tourist attractions. For a relatively small price passengers can take in the steep hills of Graça, the winding streets of Alfama, the bustling Praça do Comércio, and Chiado, a popular shopping and nightlife district. The tram's terminus, facing the Praça Martim Moniz, is at the edge of Mouraria. Travelers often pass through the long concrete plaza from either side—strolling northeast from Rossio and the Baixa shopping district or emerging from the subterranean Martim Moniz metro stop. In July, Lisbon's hottest month, one finds little refuge from the scorching sun while crossing the plaza from Rua da Palma toward the Rua da Senhora da Saúde to wait for a trip on the Eléctrico 28.

On a summer evening in 2015, Praça do Martim Moniz was bustling with tourists and locals alike. A few paused in the northern half of the plaza—the Mercado de Fusão—for a coffee or a small bite to eat. Terraces were busy as the sun set, populated by families and friends meeting for a drink. Some sported bright red sunburns from their days of sightseeing. Children played, running across artificial grass that had been laid out between kiosks and through the fountains that formed a cross from the south of the square to the metro stop to the north. In the southern half of the plaza, away from the market, others sat on public benches and under little bits of shade in limited green space.

My visit to Martim Moniz marked around three years since the debut of the Mercado de Fusão, an initiative to reimagine the use of this broad expanse of public space that had emerged under the jurisdiction of the city council's AiMouraria program. Years earlier, local production company NCS Produções had been awarded a contract from the municipal government to reimagine the space, a move widely acknowledged as a municipal endeavor to privatize a public space.[11] Accordingly, the group would manage two-thirds

FIGURE 2.1. View of Martim Moniz Plaza from vantage point of the Mercado de Fusão, 2015

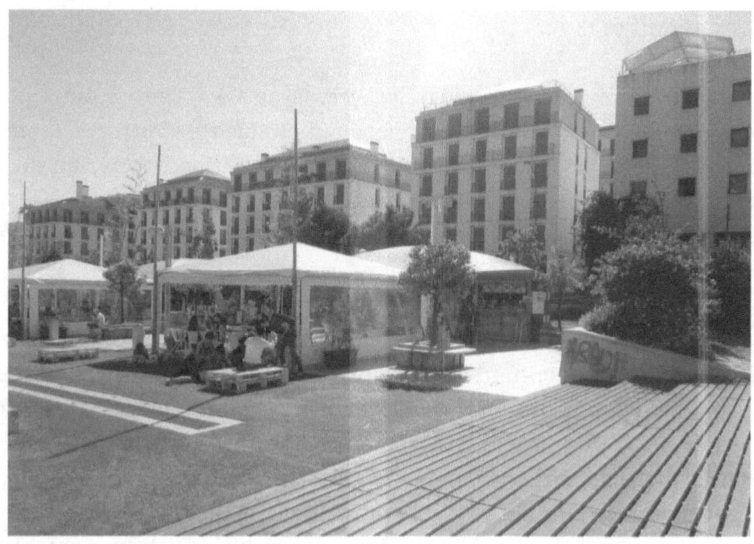

of the public square for a period of sixteen years, taking on responsibilities including sanitation services, maintenance, security, programming and a 5,000-euro monthly rent.[12] The company, led by José Filipe Rebelo Pinto, set out to reimagine the space as the Mercado de Fusão, made up of ten "multicultural" food and drink kiosks, a three-hundred-seat terrace, and a weekend market offering goods from neighborhoods including Bairro Alto, Baixa, and Mouraria.[13] In addition to this offering, the group planned to schedule frequent programming including concerts, film screenings, and festivals to compliment the multicultural theming of the space. On the eve of the Mercado de Fusão's debut in 2012, Rebelo Pinto shared his hope that the newly renovated area would "bring new blood to the plaza" while also emphasizing that new rendition of Martim Moniz had been created with Mouraria in mind, not with its back to the neighborhood.[14] While this positioning indicated that the project would be a community facing initiative, the realities of its production and the limits of its use would prove otherwise.

The Mercado de Fusão was the latest initiative in a much longer trajectory of urban interventions to shape both the Praça do Martim Moniz's physical landscape and its perception in the public imaginary. The space itself may be envisaged as a type of *terrain vague*, first forged under the Estado Novo during the twentieth century when the regime raised a broad expanse of the neighborhood's lower district, the Baixa da Mouraria, under the guise of the prevailing hygiene discourse of the time.[15] Catalán architect Ignasi de Solà-Morales describes *terrain vague* as

> internal to the city yet external to its everyday use. . . . These strange places exist outside the city's effective circuits and productive structures. From the economic point of view, industrial areas, railway stations, ports, unsafe residential neighborhoods, and contaminated places are where the city is no longer. Unincorporated margins, interior islands void of activity, oversights, these are simply *un-inhabited*, *un-safe*, *un-productive*.[16]

As Solà-Morales's definition stresses, *terrain vague* exists on the margin (either spatial or conceptual) of a city because of its lack of social and economic productivity. To this end, industrial districts, and contaminated places, largely devoid of human life, are frequently grouped together with unsafe residential districts, which are in fact inhabited, because they both exist outside of acceptable "productive structures"—that is, the social and economic systems—that give the city its desired form. Frequently, such spaces are reappropriated by the populations who live (conceptually, and sometimes literally) on the margins of urban landscapes, a tendency that will be illustrated in later stages of Martim Moniz's evolution. Provocatively, in the case of the Praça do Martim Moniz, the government had a hand in creating this *terrain vague* in their ideologically driven attempts to control the Mouraria district and its inhabitants through urban redesign.

After its demolition, the paved-over area of the Baixa da Mouraria would be used as a parking lot until it was finally earmarked for rehabilitation during the Estado Novo's final years, now seen as a blemish on Lisbon's broader urban landscape. Despite increased attention to and resources directed at reshaping what was known as the Largo do Martim Moniz, its unexploited potential increasingly evident in an otherwise-bustling city center, it was not until 1982, following the nation's transition to democracy, that any plans came to fruition. At this moment, the Empresa Pública de Urbanização de Lisboa (EPUL, Public Urbanization Company of Lisbon), an auxiliary service to Lisbon's municipal government, led the charge.[17] In a public contest, the group selected the *Plano de Renovação Urbana do Martim Moniz* (Martim Moniz Urban Renovation Plan), designed by Carlos Duarte and José Lamas, an ambitious effort to transform the vacant lot through updates to its infrastructure and the construction of commercial, cultural, and residential spaces.[18] While the group did manage to bring a few of their proposed changes to fruition, including erecting two malls, the Centro Comercial da Mouraria and Centro Comercial do Martim Moniz, the brunt of these plans were never completed. The unfinished Largo do Martim Moniz would remain widely considered an eyesore, with Lisboners describing the new malls as *mamarracho*, a term wielded to describe poorly formed, exceedingly large, and aesthetically unappealing buildings.[19]

Despite the stalled initiative, the area surrounding Martim Moniz, including the malls constructed under the auspices of Duarte's and Lamas's plan, evolved during these years into a hub for wholesale commerce largely operated by proprietors hailing from regions of Africa, South Asia, Brazil, and China.[20] These businesses attracted a wide range of clients—newly arrived to Portugal and long-term residents alike—fostering the neighborhood's budding reputation as a cultural melting pot.[21] Meanwhile, the lot became a center of unsanctioned activity involving marginalized groups including sex workers, drug dealers, and the unhoused. For these populations, the space held value despite its perceived lack of productivity within the accepted norms of public space use. These informal spatial practices would continue as the government's plans for intervention remained stagnant for more than a decade.

In 1997, eyes fell once again to Mouraria's unexploited exchange-value as the city prepared for Expo '98. In this climate, the redevelopment of the vacant lot followed the dominant urban design strategies of the time, aimed at attracting international capital through tourism and investment. This developmental upswing aligned with the spirit of the World's Fair, which sought to portray the Portuguese as "sophisticated brokers of transnational cultural flows" drawing on their history as an ultramarine empire.[22] That year, the Largo do Martim Moniz was converted into a demarcated plaza with a subterranean parking garage, providing new infrastructure for the influx of international visitors who were to descend on the capital during the mega-event. These renovations also set a precedent for expressing the space's utility in terms of its relationship to cultural heritage. This was evident in such features of the newly designed space as the fountain set on the southernmost portion of the plaza, composed of a stylized fortress wall decorated with helmets and grate in the shape of a crossbow, giving spatial form to the foundational myth of Martim Moniz. In another more explicit appeal to the city's expected visitors, the Câmara Municipal added forty-four steel kiosks to the central portion of the plaza in the months leading up to the Expo, which would house vendors specializing in regional articles, antiques, and artisanal goods.

While the interventions enacted during this period aimed to integrate the plaza into the city's tourist and leisure infrastructure, the kiosks were unsuccessful in drawing significant consumer traffic to the stigmatized district, and gradually shuttered in the years following the event. This failure was due in large part to the continued presence of marginalized groups that had staked a claim to the space in years prior, whose ongoing use of the area was met with discomfort and conflict, hindering the plaza's intended function as envisioned by the government. In turn, the northern portion of Martim Moniz grew to become the hub of a thriving clandestine market where groups of African and Indian immigrants commonly referred to as "cell phone gangs" sold low cost international phone calls to tourists and locals alike.[23] In an attempt to suppress such activities, the Câmara Municipal installed a video surveillance system run by Prosegur-Security Systems and erected a checkpoint in one of the vacant World's Fair kiosks.[24] Meanwhile, public discourse increasingly turned to the unsanctioned use of this space by different immigrant groups, stoking anxieties regarding these populations and positioning them as a mounting threat to the well-being of autochthonous Lisboners. Ahmed describes such a process as the way in which certain objects become "sticky," taking on affective meaning through narrative patterns.[25] In this case, the associations between immigration and danger, racialized bodies and crime—reinforced through public discourse—would have social and spatial consequences.

Consider, for instance, the media coverage of Operação Caril (Operation Curry), a covert operation in which police detained fourteen individuals involved in an underground cell phone market operating in the plaza. The name itself, chosen by law enforcement, highlights the racialized framing of the operation, as several of the presumed perpetrators were of South Asian descent. In an article published in *Público* titled "Cerco ao Martim Moniz" (Siege on Martim Moniz), journalist Ricardo Dias Felner employs a muddy allusion to the mythical siege of the Castelo São Jorge to describe the arrest of this group of "estrangeiros ilegais" (illegal immigrants), emphasizing the role of legal documentation in one's right to public space. His account frames the situation as an "invasion" of the plaza, inverting the memory of the Siege of Lisbon, in order to cast racialized suspects as a modern-day enemy.[26] In the same piece, Dias Felner cites a statement from the Comissão de Lojistas do Martim Moniz (Martim Moniz Commercial Association) to the Câmara Municipal, in which the group complains of a hostile environment stemming from "um negócio liderado por 'indianos, paquistaneses, asiáticos e africanos,' que se dedicam em exclusivo, 'e com toda a tranquilidade que a indiferença das autoridades competentes lhes permite,' a vender chamadas aos conterrâneos e a turistas" (a business led by 'Indians, Pakistanis, Asians, and Africans,' devoted 'calmly, with the peace that the authorities' indifference permits them,' to selling phone calls to our fellow countrymen and tourists). The complaints launched throughout the article, both in Dias Felner's narrative and in his sources, exhibit an "us" versus "them" attitude colored by the fact that the majority of those involved in the unsanctioned commercial activity, and thus seen as disrupting the peace, were not of Portuguese origin. Although those participating in the clandestine cell phone market operating within the plaza represented only a small fraction of the immigrant population living and working in Mouraria, the framing of this struggle for space in pieces like "Cerco ao Martim Moniz," and in the name of the police operation itself, reinforces negative perceptions of the district's evolving demographic landscape, with racial Otherness at the forefront. Texts of this sort were part of a broader affective process through which the racialized immigrant community and others who diverged from homogeneous notions of Portuguese identity became "sticky objects"—symbols of the fear and apprehension tied to anxieties about invasion on a larger scale, far beyond the commercial activities of the plaza.

After the majority of the kiosks that had opened during the Expo era had shuttered, the Câmara Municipal made a new deal with Mouraria's Asociação Comercial China Town (China Town Commercial Association) to once again reimagine the use of Martim Moniz as a commercial space, this time centered on businesses selling electronics and imitation designer products.[27] The association also proposed rebranding Martim Moniz as a Chinatown, akin to urban centers in the United States and Europe, capitalizing on the large concentration of Chinese businesses in the area, many of which were housed in the Centro Comercial da Mouraria. The move would highlight Mouraria as Lisbon's center of Chinese immigrants and descendants, thousands of whom had worked and resided in the neighborhood since the first major waves of immigration in the late seventies.[28] Yet, the group's plan was rejected on the premise that these additions would contribute to the perception that the area was "controlled" by the Chinese. This rejection, like in examples prior, was rooted in a racially motivated view of immigrants, in this case the Chinese, as a perceived threat to Portuguese society. These anxieties, stoked by media coverage and popular discourse, would continue to influence future decisions—or the lack thereof—regarding the plaza's development. While the Câmara Municipal ultimately allowed the Asociação Comercial China Town to use the kiosks to sell made-in-China merchandise, they were explicitly prohibited from shaping the physical landscape of the space in a way that might cast

Mouraria as inherently Chinese.[29] Within months many of the vendors, struggling to attract a consistent client base, closed up shop.[30] Evidently, changing the type of products on offer was not enough to attract significant interest from outside, and even within, the district. By late 2000, the government transferred most of the plaza's kiosk structures to other parts of the city, and abandoned their attempts at intervention for several more years.

A range of studies detail patterns of use in the Praça do Martim Moniz during this period of deregulation.[31] In a comprehensive ethnography of Mouraria during the early aughts, Menezes describes the plaza as nexus of public life largely divided along racial, ethnic, and gendered lines. Accordingly, she maps out how different groups would congregate in discrete zones of the plaza, including its benches, fountains, and thruways. To support these observations, Menezes highlights three snack bars located in the space and their respective clientele: "Snack-Bar Crioula," frequented primarily by men of African descent, "Fava Rica," the establishment closest to the Baixa shopping district visited by tourists and some Portuguese clients, and "Snack-bar dos chineses," referring to its Chinese proprietors, a bar popular with a more diverse clientele including men and women of African, China, Brazil, Southeastern Asian and Romaní heritage. In addition, she explains how Martim Moniz was increasingly a site of public rallies across the ideological spectrum, particularly those either advocating for or denouncing immigration. While Menezes's study only accounts for plaza life prior to the 2008 crisis, work by scholars including António Guterres, Marta Rodrigues, and Nuno Rodrigues confirm how similar patterns continued beyond the financial collapse. Guterres, for example, describes Martim Moniz as a type of community hub, where the neighborhood's immigrant population would congregate to participate in recreational activities like football, skateboarding, and cricket, and community organizations would hold public events.[32] At the same time, these scholars note that the plaza remained an active site of unsanctioned commercial practices, particularly drug dealing, fomenting ongoing concerns about the appropriate, safe, and legal uses of public space.

Therefore, when the AiMouraria rehabilitation plan was unveiled in 2009, just a year after the financial collapse, Praça do Martim Moniz once again surfaced as a point of interest, giving way to the municipal processes that finally put the space in the hands of NCS Produções. The developmental vision for the plaza, and Mouraria in general, was clearly aligned with broader aspirations to grow the city's tourism and leisure sector given the industry's resilience following the economic crisis. Through a range of symbolic and monetary efforts, the Câmara Municipal set out to "clean up" such *terrain vague* in the city's central areas, with each intervention positioning Lisbon as a booming cultural capital. NCS Produções, in this regard, had proven itself an effective industry partner for the municipal government. The company, founded by José Rebelo Pinto in 2004, had developed a broad portfolio in music and entertainment, organizing concerts and events in the rapidly evolving Cais do Sodré nightlife district, mounting the OUT JAZZ festival in parks across the city, and setting up shop in LX Factory, an abandoned manufacturing complex in Alcântara redesigned in 2008 as a creative hub comprised of art exhibits, restaurants, stores, workshops, and offices.[33]

Overall, Rebelo Pinto's entrepreneurial model fit seamlessly into prevailing efforts to instrumentalize culture as a conduit to shaping the use and form of different urban environments. Reflecting on this moment and his work in Mouraria in an interview with *LOOKmag*, he remarked, "The crisis is excellent for seizing opportunities. When else would I have been able to work on a plaza of this size (Martim Moniz) in a European capital? That wasn't a possibility. The crisis is encouraging young and well-educated young people like lawyers and engineers to open and design a new style of hostels and restaurants for this city, without leaving behind what is authentic."[34] Here, Rebelo Pinto's comments capture an optimistic view of the crisis as not just an obstacle, but a catalyst for innovation. By celebrating the economic—and by the same token, social—downturn as a generator of entrepreneurial opportunities, his narrative aligned with broader neoliberal discourses that valorized adaptability and resilience, a perspective that looks past, or even denies, the uneven impacts of such transformations on vulnerable populations.

In another telling statement regarding his role in the Mercado de Fusão project, Rebelo Pinto noted in this same interview,

> The Martim Moniz Plaza came to be at a time that I was thinking about doing charity work. Keeping in mind that the plaza was abandoned and there were a series of immigrant communities that were being forgotten by our city, I decided that the Mercado de Fusão was my humanitarian project. The idea was to return the Martim Moniz plaza to the city with a project that sought the social reintegration of local communities.[35]

In this case, he frames the conversion of the plaza into a market as a type of humanitarian initiative, casting himself and his company as charitable figures, rather than entrepreneurs. This stance invokes the archetype of the White Savior, a messianic figure whose instinct to "rescue" racialized, disenfranchised populations frequently undermines the autonomy of these same groups. Even if one is to take Rebelo Pinto at his word that his objective was to "return" the plaza to Mouraria, NCS ultimately developed their plan without substantial dialogue with or input from the local community. As a result, the plaza once reimagined was conspicuously aligned with the interests of groups least necessitating humanitarian aid: tourists (from outside of the neighborhood and the city itself) and the spending class. The "forgotten" immigrants to which Rebelo Pinto refers in his statement, in actuality, largely served as features of the theme, rather than beneficiaries. Moreover, Rebelo Pinto's characterization of Martim Moniz as "abandoned" and the surrounding communities as "forgotten" exemplifies the predominant view of both the plaza and surrounding area as a *terrain vague*, despite the many social actors who had long found a use, desirable or not, for the space, and would likely defend this claim.

The tensions that emerge in Rebelo Pinto's commentary on his role in the project are also evident in his interview with the tourism and leisure blog *Lux/Good*, in which he makes explicit the limits of his appreciation for the neighborhood's multiracial landscape that his own project was meant to celebrate. He states,

> That plaza was in bad shape. No one wanted it. Since I am always on the lookout, I took it on. I want to give it back to the Lisboners it belongs to. I want to make this an authentic space. It was painful to watch an old *cinema piolho* become Chinese, the Império . . . Lisbon's theater . . . it doesn't make sense! All of this is ours; it is part of our history, and it needs to be reintegrated in the city.[36]

In these declarations, Rebelo Pinto expresses anxiety regarding the ownership and use of historic buildings in and beyond the Mouraria district, referencing the Cinema Império and the Salão Lisboa, both of which had ceased to operate according to their original functions since well before the turn of the twenty-first century. He laments the repurposing of such spaces by Chinese investors, cultivating the sense of an urban conquest and subsequent loss of traditional modes of life at the behest of racialized invaders. The "our" invoked and defended by Rebelo Pinto is constructed in opposition to this outsider, reinforcing the racial limits to belonging in this vision of Portuguese society. Additionally, these sentiments contribute to the sense that racial plurality begets precarity, a position that Rebelo Pinto will then go on to contradict in his proposed celebration of multiculturalism. The decision to center racial and ethnic difference, a point of anxiety and resistance, might seem contradictory at surface level, but its logic runs deeper than representation.

In practice, Mercado de Fusão project was an opportunity to stake a claim to the expression of racial and ethnic difference in Martim Moniz, mitigating the autonomy of the Other to shape such a space going forward.

As we turn to how Otherness was metered through the production of the Mercado de Fusão, we may first assess its presentation on the NCS Produções website, which announced to potential visitors:

> Sample flavors and breathe in culture in Martim Moniz Plaza. The starting premise is that this is a dynamic space, a point of contact and bridge through gastronomy, art, installations, cinema, expositions, workshops, music, celebrations, and lots of entertainment. The project is oriented around ten kiosks offering cuisines from around the world: we can fill our souls and comfort our spirits with the most tempting delicacies from here and overseas. Colors and scents bring us from China to Argentina, from Japan to Brazil, with an obligatory stop in Africa and Bangladesh. Portuguese snacks also have a special place in this cornucopia of flavors.[37]

This framing of the Mercado de Fusão is emblematic of the tendency highlighted in Chapter 1 for branding and tourism initiatives to draw from the World's Fair model popularized in the nineteenth and early-twentieth centuries, when designated precincts were designed as virtual worlds for visitors to comfortably engage with, and make sense of, racial and cultural Otherness.[38] In the Mercado, however, these displays were not limited to the pavilions and ephemeral events of years past. Rather, the existing landscape of Mouraria was "Imagineered" as an ongoing, live display of metered diversity.[39] Here, I refer to the practice popularized in the production of Disney's theme parks to balance illusion and reality through the creative engineering of goods, services, and spaces such that fantasy feels real. To this end, the Mercado de Fusão development offered a comprehensive sensory experience that celebrated real and imagined features of the district in such a way that forged a marketable display. Moreover, the festive tone employed in the description and presentation of the market encouraged positive feelings regarding this view of Mouraria as an aspirational model of globalized modernity.

Overall, the multicultural fantasy as articulated through the Mercado de Fusão's culinary landscape departed from more established hybridity narratives in the Portuguese context, which tend to organize racial and ethnic plurality through nostalgic recourse to the nation's imperial past (think, for example, of how the Expo '98 was planned as a commemoration of the anniversary of Vasco de Gama's voyage to the Americas). This is not to say that the presentation of cultural contact in interventions like that of NCS are not heavily influenced by the legacy of discourses that position miscegenation as integral to a distinct Portuguese character. Rather, the way hybridity was articulated in the market embodied a contemporary extension of this framework that coped with transnational migrations beyond Portugal's direct colonial network by celebrating Mouraria, and the plaza more specifically, as a hub for intercultural exchange, with little fidelity to historical context.

Likewise, while Mouraria's diverse populace provided a clear jumping off point for the Imagineering of the Mercado de Fusão, the multiculturalism manufactured for display ultimately pointed to NCS Produções' much more ambivalent commitment to engaging with the district's demographic realities. Rebelo Pinto's own reflections on his broader aspirations for the plaza and the neighborhood provide additional insight into the gap between the Mercado de Fusão and the district it purported to represent. In one instance, he shared with an interviewer, "I want to transform the plaza into a creative hub. I want to bring chefs, restaurants, hostels, creative offices. . . . I want to bring young, creative people from the world of fashion, design, to open offices in the shopping malls here. . . . I want to bring new blood, groups of young and urban people, from Bairro Alto, Chiado, Cais Sodré."[40] Rebelo Pinto's statements, at face value, seem positive. With his optimistic view of the entrepreneurial spirit as a conduit to positive change, Rebelo Pinto sought to infuse the district with life through cultural capital, and envisioned a ripple effect through which the Mercado de Fusão would catalyze a wave of interventions at the behest of the creative industries. Mouraria, accordingly, would ascend to the level of Lisbon's most desirable and therefore touristed neighborhoods. Yet, the subtext of these statements is much more telling. Rebelo Pinto approaches the space as a blank canvas, ignoring the established populations, autochthonous and immigrant alike, who live and work in Mouraria, in his schemes for a higher use of the plaza. Moreover, his creativity-first vision for the city, a recurring trope in neoliberal urban initiatives, frames aesthetics and leisure as a type of social welfare. Consequently, the tastes and cultural practices of archetypes including "new blood," "young, creative people," and "urban people" guide the production of the Mercado de Fusão, rather than Mouraria's systemically underserved populations who purportedly inspired the intervention. As urban scholars point out, this strategic entanglement with the creative industries as an avenue for rehabilitation frequently evolves to the detriment of those who reside in increasingly attractive locales, unable to keep up with the rising costs that accompany consumer development and the pressures of speculative capital.[41] Zukin, in this regard, attributes the exodus that often accompanies the creative production of neighborhoods, where cultural forms are generated as commodities, to a lack of protections for "the small scale, the poor, and the middle class—to remain in place"[42]

With Rebelo Pinto's audience in mind, consider the selection process for the ten food kiosks included in the development. NCS evaluated proposals based on three primary criteria: if they believed the project to be "unique," if the concept was aesthetically appealing, and if the country was not yet represented in the market, a final standard that recalls the logic of the decision years prior to reject a local association's proposal to convert Martim Moniz into a type of Chinatown on the grounds that it would "alienate" other populations.[43] Once chosen by the company, establishments were awarded year-long contracts at a rate of 1500 euros per month to rent their kiosk.[44] By restricting the type of cuisines included in the space, the company exercised its power as a private entity to control the perception, organization, and presentation of cultural plurality in this once-public area.

From the market's debut, the rented kiosks experienced frequent turnover. One of the first groups of food stalls described on the NCS Produções website included Fusion by Viriato Pã ("Fusion food and cocktails, a true mélange of world flavors"), A Preta ("A tropical kiosk with whiffs of Africa"), Kebab Ali House ("Ali's famous samosas are irresistible"), BBQMM ("strange flavors in Lisbon like shellfish Korean pancakes"), BBTMX ("Asia in Martim Moniz!"), Botequim do Moniz ("Inspired by Rio de Janeiro's beach kiosks"), Wasabi ("for lovers of delicacies from the land of the setting sun"), Erva ("Health food"), Xico Experto ("Portuguese snacks"), and El Cartel ("South American flavors . . . be careful, don't come armed!").[45] By and large, the descriptors published by NCS showcase the group's reliance on cultural stereotypes in designing and promoting this space, including couching references to South America in relation to violence and drug trafficking, and emphasizing the "strangeness" of Asian food. Some of their selected kiosks, like Erva, were detached entirely from a geographic point of origin, further signaling the ambivalent relationship between the development and the communities it purported to represent. Evidently, NCS Produções' entrepreneurial vision, and the group's judgement calls regarding which cultures and cuisines were most aesthetically appealing, superseded the party line that the project would "reintegrate" the surrounding community into this plaza. In fact, only one establishment founded by an entrepreneur from the surrounding neighborhood, Kebab Ali House, continued to renew their contract past the first few years the Mercado de Fusão was in operation.[46]

The company's concurrent decision to nickname the plaza "The Dragon Square," and decorate the space accordingly, further highlights their prevailing practice of invoking the neighborhood's racialized populations to the extent that they served as aesthetic objects. For this specific design detail, NCS Produções took advantage of the fact that the market's debut coincided with the year of the dragon according to the Chinese Lunar Calendar. Their explicit commemoration of the Chinese tradition through naming and ornamentation, on the surface, seemed to step away from the Sinophobic anxieties that had influenced the management and policing of the plaza in past decades. At the same time, these feelings were certainly alleviated by the fact that the plan was executed at the behest of a company run by Portuguese nationals who would measure the extent to which Martim Moniz would be articulated as a Chinese space. While Rebelo Pinto, himself, had expressed concerns about the Chinese population staking a claim to historic buildings like the Salão Lisboa, the Chinese *as objects* were useful to the theming of the plaza. In addition to BBTMX, the single Chinese food stand permitted through the company's selection parameters, NCS Produções gave form to the theme by erecting a small booth emblazoned with the plaza's nickname, adding a few Mandarin translations to signage across the market, and unveiling a large dragon sculpture made of spare cell phone and computer parts at the center of the plaza, weaving around a water feature. This handful of cultural signifiers, together, served as décor in a landscape otherwise largely disengaged from Mouraria's Chinese community.

Ruth Meyer, who studies the Chinatowns of the United States and Europe as sites of myth and transnational urbanisms, argues that the reduction of such precincts to this type of stereotypical representation underestimates the "extent of agency and self-determination in the daily lives of Chinese expatriates and migrants."[47] The "Dragon Square" moniker and its accompanying spatial counterparts were precisely the reduction Meyer warns of in action.

A closer look at the dragon installation, which drew on speculative notions of Asia and Asians, further illustrates how the Chinese were cast as aesthetic objects within the parameters of the Mercado de Fusão. This blurring between personhood and objecthood encapsulates what Anne Anlin Cheng terms *ornamentalism*, that is, an "alchemy between things and persons" where one's interiority is not just framed but "*infused* by the built environment."[48] In this piece, the ancient mystique of the dragon as a symbol of

FIGURE 2.2. Dragon sculpture display in the Mercado de Fusão, 2015

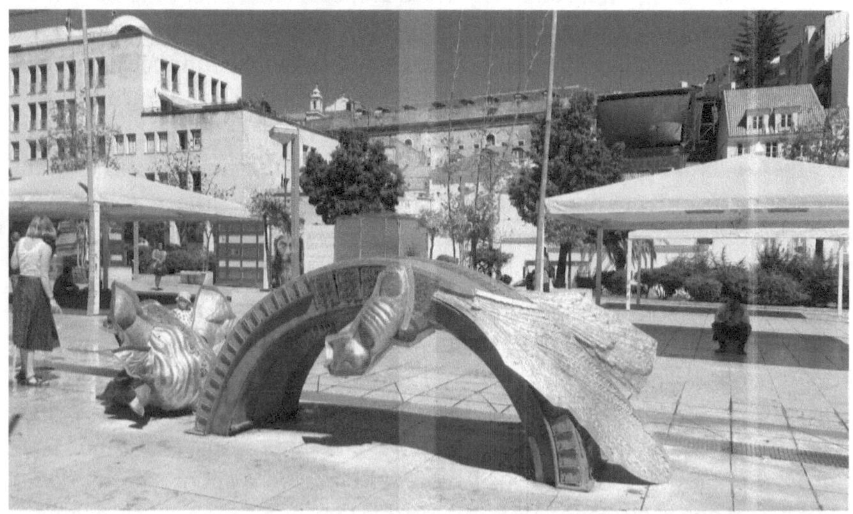

China is collapsed with views of Eastern Asia as a site of technological innovation.[49] This occurs through the statue's material form, which weaves the premodern imagery of the dragon together with modern technology of the cell phone and computer, objects often designed and manufactured in China. Intriguingly, and certainly unbeknownst to most who would come across the Dragon, the structure was erected on the site of strife related to the plaza's former unsanctioned cell phone market. This now-positive depiction, built with some of the same objects that were once a motor for conflict, is another instance in which the optimistic lens of a branding effort is overtly contradicted by the realities of diversity as lived in Mouraria.

As another point of comparison between diversity-as-imagined versus diversity-as-lived, one may juxtapose the display of "Chinese-ness" in the landscape of this plaza with the Chinese restaurants that had popped up in the years prior to the debut of the Mercado de Fusão on Rua do Benformoso, just north of Martim Moniz. There, several immigrant families had started running unlicensed operations on the second floors of residential buildings, known by word of mouth as "home-restaurants" by the Chinese community and "Chinês clandestinos" (Clandestine Chinese) by a growing clientele of locals and tourists.[50] These establishments, at their onset, catered primarily to the Chinese workers in the area, offering non-Westernized dishes to their patrons. As knowledge of the restaurants spread as an open culinary secret, locals and tourists alike flocked to them, attracted by their secretive nature and eager to try regional cuisines offered at locales like Zhiaming Lu, which offered regional dishes and ingredients from the Shandong province of China.[51] The speakeasy format of these establishments, enhanced by Western notions of stereotypes of the Chinese in Portugal as "mysterious" and "closed-off," certainly motivated visitors to make a trip to the so-called "clandestine" restaurants.[52] Yet, once inside, patrons could sample from a menu that did not pander to pan-Asian culinary tropes, a stark difference from the "Noodles-in-a-box" and "Dumplings-in-a-bag" on the menu blocks away in Martim Moniz.

In the years following the remodeled plaza's debut, NCS Produções continued in their efforts to attempt to situate and promote the Mercado de Fusão as a center of creative, globalized modernity through a range of spatial strategies. For example, in 2013, they invited local artist Rui Miragaia to install a large sculpture titled the *Ressureição do Galo* in the northernmost portion of Martim Moniz, a modern take on the Rooster of Barcelos, a Portuguese national symbol and object of seemingly inexhaustible kitschy reproductions including corks, key chains, magnets, and t-shirts.[53] In another instance, the Mercado de Fusão hosted Writer's Delight 2014, an urban art gathering where the public was could watch a selection of graffiti artists from countries including Portugal, Spain, and France as they painted different sectors of Martim Moniz.[54] The sustained effort to promote the Mercado de Fusão, and Martim Moniz more broadly, as a cultural hub was further fomented by complementary free events like Open Air Cinema, a family-friendly film series, and Bollywood Holi, an annual music and dance event in honor of the Hindu festival.[55]

Impressions of the Plaza

I returned to Martim Moniz another summer afternoon in 2015 to take a closer look at how the market was running. The plaza was much emptier than my evening trip, as there was little refuge from the scorching sun at this hour of the day. Even with the reduced crowd, music continued to play over the speakers, a playlist comprised of mostly English-language music including the hip hop duo Outkast and singer-songwriter Barry White. A few patrons were having a snack or drink in the covered seating adjacent to the kiosks. Others eschewed the paid option, but still took advantage of the shade provided by the kiosk's tents, relaxing on the artificial turf adjacent to their patios. Signs in English, Portuguese, Mandarin, and Hindi indicated where patrons

FIGURE 2.3. Rui Miragaia's "Resurreição do Galo" in the Mercado de Fusão, 2015

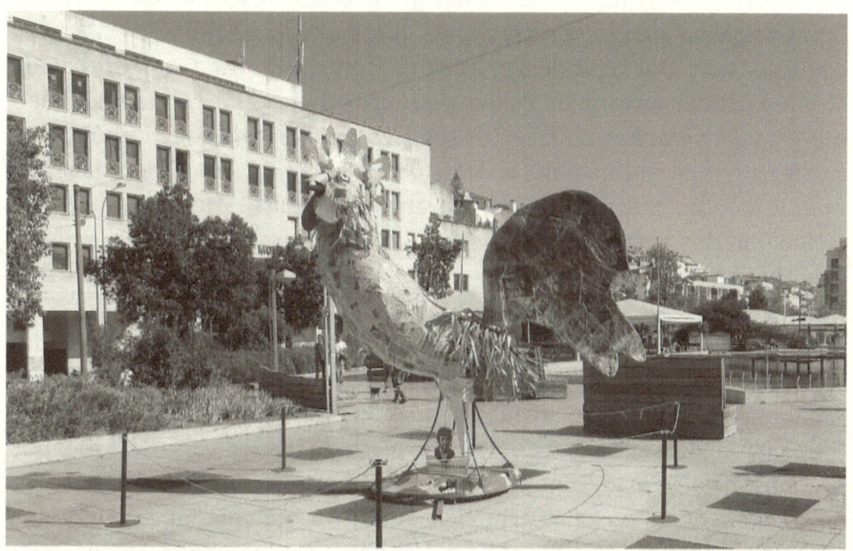

should dispose of their trash. These deracinated invocations of Otherness in the market's visual and sonoric landscape felt clunky in their application, overtly on display rather than blending seamlessly into the surroundings.

A general sense of artifice extended to the kiosk structures, which housed Dog Tails (Hot Dogs and Cocktails), Pizza Fina (Italian), Bolo do Caco (gourmet hamburgers), BBTMX, Wasabi (Sushi), Erva, El Cartel, Moules&Gin (Belgian-style mussels and gin drinks), and the recently opened Markt7 (German cuisine). A beer pong table was set up next to Dog Tails, available to patrons to play the drinking game popularized in the United States. One side read "Ketchup team" and the other "Mustard team." The wall between Moules&Gin and Wasabi featured a larger-than-life image of a woman in a headscarf, presented without context. As a whole, the largely disjointed selection of images and references within the space contributed to a cosmopolitan-seeming attraction. However, the demonstrable lack of a logical through line pointed to the underlying aim of the market: to present multiculturalism in such a way that Martim Moniz would *become useful* to the broader reimagination of Mouraria as a center of globalized modernity.

My conversations with area residents around the time of this visit pointed to an ongoing detachment between the space as manufactured by NCS Produções and Mouraria's community life. Augusto, a local originally from

Salvador da Bahia, explained, "I like how the Martim Moniz plaza is structured. What I don't like is that things in the plaza are expensive. This really influences who goes to Martim Moniz, it became more elitist. It's chic, you could say that. But right nearby Martim Moniz, near the Largo de Martim Moniz and the Mercado de Fusão, there are other options."[56] In this reflection, Augusto emphasizes how the services provided in this once-public leisure space, though appealing in design, were largely inaccessible to low- and middle-income individuals from the surrounding area. He was a long-term resident in this area of the city, having lived for more than eight years in the neighboring Intendente district, a five-minute walk to the plaza, before purchasing a home in Mouraria with his partner. Augusto's mention of "other options" as an alternative to frequenting the space also underlines the disconnect between the Mercado de Fusão and the leisure practices of the surrounding community from which its theming was derived. While critiquing the changing use and perception of the plaza via the Mercado de Fusão renovations, he also made a point to note the efforts of Tom, the owner of the newly opened Markt7 kiosk, who he credited for both his "open mind" and for being a driving force of public programming, like concerts, which were successful in bringing the community together without monetary obstacles.[57]

In contrast to Augusto's statements, Carole, who had moved to Mouraria from England in the seventies, shared a much more critical perspective regarding the experience on offer in the reinvented corner of Martim Moniz, asserting, "I certainly don't want to go there and enjoy myself in this sort of little Disneyland, having a little bit of Chinese, and then a little bit of this, and a little bit of that." As a counter point, she shared her memory of the culinary landscape of the plaza during the period of deregulation years prior,

> You know, before they did this incarnation, this sort of mini little whatever, we had a kiosk of Cape Verdeans, then we had a Chinese kiosk, and there was a Ukrainian kiosk. So, you would have tea and a few Ukrainian things at the Ukrainian place, and it was served by Ukrainians. The Cape Verdean place was delightful. At the beginning we had little Cape Verdean finger food, but then the EU and the AISAYA [Portuguese Food and Hygiene Department] closed that down. There was a lot of other very interesting things in that neighborhood, in that particular café. Sitting there was an absolute joy most of the time.[58]

Carole's first comments regarding the "little Disneyland," demonstrate how community members were hyper-aware of the extent to which multiculturalism was being expressly constructed in the renovated space. She contrasts her critique with what she positions as a more authentic expression of the local community, giving examples of culinary diversity that was not explicitly fashioned by a municipal or private entity. Carole's memories of a real *with* origin, furthermore, contradict the prevailing framing of Martim Moniz as an abandoned space according to developmental discourse. In general, her reflections and discontent with the space are well supported by Solà-Morales' assertion that, "When architecture and urban design project their desire onto a vacant space, a *terrain vague*, they seem incapable of doing anything other than introducing violent transformations."[59] Carole's comments reiterate the fact that prior to the NCS project this space was not actually vacant. Yet, it was cast as such in the public imaginary due to its association with social actors viewed as undesirable for intersecting racial, legal, and social reasons, facilitating a *tabula rasa* narrative in discussions regarding its redesign. In turn, through collaborations between the public and private sector, the market development pushed a more tourist-centered model of use for the plaza, functioning under the assumption that unwelcome social and economic networks would fall in step, or be eradicated, with these changes.

Finally, a more negative attitude toward the diverse populations the Mercado de Fusão purported to celebrate was evident in my conversation with Amália, a seamstress who had moved to Mouraria from the Algarve fifty years prior. She shared,

> We wanted to feel like Martim Moniz was really a part of Mouraria. But in reality, when we are there we don't feel like that. Because the plaza is so full of immigrants, that when you're there, it's us who feel like we don't fit in. No one does anything bad to us, no one treats us badly, just that when we get there, all of those little kiosks that were opened, I don't think any of them is run by a Portuguese person. And because, because of the prices you have to pay there, when you go you see everything except Portuguese people.[60]

Amália's commentary grieves the loss of a culturally and racially homogeneous expression of Portuguese identity. Immigrants, tourists, and "everything except Portuguese people," in her view, were encroaching on the spaces and lifestyles of Mouraria's autochthonous population which, one can safely predict, looks like, speaks like, and shares the same cultural practices as Amália herself. Unlike Augusto and Carole, who capture the juxtaposition between the immigrant groups who are mobilized as décor in the space and those who really had access to the market, Amália conflates the two as a monolithic threat to her notion of cultural authenticity, and, in consequence, disregards the space as a viable option for people such as herself.

As these three reflections indicate, the Mercado de Fusão development brought a range of feelings to the fore regarding race, citizenship, and the right to public space. This circumstance was market driven, given that the impetus of manufactured multiculturalism was entangled with the expansion of consumer markets in the post-crisis era to formerly unexploited areas of the city. Through the NCS Project, ideological leanings became exposed as they took on form, narrative, and place within and in relation to the plaza. The group's top-down approach to rethinking and reshaping the city engaged with Mouraria's populace to the extent that they provided inspiration for a display that would—aspirationally—attract a different profile of urbanite to areas like Martim Moniz. Yet, where this strategy for urban design took off in other sectors of Lisbon, the Mercado de Fusão faltered.

By 2017, due to ongoing financial challenges related to the Mouraria development, NCS Produções transferred ownership of the plaza to another private company, Moonbrigade Limitada.[61] The new group, who then negotiated an even longer contract for rights to the space, soon erected barricades where the Mercado de Fusão had once stood, bringing the project to a close after five short years.[62] Though the primary source of funding had changed, Rebelo Pinto remained involved in the maintenance of the now-shuttered plaza, and frequently spoke on the behalf of the new company regarding their next stage of plans for the space. Accordingly, the group shared their ambitious vision of populating the privately held segment of Martim Moniz with fifty shipping-container style structures housing restaurants and shops. While the scope of the initiative had changed, its logic remained the same: promote and design this sector of the city in terms of its exchange-value.

By this point, however, enough time had passed that locals were increasingly attuned to the more detrimental outcomes of the post-crisis push for consumer-oriented development, increasingly correlating consumer-facing initiatives with a lack of affordable housing and a skyrocketing cost of living in the city center. Only steps from the plaza, residents at 25 Rua dos Lagares were fighting against their impending displacement by developers who wanted to convert their building into tourist rentals. Organizations like Morar em Lisboa were leading the charge against these increasingly unpopular development trends, bringing together associations and individuals demanding for the state to mitigate the impact of Lisbon's promotion as a site of tourism and investment. The narratives that had driven interventions only years prior—smiling, creative, cosmopolitan cities—were visibly losing their affective weight. In this climate, the newest attempt to shape Martim Moniz was met with unprecedented grassroots resistance, and negotiations over how the space would be developed dragged on. In February 2019, with the fence erected at the behest of Moonbrigade still standing, a group of protestors created a human chain around the plaza as a sign of public resistance to the continued privatization of the space.[63] During the protest, the group unveiled a large sign that declared "The CML [Câmara Municipal de Lisboa] is obligated to respect democracy and the desires of Lisboners. We want a public Garden. Lisbon is not for sale. Lisbon is for everyone."[64]

The event, curiously, was organized by Renovar a Mouraria, the same neighborhood association that had listed fomenting tourism as a founding tenant of their work only a few years prior. Journalist Jõao Pedro Pincha, who frequently covered topics related to the plaza for *Público*, referred to this as "a strange gesture for them" (num gesto que lhe é raro), recognizing the shifting priorities of some of the former advocates of consumer-facing development in the area.[65] Under this immense public pressure, Fernando Medina, the mayor of Lisbon, announced that the project would not go forward as planned. With the future of the Praça do Martim Moniz still in the balance, Mouraria would continue to take shape as contested terrain.

CHAPTER 3

Capturing Community in Lavapiés and Mouraria

In front of the lens, I am at the same time: the one I think I am, the one the photographer thinks I am, and the one he makes use of to exhibit his art.

—ROLAND BARTHES, *Camera Lucida*

This chapter turns to the power of documentary-style photography in shaping how the populations of Lavapiés and Mouraria were recast in the public imaginary during the post-crisis era of branding and development. Departing from the understanding of the photograph as a powerful tool in the process of knowledge generation, and therefore influential in the reciprocal conception and production of lived environments, I study how different social actors forged a sense of place both grounded in and extending beyond the material landscape by framing, shooting, and sharing scenes of these neighborhoods and their inhabitants with the objective of changing their perception in the public imaginary. With this consideration as the forefront, I evaluate the affective implications of such initiatives, while remaining aware of the problematic implications of presenting photographs as unobstructed representations of the real.

Indeed, before turning to this chapter's case studies, it is imperative to note how the practice of visual documentation itself is informed by societal values and life experience, from those of the photographers to the subjects themselves. Critically, the photograph transcends the framework of its production, including the photographer's intentions, as it is interpreted and consumed by different publics. Therefore, despite its utility for documentation, my analysis to follow hinges on the understanding that a still image is never a neutral depiction of the world. Barthes describes this as the photographic paradox, referring to how both culture and ideas are encoded in the production of images.[1] Tina Campt, in a similar vein, speaks of the "social life of the photo," the relationships in and beyond the frame of an image that contribute to its creation.[2] This life, she argues, is informed by the intentions of both subjects and photographers, and the broader implications of the stories told by the images captured. These issues of connotation, intention, and life beyond the image will be central considerations in this chapter's analysis of distinct efforts to establish, through photography and curation, an organized narrative regarding Mouraria's and Lavapiés's respective populations in a climate of consumer-oriented development.

Bearing in mind the prevailing discursive trope of manufactured multiculturalism as explored in prior chapters, the present analysis focuses on two interventions that situate race at the forefront of their visual construction of the quotidian in Lavapiés and Mouraria. The first case study is *Nosotros: Un album colectivo del barrio de Lavapiés* (2009), a book and public exhibit by Spanish photographer Juan Valbuena, described by the artist as a "collective photo album" of Lavapiés and its inhabitants.[3] One of the earliest texts studied in this manuscript, the project was not explicitly positioned as an effort to foment interest in the neighborhood in terms of its potential for capital accumulation. Yet, the series has curious parallels to the later intervention of Portuguese photographer Gonçalo Gaioso in *All Around Us* (2013), which was explicitly attached to the branding and promotion of Mouraria as a multicultural hub. While Gaioso took on the role of documenting the broader Mouraria community through his lens alone, Valbuena situated himself as a curator and cultural broker, organizing residents' personal photographs into a single community album. Therefore, I study Gaioso's piece, which was commissioned as part of the Mercado de Fusão, as an evolved stage of a culture-as-resource paradigm that Valbuena's intervention captures in a more nascent form.[4] While each of these texts embodies different notions of viewing and visual production, and develop from distinct social and geographic contexts, I also find that they converge in their approximation to race. Therefore, I assess the similar ways of looking that surface in these projects as evidence of a broader trend in racialized viewing: the didactic power of producing race and racial difference through image-making, collecting, and consumption.

More specifically, in both *Nosotros* and *All Around Us*, a White mediator employs visual strategies to advance a narrative of celebratory multiculturalism grounded in the notion that proximity to a racial Other begets conviviality. This rhetorical approach, similarly to prior chapter's case studies, depends on the public recognition and optimistic recasting of demographic realities that are frequently the source of feelings of discomfort and anxiety. By attributing cultural and racial difference a positive value—in terms of both emotion and capital—a mitigated vision of Otherness is cast as a collective desire. As I evaluate the affective implications of what is made visible in both Valbuena's and Gaioso's interventions and how it is framed, I consider both formal and narrative qualities of each photographic project, and, more broadly, the spatial and cultural networks invoked in each piece. Despite the celebratory depiction of a multiracial populace articulated in these two interventions, this analysis illustrates how, and to what end, these mediators advance a contemporary form of racialized viewing in their optimistic representations of community.

I conceive of racialized viewing as a variation of what Nicholas Mirzoeff defines as visuality, which he explains as the authority to look and to shape how things are seen, "the visualization of history."[5] While this practice, as a form of visuality, is not limited to seeing in its literal sense, it is greatly emboldened by visual modes of knowledge production. This way of envisioning the world has a long legacy in both Spain and Portugal, having been wielded with particular prominence during the era of Imperial expansion. In this regard, one may deliberate contemporary forms of racialized viewing and their affective implications as they relate to viewing practices established during that same period. At the time, visual culture was an effective tool for communicating hierarchies of power and expressions of Otherness. Take, as an example, the *casta* paintings produced following the conquest of the Americas and distributed in Spain, which organized social stratification according to physical appearance and blood lineage.[6] In Portugal, too, portraiture was used to communicate the correlation between phenotypical and social difference among subjects in the overseas colonies, such as in José Conrado Roza's "The Bridal Masquerade," (1788) an allegorical depiction of a wedding between enslaved Black and Indigenous members of the Portuguese court.[7] Visual epistemologies as a means by which to understand the Other were further strengthened with the advent of the photograph and film, with still and moving images giving a more realistic face and form to the ongoing colonial exercise in racial thinking. Indeed, the emergence of these technologies provided a renewed vocabulary for capturing, organizing, and sharing the visible surface of the world, and expanded a prevailing methodology through which fantasies, ideas, and feelings about the racialized Other could be framed as fact.[8]

Racialized viewing, emboldened by such narrative tools, continued well into the contemporary era as an expression of hegemonic power that, as

Quijano argues, "presupposes an element of coloniality."[9] This was especially evident in the late twentieth century when increased immigration to both Spain and Portugal, tied to the nations' relative economic prosperity, destabilized prevailing understandings of the axis of power. The racialized Other, instead of an overseas entity relegated by European powers, was now increasingly visible on Iberian shores, thus inverting the former colonial order. Mounting racial anxieties and volatile reactions to such demographic change were anticipated and discussed across cultural mediums, with racialized viewing frequently employed as an instrument of national and self-understanding in visual genres as film, television, and performance arts.[10] Characters from Ngé Ndomo, a shock-inducing Black man from La Mancha featured in *Amanece que no es poco* (Cuerda, 1989) to the disenfranchised children of Angolan immigrants in *Zona J* (Vieira, 1998), were didactic figures, training audiences in how Spanish and Portuguese identities could be understood through encounters with and against these racial Others. In others, like *Flores de otro mundo* (Bollaín, 1999) and *Ossos* (Costa, 1997) cultural producers explored the different forms of violence suffered by what Luis Martín-Cabrera has called the "postcolonial subject," those whose very presence was increasingly cast in public discourse as a threat to the prosperity correlated with Europe.[11] Throughout these pre-crisis decades, the Iberian nations' relative economic prosperity served as a critical touchstone according to which they could still articulate their power and proximity to the perceived Whiteness of European modernity.

Following the financial crisis, as the Iberian nations' gloomy economic climate blurred the lines between socioeconomic superiority and inferiority, the racial standards according to which these parameters were drawn became further entrenched. Now, the racial axis that was once forged as a justification for power and influence was the rationale against which authority would be reclaimed—an invocation of the "public and psychological wage" of Whiteness.[12] Racialized viewing adapted to these changing circumstances, with cultural producers depicting the loss of the power and prosperity once thought to be granted by this racial category. Post-2008 pieces like Icíar Bollaín's *En tierra extraña* (2014), as one example, painted a picture of Spanish emigrants both in solidarity with yet distinct from their racialized counterparts in their home country, their mounting precarity lamented as a temporary condition rather than their common place in society.[13] In Marco Martins's *São Jorge* (2016), a former Portuguese boxer's slow descent into a world of crime was catalyzed by his efforts to support his Afro-Brazilian partner and child in the wake of the crisis. This somber depiction of a world turned upside down was further accentuated by the partner's desire to return to Brazil with their son, a palpable shift in migratory currents, and evolving expression of a colonial legacy in the former metropole.

This trajectory of visual culture as medium for racialized viewing within and beyond the Iberian Peninsula is critical to my understanding of the visual construction and deliberate celebration of racial diversity in *Nosotros* and *All Around Us*. Namely, the prior examples provide necessary context for the genesis of layered racial thinking that would lead to casting the Other as useful to a themed depiction of a given Spanish or Portuguese neighborhood, while simultaneously distinguishing these same subjects from standards of national belonging framed in proximity to Whiteness. With that, we may turn to Valbuena's intervention, a significant example of a photographer's attempt to construct a convivial narrative that would mitigate the ongoing stigmatization of Lavapiés and its inhabitants. While this piece was explicitly framed as an empathetic effort and platform for community self-expression, I delve into some of the more the problematic implications of the project's framing and, at the level of the image, Valbuena's recourse to *castizo* markers of identity as an orienting pole for expressing kinship between community members.

Juan Valbuena's *Nosotros*

A photo album transports viewers through space and time. It is with this premise that Juan Valbuena introduces *Nosotros: Un álbum colectivo del barrio de Lavapiés*. The photography project was spearheaded by the artist in 2008 with the financial support of Lavapiés's Casa Árabe, a government-funded cultural center with the stated mission of fostering connections between Spain and the Arab world.[14] Valbuena, a native of Madrid, has a body of photographic work that includes both personal and commissioned multimedia projects that interrogate notions of territory, memory, and identity. For example, his piece *Noray: Libro de viajes por la ancha frontera* (Noray: Trips around the wide border), which was developed over the course of a decade (1999–2009), explores the far corners of the Mediterranean Sea via images of its port cities.[15] For *Nosotros*, Valbuena took a step away from his place behind the camera, opting instead to curate a compilation of personal photographs contributed by residents of Lavapiés for a month-long exhibition in December 2009 at the Casa Árabe and a corresponding published collection, which extended the exhibit's life and circulation beyond the ephemeral display. The selection of images featured in the final *Nosotros* volume, bound as a book, are primarily vernacular photographs depicting ordinary and domestic scenes including family snapshots, vacation photos, and photo-booth images. The timing of this piece is of particular note in that it signals mounting attention to Lavapiés's population as a type of cultural resource that, propelled by the atmosphere of a society in crisis, would evolve in the service of branding and consumption in the years to follow.

The *Nosotros* book features more than one hundred photos presented without captions on blank white backgrounds. The selection of images is preceded by four introductory narratives written by leadership from the Casa Árabe, an art historian, and Valbuena, and followed by an index including dates, locations, brief descriptions, and attribution for each image in the volume.[16] These auxiliary sections, and in particular the essays, guide the reader's interpretation of the album and make explicit the prevailing vision for the intervention: using the format of a family album to celebrate and map Lavapiés as a type of global village. Administrators Gema Martín Muñoz and Nuria Medina from the Casa Árabe, to this end, speak to their personal and institutional investment in casting a positive light on the neighborhood's diverse populace.[17] In the first of the two texts, Martín Muñoz emphasizes the global quality of the district, describing it as "without borders, intercultural, dynamic." Medina's piece, similarly, invokes the notion of borders when describing the genesis of the project, explaining "it's about opening ourselves to mutual understanding and coexistence in a society, ours, the one of *Nosotros*, that is increasingly intercultural."[18] These reflections are indicative of an empathetic effort to push back on the ongoing stigmatization of the district by sharing positive representations of contact between community members. Yet, both authors depend on a misleading equivalence between proximity and harmony to make their points, overlooking the more pervasive xenophobic and race-based anxieties that persisted in community relations. This representational tendency, again, captures a more troubling pattern of engaging with racial plurality to the extent that it may be represented as a perennially positive feature. Even when executed from a place of compassion, denying this reality its necessary complexity does the affective work of recasting different groups' ongoing categorization as racialized Others (defined in difference to an established norm) as a desirable, happy position, thereby obfuscating the violence inherent to the process of race creation.

Framing Lavapiés as a rosy melting pot is further buoyed by positioning the project as a family album. Returning to the volume's introductory texts, in another, Professor Aurora Fernández Polanco comments that Valbuena "extends the soul of the family album to the entire neighborhood's big family."[19] This reference to the genre foments the sense of community as a type of metaphorical blood lineage, which Fernández Polanco points to as evidence of the positive atmosphere the project purports to represent. Yeon-Soo Kim, who studies the prevalence of the album as a text type in contemporary Spanish cultural production, explains that this form "lies on the interstices between experience and fictional memory: while it documents actual events, it presents them in a selective way so that a subjective reading of the past is embedded in the act of photographing, preserving, and organizing."[20] Likewise, Kim emphasizes the narrative power of the organizer of a family album who takes on the authority "to manipulate, accentuate, or erase certain memories."[21]As we have previously touched upon in the discussion of recurring tropes such as *Hispanidad* and *Lusotropicalism*, recourse to fraternal bonds by narratorial authorities addressing cultural and racial plurality has been extensively critiqued for reinforcing systems of race and power established in the colonial era. Given the project's alignment with this pattern from the outset, *Nosotros* can be understood as an exercise in racialized viewing obscured, like other fraternal narratives, under the guise of kinship.

In his introduction to the volume, "Una máquina para viajar por el espacio-tiempo" (A space-time machine), Valbuena takes the opportunity to both situate himself within the community depicted in the album and minimize his authority as curator. He writes,

> The *Nosotros* project is a collective album of the residents of Lavapiés comprised of a collection of photographs and corresponding stories. Nowadays, communities are known according to the images shared of them. It seems appropriate not to always leave the creation, selection, and dissemination of these images to another group and, out of all the other options available, opt for those of us as we see ourselves.[22]

Here, Valbuena recognizes the hierarchical dynamic that emerges in the process of image creation and dissemination, arguing for self-representation as a viable alternative. At the same time, he assumes the first-person plural in this position statement, in which he as author and curator is situated on the same plane of subjectivity as others included in the collection. Through this rhetorical strategy, the artist reinforces his inclusion in the community to be depicted in the piece, thus lending himself the positionality needed for self-representation. As the introduction unfolds, Valbuena works to distance himself from any hierarchy implicit in the role of curator, asserting that the album came to life naturally, "It was just a question of finding photos and stories and putting them all together. The sum of individual parts will unfailingly take a pluralistic form."[23] Yet, "just" finding stories and putting them together is, as Kim emphasizes, the crux of the narratorial power of the album curator. While the images are not Valbuena's, the way he organizes them produces a subjective narrative, a fact he minimizes in this reflection. Instead, Valbuena ruminates on the incomplete nature of what he sees as an "imperfect" map of Lavapiés, "made at human scale, 1:1 ratio, specifically, *Nosotros*," limited by the fact that only those who agreed to participate were included in the piece.[24] Such reflections allude to the author's implicit vision of what a complete representation of the neighborhood would entail. Overall, by emphasizing the role of the community in the piece, along with his relationship to its members, Valbuena positions the intervention as the result of a simple exchange between neighbors provided with a platform for self-expression. Yet, the stickier elements of constructing such an archive, including authorship, curation, and the gaze of the White mediator, complicate how the past and present of Lavapiés's population is woven into a cohesive tale.

Even if one is to look beyond Valbuena's role as curator, his emphasis on self-representation as a more legitimate frame for viewing Lavapiés merits inquiry. Scholar and artist Coco Fusco, in particular, speaks to the trend of self-imaging in photographic exhibitions of race, which are frequently positioned as more authentic, superior, or self-reflective than what is generally identified as colonialist photography.[25] Although Fusco acknowledges that these efforts yield interesting exhibitions, she stresses that "attributing 'master' status to a handful of nonwhite photographers based on the 'discovery' of the quality in their work" obscures a critical analysis of Western forms of racial thought and how those perspectives are manifest in cultural production.[26] Fusco's observations also bring to the fore how images produced by racialized groups, given a life and circulation through a framework born of the White gaze, often serve as an appeal to or confirmation of different types of racial thinking. Similar to the self-fashioned representations that Fusco critiques, Valbuena's decision to use vernacular photography may be perceived as more authentic than fine-art or professional portraiture. Yet, untrained imaging, regardless of its purported legitimacy, is just as much a tool for ordering what is seen as any other visual medium. These questions of form and design are necessary to keep in mind when critically assessing a piece such as *Nosotros*.

With the critical implications of the project's framing at the forefront, we may move on to some of the details of the photos themselves, focusing on Valbuena's frequent use of hegemonic symbols of Spanish identity as an orienting pole when expressing kinship between neighborhood residents. In

FIGURE 3.1. Image of the Corrala de Sombrerete included in *Nosotros*. Courtesy of NOSOTROS Project / Casa Árabe & Juan Valbuena (ed.)

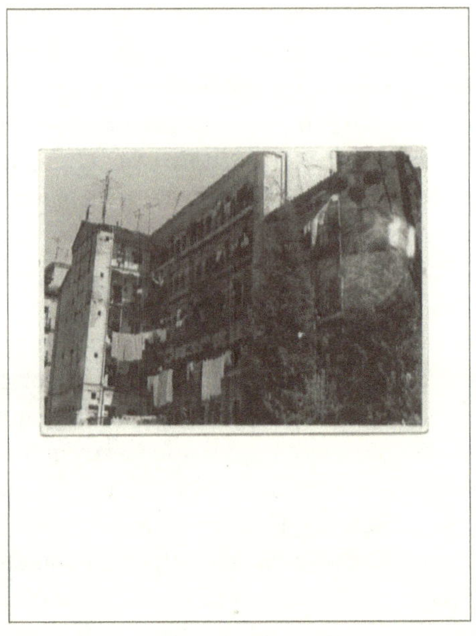

my assessment of this tendency, I return to Ahmed's observation that multiculturalism is often "made happy" through its approximation to national ideals. By celebrating difference to the extent that it approximates an established identitarian standard, this pattern implicitly reinforces a monolithic archetype of Spanish identity against which expressions of difference can be measured. The tendency is evident from the first page of the album, which opens with a sepia toned image of the Corrala de Sombrerete, a landmark in Lavapiés declared national patrimony in 1977. This style of building, distinguished by its open-air hallways oriented around a patio, historically housed the city's working poor. Many of these structures date to the industrial boom of the nineteenth century, when internal migrants from the country's rural regions sought economic opportunity in urban centers like Madrid. During this period, life in the *corrala* was one of destitute poverty, where inhabitants navigated most of their daily lives in the buildings' open patios due to their limited allotments of private space.[27] Yet, like many *castizo* symbols, these harrowing details are often softened in public discourse, particularly when lamenting the loss of urban practices popularized prior to Madrid's globalization. Consequently, life in a *corrala* relates to *lo castizo* as a type of aestheticized symbol—a snapshot of community in a growing city that embodies a challenging yet, in some ways, more authentic existence. By beginning the album with an architectural emblem specific to the district, Valbuena highlights the close (and sometimes uncomfortable) spatial relationships within the community as a tenant of Lavapiés's exceptionalism. Moreover, the image serves as a marker of an imagined national original to which the Other will be compared to throughout the piece, drawing on standards for belonging that maintain entrenched social hierarchies.

As *Nosotros* unfolds through Valbuena's curation, the artist continues to situate displays of difference in parallel to national symbols and social practices. In one such example, he features a photograph of the neighborhood's Lunar New Year celebration. In the foreground of the scene, a group performs the dragon dance, a typical act during Chinese New Year festivities in which entertainers manipulate the mythical creature with poles. Spectators stand primarily along the perimeter of the patio, which is decorated with red balloons and banners, a color used to represent luck and good fortune during New Year celebrations throughout China and among diasporic Chinese communities. On the next page, the reader is witness to another commemorative display: Lavapiés's San Lorenzo festivities in 2003. The featured image is an aerial shot of the street, capturing a crowd of spectators that watches the procession honoring Saint Lorenzo, for whom the celebration is named.

FIGURE 3.2. Two-page spread of *Nosotros* as curated by Juan Valbuena. Courtesy of NOSOTROS Project / Casa Árabe & Juan Valbuena (ed.)

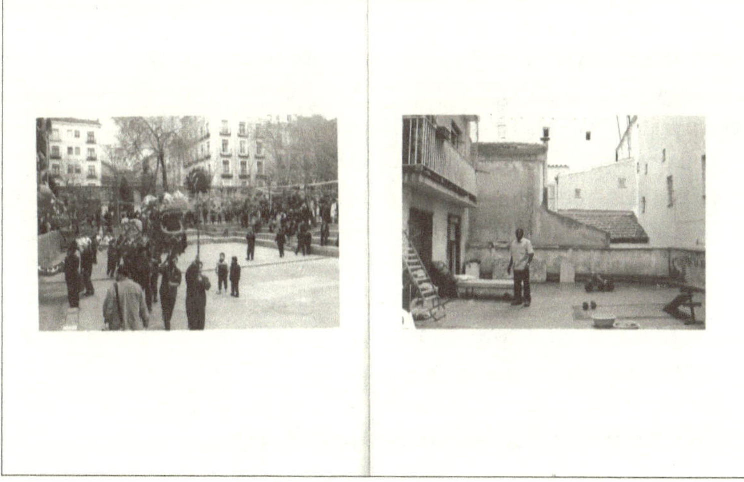

FIGURE 3.3. Two-page spread in *Nosotros* as curated by Juan Valbuena. Courtesy of NOSOTROS Project / Casa Árabe & Juan Valbuena (ed.)

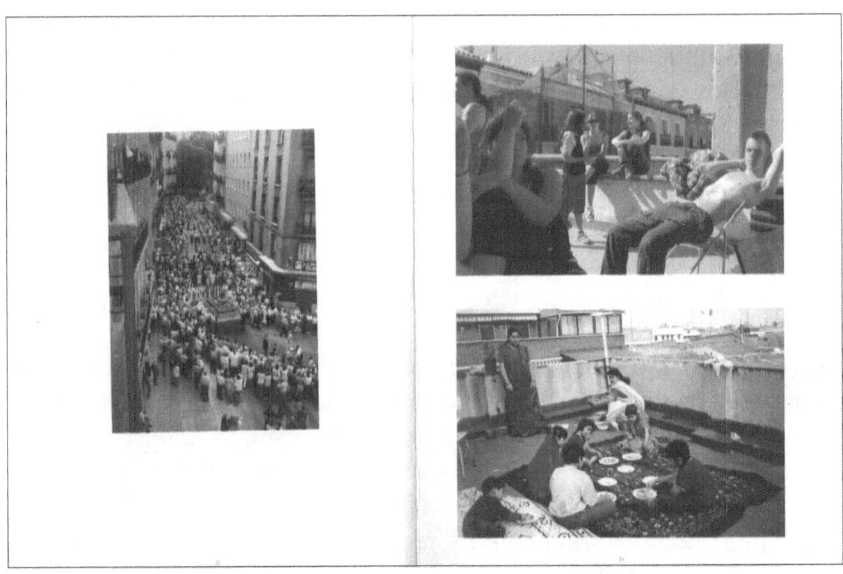

The event accompanies the Paloma and San Cayetano festivities each August, a markedly *castizo* tradition observed in Lavapiés and the neighboring La Latina neighborhood. The quick succession of these images accentuates similarities between otherwise disparate celebrations. The San Lorenzo procession therefore provides a *castizo* parallel for the Chinese traditions featured on the previous page, the more recent presence of which is emphasized in the index where the person who shared the photograph comments, "It looks like they're going to do it again."[28]

These parallels are also evident in the three different terrace images that Valbuena pairs with scenes of public celebration. The first, set adjacent to the photo of the Lunar New Year festival, is a shot of a single Black subject pictured on a patio filled with bed parts, exercise equipment, and a child's tricycle. The man is captured from a distance, dwarfed by the enclosure of walls that surround him, a sliver of sky visible in the top right quadrant of the image. In the second spread, adjacent to the San Lorenzo aerial photograph, Valbuena includes snapshots of two different groups caught in medias res. In the top photograph, a group of young men and women relax under a sunny sky. All but one subject look away from the camera, caught up in

FIGURE 3.4. Spread of wedding photographs in *Nosotros* as curated by Juan Valbuena. Courtesy of NOSOTROS Project / Casa Árabe & Juan Valbuena (ed.)

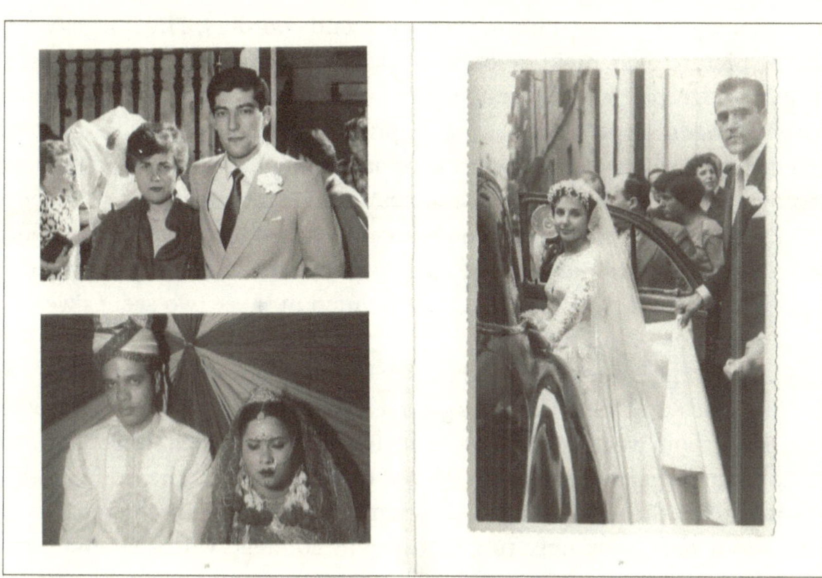

conversation or peering into the distance. The man that returns the camera's gaze is shirtless and holds his arms behind his head, teetering on two legs of a chair in a posture of repose. In the scene captured below this image, two women dressed in saris watch a group of children who dine in the foreground of the photo. They sit cross-legged on a pair of blankets, engrossed in their meals as their caretakers look on. Though the subjects of each photograph are dissimilar, the built environment of Lavapiés's terraces ties the scenes together: red concrete and tile floors, worn stucco walls, and the barrel roof tiles of surrounding buildings, each visual parallel fomenting the sense of cohesion advanced through the album's design.

Even as the album evolves beyond Lavapiés's built environment, Valbuena continues to weave distinct characters together through milestones and visual parallels. As a result, the reader is given the sense of a common life experience among subjects that informs their place in the neighborhood. The nuclear, heteronormative family is a primary touchstone in this process of expressing community, as the display of photographs is organized in a way that mimics such a family's records of life events: beginning with marriage, then birth, and continuing to milestones including communions, trips, and celebrations.

A spread of wedding photographs, for example, features three different couples, two photographed in Madrid and one in Bangladesh. Together, the series positions marriage ceremonies as a commonality between these distinct subjects, a social norm that transcends borders. The images set in Madrid picture pairs dressed for the occasion in formal wear. The largest of these photographs is a black and white image dated to 1959. In it, a woman in a white wedding dress smiles for the photographer as she enters a car, followed closely by her partner. On the opposite page, a woman and man are photographed together outside Lavapiés's San Cayetano church. The index reveals that the photo was taken in 1987 on the wedding day of the donor Isabel's son. Behind the duo one can make out the white veil of the bride speaking to an older woman. Each of the men in these two scenes wears a white carnation on his lapel.

A photograph from Bangladesh, taken in 2006, completes the spread. The medium close-up of the bride and groom showcases their dress for the occasion. The groom wears a white *sherwani* (a dress coat typical to South Asian formal wear) and *pagri* (turban) with red ornamentation. The bride's outfit, which matches the red on the groom's pagri, includes an embroidered *dupatta* (veil) and *noth* (a hoop nose ring that usually connects with a chain pinned behind the ear). The outfits in this photo contrast starkly with the Western dresses and suits featured in the other two scenes. Cultural and racial differences between the three couples depicted are thus inferred through these visual markers, both phenotypical and material, that distinguish the subjects from one another. The image of racial Other is mediated by the hegemonic references that orient it: Western formalwear, Catholic churches, and the streets of Madrid.[29] It is the affinity for the institution of marriage that ties these scenes together, ordering and understanding the experience of another through personal identification with and proximity to an established national ideal.[30] This pull toward sameness seems antithetical to the celebration of diversity, yet it serves as a way of metering and accepting the Other (in the pursuit of conviviality) while remaining faithful to hierarchies of belonging.

These assemblages continue throughout the album: a girl at her first communion, with a doll of baby Jesus in hand, is set alongside a portrait of a child wearing a *chedda*, a ceremonial Moroccan dress. On the corresponding page, another young girl is pictured with flowers and customary dress for the Fiesta de las Mayas, a celebration of spring designated as cultural heritage in the Province of Madrid.[31] She appears alongside a tile display of the city's coat of arms, a folkloric icon next to a herald of Spanish territory. In another spread two

FIGURE 3.5. Images of children in *Nosotros* as curated by Juan Valbuena. Courtesy of NOSOTROS Project / Casa Árabe & Juan Valbuena (ed.)

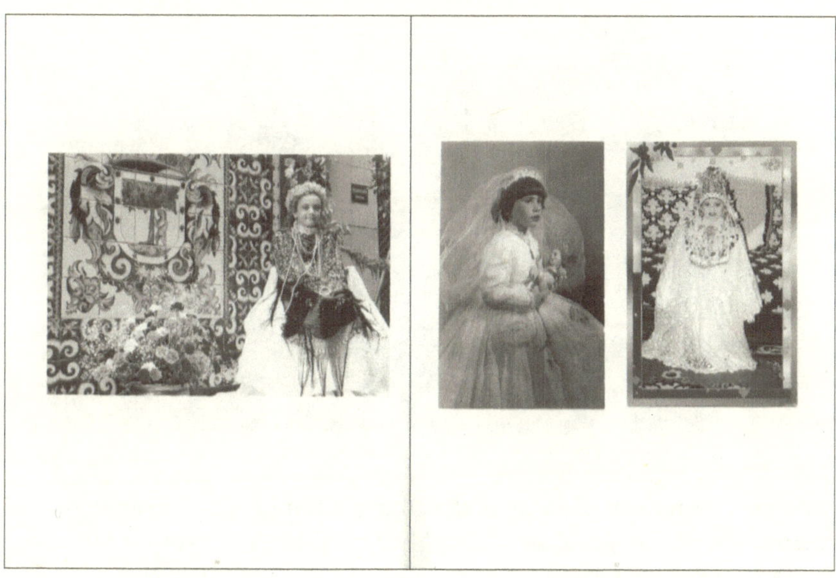

children dressed as a *chulapa*, an outfit typically worn during celebrations of the city's patron saints, and *gato madrileño*, the affectionate term for multi-generation residents of the city. These pairs are juxtaposed with different duos: the first, two soccer players from Senegal, and below, a mother and son pictured in Beijing. On a later set of pages, portraits of four female subjects are united by an article of clothing: the first, an Italian woman wearing a shawl, the second, a baby dressed as a *chulapa* with an embroidered *mantón*, a Senegalese subject pictured in a hijab, and a Spanish woman with a neck scarf. The Spanish and *castizo* counterpoints for each invocation of diversity stand as a recurring reminder of the prevailing standards according to which racial difference is perceived and expressed. Consequently, framing these social bonds according to nostalgic invocations of historic traditions and effectively relegates those diverging from more established national norms to the place of Other.

As a final point regarding my reading of *Nosotros* as an exercise in racialized viewing, let us return to Valbuena's assertion that the album presents Lavapiés "as we see ourselves." In actuality, this vision statement minimizes the myriad gazes present in the series. In this regard, we may return to the

FIGURE 3.6. Eleanor's photograph of Maxime in *Nosotros*. Courtesy of NOSOTROS Project / Casa Árabe & Juan Valbuena (ed.)

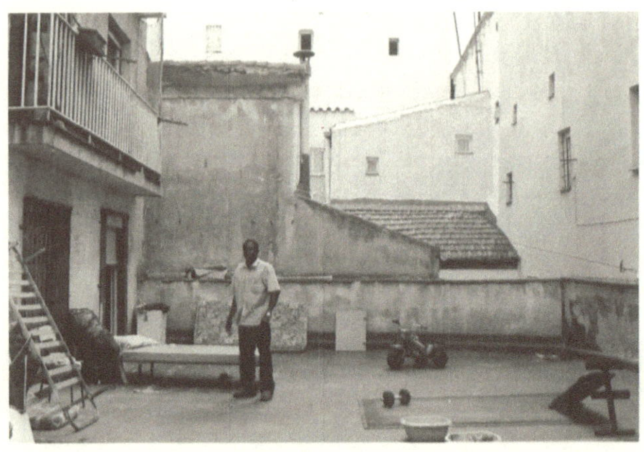

terrace scene at the beginning of the album, submitted by a woman named Eleanor, who photographs her neighbor Maxime. The caption furnished by the contributor provides insight into the dynamic behind the image. She writes, "Madrid is where I realized for the first time how lucky I was for having been born in Great Britain, for being able to travel easily with a passport easily attained. As I took photographs of my neighbor Maxime for days, I felt that our situations, which on the one hand were so distinct, were also similar: both having recently arrived to Madrid, with French as our common language, and without knowing almost anyone."[32] Eleanor's statements demonstrate how she approached image-making as a form of personal knowledge production, learning about herself by way of her understanding of the Other. This more informal process of observation and analysis curiously echoes traditional ethnographic approaches where, as Deborah Poole explains, the native was constituted as an object and the ethnographer a reasoned, thinking subject.[33] This dynamic thus established a centralized authority that applied their world view to the unknown that they seek to organize. In her empathetic effort to depict a shared life experience between herself and her neighbor, Eleanor emphasizes common ground as a path to conviviality. However, by reducing her and Maxime's experiences to those of two individuals navigating unfamiliar territory, glazing over issues of race and legal status, her reflection minimizes the significant impact of these factors on the migrant experience. This specific expression of solidarity is both a product of and produced for the White gaze. By minimizing the nuances of the migrant experience in pursuit of solidarity, Eleanor effectively places herself on a similar plane as her neighbor, a discursive maneuver that, regardless of intent, obscures other pervasive issues, like systemic racism, that inform the ongoing disenfranchisement of racialized migrants and their descendants in this neighborhood.

The White gaze is also palpable in the formal qualities of Eleanor's image, a scene that captures a courtyard terrace surrounded by the walls of neighboring buildings, a sliver of sky, and Maxime as a small figure swallowed by his surroundings. These details call attention to difference and transience, with Maxime's presence informed by the materiality of his circumstances. He stands off-center at the foot of a small cot and mattress with a black garbage bag at its head. Another empty bed frame is propped against the building wall, and a mattress leans against the back barrier of the terrace. In the right half of the image there is a small workout area including a dumbbell and bench, and a red tricycle. With this framing, the viewer is led to conceive of subject of the photograph in terms of his environment, a distant figure among a sea of items and walls.

I evaluate this portrayal of Maxime's circumstances according to what Nicole Fleetwood terms "photographic icons," that is, the images circulated in popular culture that convey dominant narratives regarding Blackness.[34] These observations do not serve to deny the very real struggles faced by racialized migrants to Spain, but rather highlight the way that the White gaze recurs to iconic ways of seeing the racialized Other. The icon, Fleetwood argues, "produces affective responses by 'sticking' the thing or person signified to normative codes, meaning, and values."[35] In effect, "iconic" representations tend to reinforce the sense of Blackness as a state of enduring spectacle whether in duress (the oversexed body, the enslaved, the incarcerated) or against it (the venerable activist, the remarkable athlete, and so on). Fleetwood, in this regard, argues that the response to Blackness as spectacle is non-iconicity, which is to say, interventions that "lessen the weight on the Black visual to do so much."[36] In Eleanor's image and description, she couches the icon of the fraught Black migrant in terms of her personal relationship with her neighbor, situating herself as witness of the archetype in duress most frequently invoked in sensational reports of undocumented passage from Africa to Europe. As a point of comparison, consider some of the more mundane representations of Blackness included in the volume: a man posing in front of the lake at Madrid's Retiro Park, two friends relaxing on a couch in Dakar, a group celebrating a football match in the Cibeles Plaza. Each of these snapshots, furnished by the individuals pictured within, could very well be conceived as non-iconic given that they do little to nothing to portray Blackness as spectacle. While this handful of snapshots demonstrate how self-imaging can invert a hegemonic gaze, their inclusion alongside stickier photographs like that of Eleanor ultimately undermines their potential.

In sum, Valbuena depends on the presumed validity of self-imaging to build a cohesive vision of Lavapiés as a harmonious, cosmopolitan hub. Despite this framing, his role as curator undercuts the power of such images to claim autonomy from being named, categorized, and defined by a visual authority, what Mirzoeff refers to as the "right to look."[37] In turn, one must understand the broader narrative shared in *Nosotros* as one of Valbuena's making, despite his positioning to the contrary. One could undoubtedly study the photographs in isolation, like in the above examples of non-iconic invocations of Blackness shared by some contributors. Yet, when viewed as a whole, the curator's role must be taken into consideration. Moreover, specific details from the album, including the people, spaces, and practices highlighted and juxtaposed within, indicate how Valbuena's depiction of happy multiculturalism depends on nostalgic and frequently revisionary invocations of national ideals, which likewise serve to orient the reader's perception of Otherness.

This intervention exemplifies how purported celebrations of multiculturalism and diversity can reinforce racial hierarchies and a continued valorization of homogeneous national ideals, often obscured by the premise of positivity. Moreover, even though *Nosotros* was not explicitly positioned as an effort to foment consumption within the bounds of the Lavapiés, it effectively positioned the neighborhood's diverse populace as a point of interest through its celebratory tilt. This shift in the public imaginary would prove advantageous in later stages of the district's development. As a point of comparison, we will now turn to a case from Mouraria that illustrates the full expression of racialized viewing in the service of a consumer-oriented initiative.

Gonçalo Gaioso's *All Around Us*

In May 2013, Gonçalo Gaioso's photo installation *All Around Us* was unveiled in the Praça do Martim Moniz. The artist had created the piece according to a call from NCS Produções for proposals to "give more color to the Mercado the Fusão."[38] Gaioso, whose portfolio was primarily in fashion and commercial photography, shot a series of portraits of Mouraria's entrepreneurs to illustrate, in his words, "What happens around us."[39] Accordingly, he promoted the

FIGURE 3.7. *All Around Us* series as displayed in the Mercado de Fusão

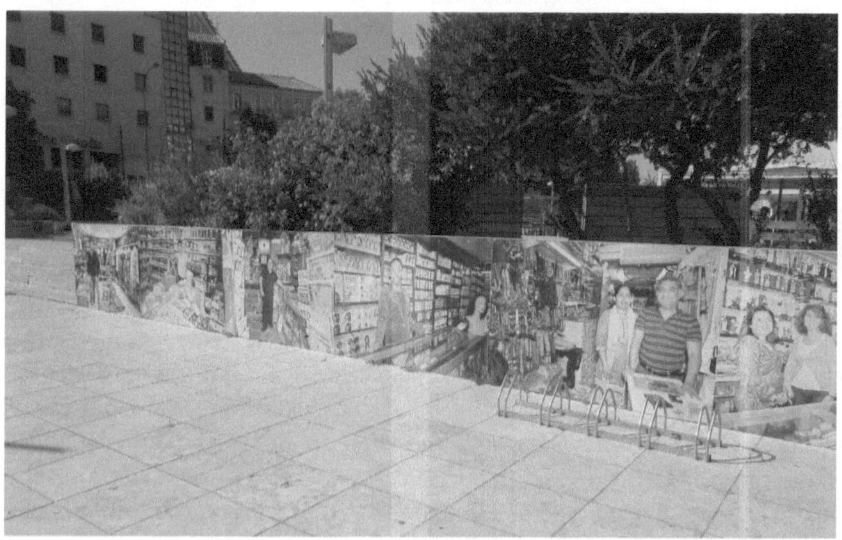

exhibit as a complement to touring the district, his view succinctly expressed in one interview where he asserted "*All Around Us* mirrors the multiculturalism and charm of the commercial district in this part of the city, which I recommend visiting with a keen eye!"[40]

In contrast to Valbuena's initiative, the "us" presented in *All Around Us* was never explicitly defined, allowing for more liberal interpretations of the exhibit's visual order ranging from residents of Mouraria looking at one another, or, a likely scenario given the English title, those from outside looking in. The display, described by one blogger as "an explosion of color, smiles, and multiculturalism," was set up as a permanent exhibit alongside the Mercado de Fusão's other decorative installations.[41] While its purpose as an auxiliary complement to a consumer-facing initiative, among other artistic considerations, distinguishes Gaioso's work from that of Valbuena, the pieces converge in their approximation to race. Namely, *All Around Us*, like *Nosotros*, advances a celebratory representation of the racialized Other in such a way that simultaneously reminds the viewer of their divergence from standards of belonging shaped in proximity to Whiteness. Accordingly, the social, and by extension, monetary, value of the diverse populace represented in the piece is conveyed while maintaining enduring attachments to racial hierarchies. This is especially impactful given the presumptive audience of this intervention—tourists and visitors to this space—who were instructed, through these visual cues, how to conceive of the neighborhood and its inhabitants.

For the exhibit, vibrant portraits were erected on two concrete barricades among the market's kiosks and leisure spaces. This creative direction was a logical choice, taking into account Gaioso's background in commercial photography and the installation's purpose as a complement to a consumer-oriented development. Likewise, such large-scale, exuberant photographic depictions of visual diversity are a common strategy in commercial spheres. Take, as an emblematic example, the advertising campaigns of clothing brand United Colors of Benetton, renowned for their glossy and attractive displays of racial difference.[42] This is an affect-driven enterprise, where racial plurality as a revenue generating product is sold through creative marketing strategies that cultivate positive feelings. Such strategic exaltations of Otherness are not a negation of racial thinking, but, as Fusco observes, "an extension of racialized discourse on beauty," and implicit reminder of the power dynamics that forge racial categories.[43] Once more, it is necessary to look beyond the positive veneer of this type of piece, bolstered by a glossy, colorful display difference, to consider the more complex messages that exhibits like that of Gaioso convey regarding the intersections between race, capital, and cultural identity in Mouraria and, by extension, contemporary Lisbon.

In the capacity of his role as a mediator, Gaioso brings to the public eye a range of semi-private spaces and atypical tourist attractions, weaving together disparate sites and subjects throughout Mouraria as accessible, attractive, and consumable components of a cohesive narrative regarding community and commercial activity. Through a taxonomic presentation of neighborhood entrepreneurs and their corresponding environments, the artist grounds his visual portrayal of racial difference in relation to networks of production and consumption, with the effect of rendering the multicultural discourse of Mouraria concrete, observable, and quantifiable. The images that make up the exhibit are middle and long shots of shop owners and employees captured in boutiques, convenience shops, and workshops, pictured behind counters, in doorways, and next to an array of consumer products. This array of quotidian settings lends an unaffected quality to the series, compelling the viewer—presumably a visitor to the Mercado de Fusão—to feel that they are witnessing life as it is lived. This sense is further fomented by Gaioso's choice to frame the portraits in a way that emulates the perspective of a client or passerby who might enter, or view from beyond its threshold, each of the stores depicted. Given that the images are presented without caption, the spectator has only visual clues to draw conclusions regarding each subject's place in Mouraria and Lisbon's broader social and economic circuits, inviting conjecture based on physical and material details. In this respect, the framing of *All Around Us* encourages the position that one may understand another based on the spaces they inhabit.

To this point, Gaioso's photographs envisage stark juxtapositions, along racial lines, among members of the neighborhood's commercial domain. Portraits of White merchants, including a seamstress, a shoe repairman, and a stationary salesman, for example, capture a small business model that predates corporate chains and global consumer trends. In contrast, non-White retailers are photographed in commercial settings that reflect contemporary migratory currents and the impact of tourist consumption on the local economy, including international grocery stores, trinket shops, cell phone outlets, and wholesale establishments. These settings are more ambivalent in their attachments to Portugal, the type of space without moorings that Marc Augé defines as a non-place.[44] Such environments are the material expression of an increasingly networked global society, where identical models for goods and services proliferate with minimal adjustment to national and geographic considerations. Notably, in *All Around Us*, these transnational, decontextualized settings are portrayed exclusively in relation to the racial Other, formal and aesthetic details that reinforce the way that the White subject conforms to and the racialized subject departs from long-established commercial conventions specifically attached to the Portuguese national and geographic context. This distinction underscores the relational, historical and identitarian details that, as Augé argues, differentiate places from non-places.[45] Presented as part of a broader didactic intervention, these images train the spectator to perceive racial difference within a contextually grounded stasis of Whiteness, where novel, itinerant figures are contrasted with those presented as more established members of Portuguese society.

Gaioso's shot of shopkeepers in a *tabacaria* exemplifies the tendency in the exhibit to situate White subjects, through compositional details, in a concrete national and historical context. In the image, the artist showcases the small-business model of the tobacconist, who sells convenience items like magazines, newspapers, and souvenirs as well as tobacco products. Gaioso captures his subjects from outside the entrance to the shop, mimicking the viewpoint of a client entering directly from the street. In the foreground of the shot, local newspapers including *Diario Público* and *Correio da Manhã* and magazines like *Lux* and *Sábado* provide visual cues to orient the establishment as a Portuguese space. The subjects' relationship to Portugal within the narrative of the scene is further accentuated by the local postcards, Portuguese

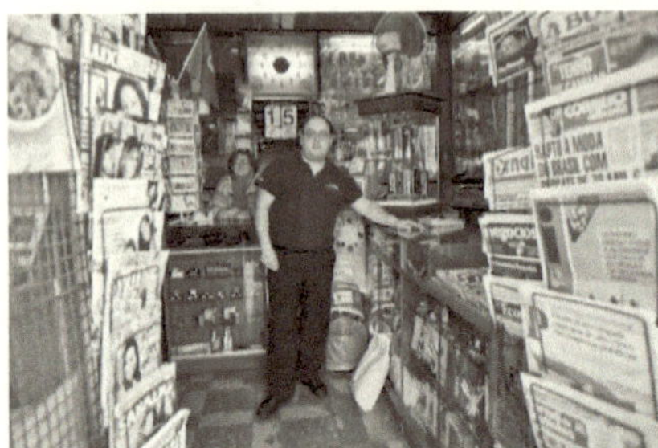

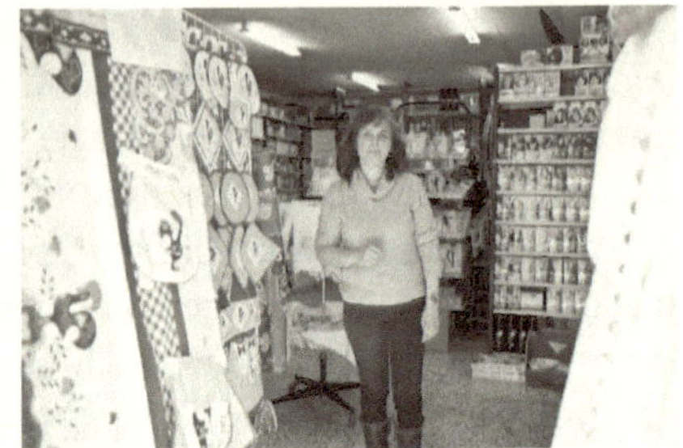

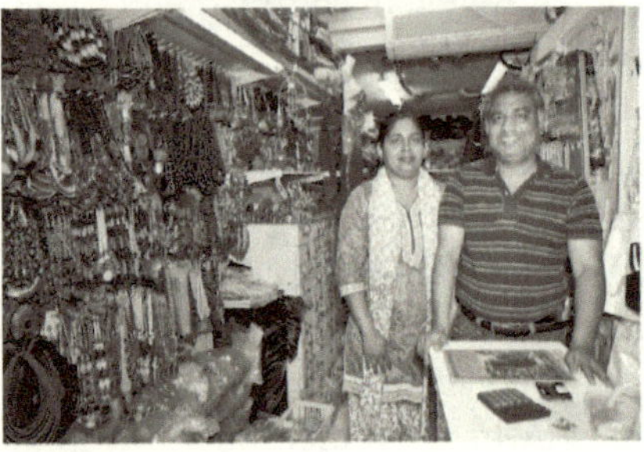

FIGURE 3.8. Tabacaria shopkeepers pictured by Gonçalo Gaioso in *All Around Us*

FIGURE 3.9. Shopkeeper photographed by Gonçalo Gaioso for *All Around Us*

FIGURE 3.10. Images of shopkeepers in Mouraria featured in *All Around Us*

flags, and souvenirs that surround them, displayed in glass cases and sturdy stands, contributing to the sense of the established presence of this type of commerce in the neighborhood. A calendar and clock, which appear in the center of the frame, likewise add to the sense that the image captures a place and time specific to Mouraria, and Portugal more broadly.

In another example, a woman is photographed from the threshold of her store, with Portuguese-themed linens and aprons on display the foreground. Behind her, one can discern a range of convenience-oriented goods from health and beauty to cleaning supplies. While a market of this sort could exist in a range of urban contexts, the abundance of items adorned with the Rooster of Barcelós that occupy a third of the portrait emphasize the place of this shop in the space and time of a Portuguese neighborhood. The handwritten signage and unrefined displays throughout the scene indicate that this is a small, independently owned operation, rather than part of a larger commercial chain or wholesale distributor. This image is also suggestive of how established businesses generate new forms of income as Mouraria is positioned as a tourist attraction. The linens, displayed on the street, contrast with the more utilitarian items in the interior of the store, alluding to the distinctive publics to whom local shops cater as neighborhoods become more touristed. These details prompt an empathetic response on the part of

FIGURE 3.11. Two portraits of shopkeepers in wholesale goods stores featured in *All Around Us*

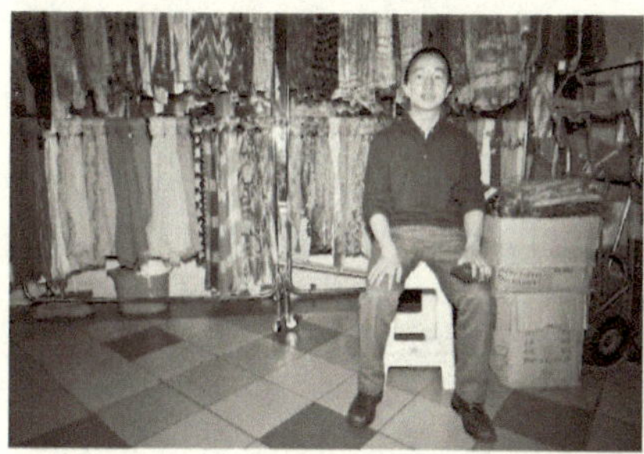

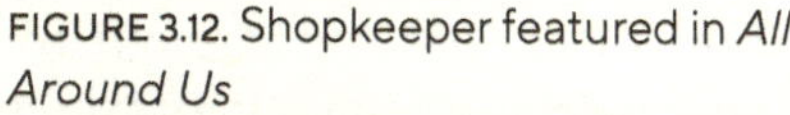

FIGURE 3.12. Shopkeeper featured in *All Around Us*

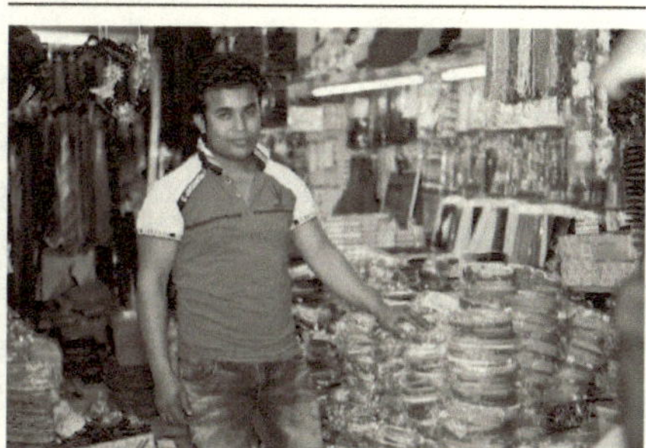

the spectator, witness to this earnest effort to maintain local enterprise under the mounting pressures of a speculative, increasingly globalized market.

In contrast, Gaioso captures the brunt of the series' non-White subjects in contextually ambiguous commercial spheres, fostering the visual attachment between racial Otherness and non-places throughout the exhibit. In one such scene, for example, a couple stands side by side in a narrow store packed with products from floor to ceiling. The improvised appearance of the shop, which is pictured with no natural light or windows in view, is accentuated by the amount of goods crowded on movable shelves. The large quantities of inventory and crates of duplicate merchandise depicted in the photograph indicate that these are wholesale goods, a category of product as unremarkable and transferrable as a non-place itself. In the foreground of the image, a large calculator rests on a standalone white countertop, both portable and compact objects, adding to the ephemeral sense conveyed by the snapshot. Effectively, Gaioso documents an atemporal and ahistorical commercial display, which out of the out context of the exhibit, could be attributed to a litany of urban spaces, from London and New York to New Delhi or Dhaka.

A return to Cheng's concept of *ornamentalism* is useful for delving deeper into how the interiority of the racial Other, like in the photos of the wholesalers, may be shaped by the depiction of their material circumstances, particularly from the perspective of a White viewer.[46] She writes, "To attend to ornamentalism is to ask how racial personhood can be assembled not through organic flesh, but instead through synthetic inventions and designs, not through corporeal embodiment but rather through attachments that are metonymic and hence superficial, detachable, and migratory."[47] This theory of being elucidates the peculiar fusion between people and objects that often underpins racial thinking and racialization. Cheng describes this process as an interplay of legal, material, and imaginative factors that help name and conceive of personhood through ornamental gestures; for example, how an Asian woman's display in proximity to china, "allows her to be read as a particular kind of surface."[48] This logic can be extended to assess the relationship between the wholesalers pictured by Gaioso, and the transient and undervalued objects that surround them. Their personhood, as conveyed in this image, is borne of an exchange between the individual and the object, with their interiority rendered as decontextualized as the space they inhabit.

A similar visual interchange occurs in several other portraits in the series. In one such image, a man sits on a plastic stool in front of two racks displaying colorful scarves. Each of the metal racks are on wheels, suggesting that this setup could be easily broken down, moved, and re-established in another location. Next to the subject of the photograph, two cardboard boxes filled with unwrapped goods are stacked atop one another, indicating the volume of merchandise that moves through the store. The large cardboard boxes and plastic packages of scarves not yet hung on racks are additional details that imply that these are mass manufactured products. In the next image, a man stands alongside a stack of plastic-wrapped merchandise in a store awash with fluorescent lights. The sheer quantity of items indicates that these, too, are likely wholesale goods, an accumulation of objects reflective of a mass consumer society. With no discernable surfaces left to display items, the products wallpaper the store's vertical space, an overwhelming demonstration of man's ability to produce and consume. Void of context, the spectator unfamiliar with these spaces and individuals is compelled to perceive these subjects in terms of their surroundings: a sea of makeshift items, goods in transit, and the exponential possibilities of machine-made apparel. They, like the products surrounding them, are movable objects, who may migrate from this scene to another, existing in a manner that transcends the geographic parameters of the exhibit and relates to the material excess and transnational flows of contemporary capitalist production.

The lack of natural light and reference to the way these shops are integrated into the neighborhood's landscape, too, contrasts with the way White subjects in the series are predominantly pictured from beyond the threshold of their businesses. Indeed, it is not immediately apparent how one would access several of the shops depicted without a discernable entryway, or if they are open to the public, especially a visiting public. This artistic choice positions the more established business models, like the market and *tabacaria* as open, accessible, and integrated in the street life of the community, while reinforcing the notion of those considered the racial Other as clandestine and isolated from the broader populace.[49] In fact, the subjects in *All Around Us* depicted as accessible and therefore connected to their neighbors via the artist's invocation of public space are exclusively White merchants. Such framing can embolden assumptions on the part of an uninformed or prejudiced spectator regarding migrants and racialized populations with a propensity to view differing models for daily life as infringing upon time-honored traditions. As looking, seeing, and knowing are interrelated acts, the observable juxtapositions in *All Around Us* between White subjects, portrayed in contextualized scenes, and non-White subjects, pictured primarily in transitory spaces, reinforce the sense of an original and an interloper in Mouraria's social and economic landscape. Accordingly, Whiteness is situated as an integral dimension of the neighborhood's origin story, to which individuals may then turn when lamenting the loss of community connections. Overall, this display of the commercial landscape of Mouraria, while positioned as a positive depiction, provides fodder for more problematic generalizations that circulate regarding race and socioeconomic proclivities in increasingly diverse communities.[50]

While Gaioso's intervention aimed to promote the neighborhood as an attraction vis-à-vis reference to its multicultural nature, his images, whether intentionally or not, reinforce standards of belonging drawn along racial lines. The celebratory tone used to frame these divisions associates implicit hierarchies with a sense of joy, fostering affective attachments that act as a shield against critiques of racial stratification. These discursive tendencies suggest that one cannot oppress another if the Other is viewed through a lens of love or admiration. Consequently, cloaking racialized viewing in positive allusions effectively leverages difference for cultural expedience, regardless of the cultural producer's intent. Such is Mirzoeff's argument that capital "has commodified all aspects of everyday life, including the human body and even the process of looking itself."[51] *All Around Us* was designed to complement a market built for consumption, a space with the explicit objective to stoke consumer interest in Mouraria. Therefore, it was imperative that the difference showcased in Gaioso's photographs was cast in a positive light, in order to facilitate its role as a commodity. Upon closer interrogation, the images fall into a similar narrative pattern as explored in Valbuena's *Nosotros*, where the belief in a mythical original is sustained as a neutral form against which the racial Other is defined and understood.

Overall, the visual narratives advanced through *Nosotros* and *All Around Us* embody a distinct form of racialized viewing deeply influenced by the socioeconomic pressures and demographic anxieties of the period following the

FIGURE 3.13. Camila Watson's *Canto do Sol* pictured on the corner of Mouraria's Rua dos Lagares, 2022

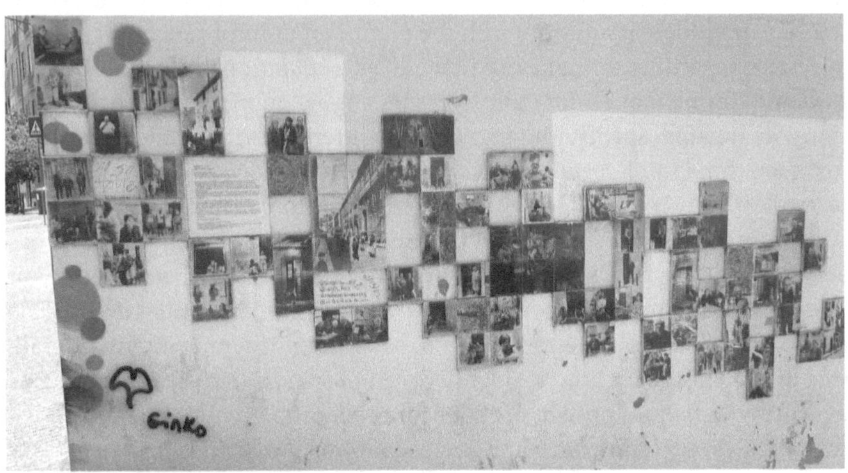

financial crisis. In both cases, White mediators advance a vision of conviviality in a purported push against the ongoing stigmatization of neighborhoods like Lavapiés and Mouraria, presented as a good-faith effort to celebrate the evolving community. Yet, as this chapter has examined, these versions of happy multiculturalism often have the converse effect of reinforcing standards of belonging forged along racial lines, the parameters of which shift according to different social, economic, and migratory pressures. And in the end, the primary benefactors of these efforts to influence public opinion regarding these spaces and their inhabitants were not the community members of Lavapiés and Mouraria, but instead the investors and entrepreneurs with the power to capitalize on the burgeoning exchange-value of the neighborhoods, and the consumers to whom their services appealed. Ultimately, the very individuals championed in projects like *Nosotros* and *All Around Us* for lending these spaces their flair would be left to grapple with the economic fall-out of their districts' newfound popularity. For many, this would result in their exodus.[52]

In 2017, with these consequences increasingly palpable, British photographer and long-time Mouraria resident Camilla Watson debuted *Canto do Sol* (Sunny Corner), a public installation positioned as a reflection on the human impact of the neighborhood's growing tourism and consumption industries. For the piece, a series of monochrome images printed on mosaic tiles were mounted on a corner adjacent to the twenty block of Rua dos Lagares, the ongoing site of a highly publicized anti-eviction struggle involving several families, a multinational developer, and the municipal government.[53] Watson, speaking to the impetus behind her intervention, explained, "In recent years the community has been under threat because many inhabitants have been asked to vacate their properties for tourists. For me this gave a sense of urgency to show that community has always existed on this corner and that we must value it."[54] While Watson's intervention finds common ground with those of Valbuena and Gaioso in that it was framed as a celebration of Mouraria's community, autochthonous and immigrant alike, it differed in its contestatory objectives. In fact, this mediation on Mouraria's residents was positioned in direct opposition to the rationale for *All Around Us*, an intervention meant to stoke interest in visiting the area.

To illustrate her point, Watson juxtaposed images of Mouraria's street life that she had taken since 2010 with historic photographs of the same area dating to the early twentieth century. By editing and printing the newer images to emulate the aesthetic qualities of the earlier snapshots, the artist created a type of visual continuity that supported her overarching narrative regarding Mouraria's long legacy of public life. This optimistic display of community was further illustrated through open-air scenes of different subjects ranging in age and racial appearance, tied together by the backdrop of public space: alone and in groups on stoops, doorways, and sidewalks. In addition to context clues within the images themselves, the tiles included names and dates in their bottom corners, distinguishing between the old and the new, and cultivating a sense of shared values across time periods and subjectivities. This visual return to the early twentieth century as a means by which to orient community values is curiously comparable to Valbuena's use of the *corrala* at the start of *Nosotros*, in that it can be read as a selective return to the aesthetics of the time before globalization, particularly in conversations regarding an ideal community. Watson, in this case, orients her explicit condemnation of impact of speculative capital on Mouraria's residents with reference to scenes from the city's past, depending significantly on images of the neighborhood from the era prior to the immigration boom. Such a nostalgic return to the past when denouncing the challenges of the present, thus, merits further inquiry in terms of the fact that it, too, is entangled with hierarchies of belonging.

Keeping this in mind, these next chapters of the manuscript turn to cultural contestations, like that of Watson, that responded to the boom of capital-oriented urban development in Lavapiés and Mouraria in the years following the 2008 financial crisis. While I acknowledge that many of the examples I have selected for study demonstrate the power of collective organization when denouncing the way the city and its inhabitants were viewed in terms of their potential for monetary gain, my focus will be on primarily on the affective implications of these contestations. In doing so, I bring to the fore the prevalent, unexpected, and often problematic social and cultural attachments that surfaced in oppositional culture during this period.

Interlude

Throughout the previous chapters, we have explored the ways in which Mouraria and Lavapiés were mobilized, through visual, digital, and embodied culture, as centers of consumption and capital accumulation in the wake of the global financial collapse of 2008. The diverse text types and actors involved in this process highlight the way that urban change is the result of broad cultural networks with explicit or passing interest in improving their social and material circumstances. By and large, the narratives explored in previous chapters cast economic growth, by way of consumer-oriented development, as a desirable avenue for reorganizing the unraveling of everyday life catalyzed by the crisis. To this point, we have focused on case studies demonstrating how this vision was achieved through a consensus among different cultural actors who built and promoted recognizable brands by harnessing, sanitizing, and recasting each neighborhoods' respective past as a hub of the working poor, and present as a center of racial heterogeneity, as a type of aestheticized trope. In the process, we have touched upon how government-supported advocacy within these neighborhoods, including the work of Renovar a Mouraria (Chapter 1) and the Casa Árabe in Lavapiés (Chapter 3), largely fell in step with the growth-oriented vision, engaging with each area's diverse populace in terms of its cultural expediency. Yet, just as the urban served as a means through which dominant social, political, and economic interest groups could control the narrative on their terms, it was also a frequent site of resistance to this predominant post-crisis urban model.

With this in consideration, the final case studies in this study turn to cultural products framed explicitly as antihegemonic activism that, too, contributed to the ongoing production of the city during the post-2008 era. I emphasize this distinction to underline not just the differences but also unexpected commonalities in narratives disseminated by cultural producers on opposing sides of the ideological spectrum as they attempted to mitigate, through storytelling, the challenges of the crisis era. Rather than assess these oppositional cultural texts in terms of the extent to which such interventions successfully impeded urban change or the exodus of certain populations (a more quantitative task), I focus, instead, on which issues and whose interests came to the fore as oppositional culture reared its head in these evolving neighborhoods. One of my central questions, in this process, is how, and the extent to which, stakeholders engaged with race and racial difference in their process of contestation. As in previous chapters, the ongoing discussion of how this manifested in two different districts serves to illuminate aspirations and preoccupations in distinct national contexts, revealing both continuities and variances in the affective negotiation of post-crisis urban development in the Iberian region.

As we turn to interventions that respond to and resist hegemonic modes of urban production, I keep in mind Harvey's argument regarding the complexities of fighting for the "right to the city." He states,

> The question of what kind of city we want cannot be divorced from the question of what kind of people we want to be, what kinds of social relations we seek, what relations to nature we cherish, what style of life we desire, what aesthetic values we hold. The right to the city is, therefore, far more than a right of individual or group access to the resources that the city embodies: it is a right to change and reinvent the city more after our heart's desire. It is, moreover, a collective rather than an individual right, since reinventing the city inevitably depends upon the exercise of a collective power over the process of urbanization.[1]

As Harvey maintains, exercising one's "right to the city" is not, alone, a question of access. Rather, it is the way that a given collective shapes processes of urbanization according to their desires and aspirations. As different interest groups seek to forge more workable geographies for these spaces and their inhabitants, they, too, disseminate narratives informed by the plurality of their desires. Indeed, the "good life" fantasies and aspirations regarding urban life, to return to Berlant, are not limited to a single political or economic ideology, but rather are as multifaceted as the stakeholders who disseminate them. By interrogating the affective attachments and implications of the anti-hegemonic alternatives presented by cultural actors in the chapters that follow, it is possible to uncover systems of power functioning both within and beyond capitalist class interests that also shape urban spaces. In this process, as anthropologist Delgado Ruíz notes, the city is not just a backdrop for protesting social woes, but also a site actively shaped by oppositional acts.[2] These are necessary points to establish in order to more effectively engage with the multiple and even contradictory ways that those fighting for Lavapiés and Mouraria expressed their vision for an alternate social and material landscape. While the brunt of contestatory interventions found common ground in that they responded to the power of predatory capital, they, like the collectives that gave them form, were not a monolithic force.

A brief return to the anti-austerity protests of 2011, to which the brunt of the activism considered in these next case studies is connected either explicitly or in spirit, aids in comprehending the wide scope of interests at play in efforts to both critique and propose alternatives to the branded city model that rapidly gained momentum in the post-2008 era. During this wave of civil unrest in Spain and Portugal, activists took to and actively occupied public spaces, calling attention through spatial disruption to their discontent with the models of governance practiced by political and economic elites.[3] In both nations, protestors advanced a range of proposals that reflected the diverse interests of demonstrators seizing their opportunity to be heard. Snyder, speaking to the Spanish context, references the form of a polysyndeton (and . . . and . . . and . . .) to understand the *indignadxs*'s varied demands for change, emphasizing how one movement could stand for a "multiplicity of concerns" from an array of individuals and platforms regarding varied and intersecting subjects including "gender equality, protections for undocumented immigrants, renewable sources of energy, election law reform, debt-forgiveness on foreclosure, precarious employment, political corruption, and so on."[4] Portugal's Geração à rasca, which took cues from the Spanish protests, may also be understood in this manner, given that its participants, too, articulated heterogeneous objectives regarding national politics, financial precarity, environmental protections, and social justice under the overarching framework of contestation.

The social, economic, and politically engaged networks born of these protests found a life beyond their initial public expression in spaces like Madrid's Plaza del Sol and Lisbon's Rossio Square. As encampments were dismantled, activism continued in the form of local assemblies and action initiatives across the peninsula. This was especially prevalent in Spain, where the nearly month-long occupation of Sol provided time for protestors to organize their actions into a model of horizontal organization and governance exportable to other areas of the city as neighborhood assemblies.[5] In Madrid, the Indignadxs established over one hundred local *asambleas* with the objective of uniting neighborhood-specific stakeholders in spearheading initiatives related to evolving needs not met through the political establishment's approach to governance.[6] Lavapiés, in this regard, was an especially prominent site for these activities, given the ongoing social and economic challenges faced by members of its populace, and established networks of community solidarity and support that predated the 15-M Movement. Moreover, the district's historic alignment with left-wing resistance, from Republican solidarity during the Civil-War era, to the more recent Okupa movement, served as a useful point of reference for collectives established in the wake of the 2011 protests, including the new progressive political party Podemos (We Can, founded in 2014), which elected to open their headquarters in the district. Though Portuguese anti-austerity received less global attention than the Spanish protests, it, too, lived on through the continued actions of platforms and organizations both born of and predating the demonstrations including Cidadãos por Lisboa (Citizens for Lisboa), Associação de Combate à Precariedade (Association to Fight Precarity), and Primavera Global Portuguesa (Portuguese Global Spring).

Of necessary emphasis is the fact that these networked social movements, to employ Castells's summation of the period, surfaced and expanded *in tandem with* the post-crisis drive for consumer-oriented development explored in preceding chapters.[7] This ongoing tension would reinforce one of the primary claims of those demanding "Real Democracy Now": that their governments did not representing the will of the people, and would inform the way that anti-hegemonic grassroots actions would shift according to subsequent actions by the political and economic elites.[8] In terms of the urban as a site of affective expressions, it is also logical that the accelerated drive to mold the landscape of Spanish and Portuguese cities in terms of their exchange-value rather than the social welfare of their inhabitants would be accompanied by mounting expressions of discontent in a range of discursive and spatial forms, from artistic and material interventions, to the rise of municipalist parties in local government.[9] Moreover, this range of reactions were further evidence of the different "patterns of adjustment," behaviors Berlant describes as "toward and beyond survival," that surfaced as societal agents felt their way through the affective impact of the financial collapse—some imagining radical alternatives to the status quo, and others doubling down on their optimistic attachments to the promise of capital accumulation.[10]

Shifting focus to interventions presented as an alternative to or contestation of the status quo, the next chapter looks at the grassroots-led redevelopment of Lavapiés's Mercado de San Fernando as a counterpoint to the spatial production of manufactured multiculturalism in Mouraria's Mercado de Fusão, studied in Chapter 2. There, I examined how branding practices, fomented through strategic partnerships between the public and private sector and buoyed by local stakeholders, came to fruition in the built environment, drawing from both Lefebvre's foundational theorization of space is a social product and Harvey's supporting argument regarding the centrality of political and economic agency to urbanization processes. Now, informed by the same theoretical underpinnings, I assess which meanings and values were given prominence in an intervention explicitly positioned as an alternative to neoliberal urban models, and weigh the extent to which the redeveloped space broke from the social and economic paradigms that oriented dominant modes of urban and cultural production in the Iberian nations during this period. As a point of entry into this case study, we will first consider the symbolic weight and the declining state of Madrid's municipal markets at the turn of the twenty-first century, a review of which informs my assessment of how the Mercado de San Fernando was imagined as a space for alternative social and economic possibilities by oppositional stakeholders.

CHAPTER 4

Markets and the Limits of Opposition

In "Mujeres del mercado," Ángela Figuera Aymerich engages with the character of the female shopper as a means by which to denounce the impoverished condition of the lower classes in the aftermath of the Spanish Civil War. The powerful imagery of this piece, in which the "market woman" purchases wrinkled tomatoes, moldy oranges, and over-ripe vegetables with the filthy change in her worn-out coin purse, renders tangible a relationship between poverty and decay. The significance of this site, beyond brick and mortar, is central to the author's narrative.

> They are of lime and brine. Forever old.
> Rusty armor lined with muck.
> Their eyes hard like cold sleet.
> Hair withered like stomped grass.
> And a malignant vinegar courses through their veins.
>
> They go to the market early. They snoop around the stands.
> Almost investigating. They choose rotten tomatoes.
> Moldy oranges. Macerated vegetables
> that already smell of dung. They buy cooked blood
> in dark cylinders like sludge cheese
> and those lungs they display, rosy pink and timid,
> an obscene illusion.

When paying, a breath parts their lips
slowly exploring the filthy womb
of an enormous threadbare purse without straps
with a furious fear of running into the unforeseen
at its depths the last grimy coin.[1]

Through reference to the market's unpleasant qualities, demonstrated through a reciprocal exchange with the shopper herself, Figuera Aymerich calls attention to the connection between space and identity: you are what—and where—you consume. Her spatially engaged depiction of Spain's working poor as they exist within and in relation to the market brings to life Zukin's description of such locales both as tangible sites of commercial activity and "symbolic thresholds," traditionally bound with local communities.[2] Accordingly, the market exists simultaneously as a physical place that houses the exchange of goods and services and as a more abstract and evolving social institution, reflective of changing modes of production and consumption. In Figuera Aymerich's poem, the *mercado de abastos*, a covered building comprised of stalls rented by small retailers offering foodstuffs and quotidian services like tailoring and repairs for mainly local clients, takes on symbolic weight as the domain of a specific social class moving forward in the wake of the devastation of war.[3] Yet, as modes of production and consumption changed over time, so too would the affective implications of these types of spaces.[4]

Most critically, as cultural conversations regarding the *mercado de abastos* have evolved over the decades, these spaces are increasingly discussed in relation to positive and prideful emotions, eclipsing the more drab and unceremonious perspective shared in Figuera Aymerich's poem. This shift, provocatively, occurred in tandem with the declining use of the market model during the late twentieth century and the corresponding degradation of such environments, changes fueled by evolving consumer habits, globalized commercial institutions, and the advent of new technologies. Increasingly, the arrival of supermarkets to Spain backed by multinational corporations offering extended hours, a broader selection, and lower prices would draw clients away from the more limited goods and services provided by independent proprietors in *mercados de abastos*. The newer establishments complemented evolving household practices, with both men and women now working outside of the home, and the large brunt of shopping occurring outside of office hours. The market timetable—opening early, closing after lunchtime for rest, and opening once again in the late afternoon—was better suited for the dwindling number of households where a member of the family or hired help cared for the home as full-time labor. Urban planning, too, took a toll on the use and infrastructure of *mercados de abastos* throughout the Iberian Peninsula. In Madrid as the local government steered growth toward burgeoning suburbs, consumers increasingly opted for the one-stop, car-oriented shopping experience available at the growing number of commercial centers and box-stores dotting the highways on the city's periphery.[5] This convenience-driven model of business was also brought to the city center, as supermarket chains like DIA and Carrefour opened neighborhood outposts.[6] Amidst these shifts, the downturn in *mercados de abastos* clientele was accompanied by a similar decline in maintenance of Madrid's forty-six municipal markets, further compromising their commercial viability.

The evolving affective weight attached to such environments became increasingly evident in the late twentieth and early twenty-first century as social actors began to address their steady abandonment. In academic forums like *Distribución y consumo*, scholars discussed steps for remodeling, renovating, and rethinking consumption practices to ensure the continuity of *mercados de abastos*, given mounting obstacles to the success of this traditional commercial model.[7] In the process, those lamenting the loss of the market made explicit the way in which these spaces had become entangled with social values. In a 1997 article on the subject, for example, economists Javier Casares Ripol and Alfonso Rebollo Arevalo state, "Municipal markets have and continue to be a unifying base for cities. Pirenne wrote that cities are the children of commerce, and within that one must highlight the important role of *mercados de abastos* as a type of glue for traditional urban life."[8] Such assessments underline how the material space of a *mercado de abastos* had become enmeshed with a sense of origins, a powerful relationship that could be invoked according to different ideological perspectives, particularly in moments of increased tension over the future of urban spaces and their populations.

The social value assigned to *mercados de abastos* is also perceptible in the later work of anthropologist Juan Ignacio Robles.[9] In a 2008 article dedicated to the subject, he writes, "The market is meeting place, where neighbors exchange information, favors and goods, bolstering mutual social relations. Markets are convivial spaces, where the long history of buying and selling between customers and merchants, sometimes across generations (from parents to children) forges strong reciprocal relationships between merchants and customers based on mutual knowledge and trust."[10] By emphasizing conviviality, familiarity, and trust, Robles paints a picture of a space characterized by mutual acquaintance and intergenerational community ties. These descriptors, associated primarily with positive feelings, situate this model of market as a desirable and thus defensible institution. Likewise, this reflection recalls what Zukin describes as the "moral right to the city," a sense of authenticity forged through "a continuous process of living and working, a gradual buildup of everyday experience, the expectation that neighbors and buildings that are here today will be here tomorrow."[11] The value placed in such practices perceived as a constant thus illuminates why sites like Madrid's markets, and those who make use of these spaces in the manner most consistent with the prevailing public imaginary, would be powerful and hotly debated symbolic thresholds during periods of accelerated urban change.

Prior to the financial crisis, government officials in Madrid had already begun to direct substantial attention to renovations of the city's markets according to the Plan de Innovación y Transformación de los Mercados de Madrid (2003–2011) (Plan for Innovating and Transforming Madrid's Markets).[12] Accordingly, this plan sought to reposition these spaces, through rehabilitation and strategic branding, within a commercial landscape that favored multinational supermarkets and box stores.[13] Points of action included updating both the physical structures and commercial offerings of thirty-nine of the city's network of markets, streamlining their management through dedicated courses and municipal ordinances, and fomenting interest in these sites as a cohesive point of social and cultural value through the "Mercados de Madrid" marketing initiative. In general, these plans sought to combat the ongoing degradation of the city's network of markets by rethinking the parameters of their design, aiming to convert many into mixed-use shopping, dining, and leisure destinations. Given the substantial funds required for the undertaking, ongoing collaborations between the local government, small-business owners, and economic agents including supermarket chains and hoteliers were at the core of bringing these plans to fruition. The economic downturn following 2008 crisis, in turn, would accelerate the transition of many of these spaces in full or in part to private ownership, a process already mapped out in the city government's designs.

Take, as an example, the second life of the Mercado de San Antón, a municipal market located a short five-minute walk north of the Gran Vía thoroughfare in the Chueca neighborhood of central Madrid. Its redesign, described by then-mayor Alberto Ruiz-Gallardón as a response to the "Anglo-Saxon commercial model" included demolishing and rebuilding the building itself, a project subsidized by both the municipal and provincial governments.[14] SuperCor, a supermarket chain within the El Corte Inglés department store conglomerate, absorbed a significant portion of the costs not covered by government subsidies, and in return was granted management of one-third of the newly constructed space.[15] The renovation process extended over a period of four years, from breaking ground in 2007 to reopening the market to the public in 2011. Over this time, the majority of San Antón's Asociación de Comerciantes (Shopkeeper's Association) were bought out from the project, with only eleven original vendors remaining at the end of the protracted period of reformation. The space that debuted in May 2011 was a far cry from the small-scale commerce typical of markets of decades past, offering, instead, a full-fledged gastronomic experience including restaurants, wine bars, terraces, and take-away food stalls. While some grocery stands remained, only one per genre was permitted (a single fruit stand, a single bread stand, and so forth) in a stated effort to facilitate a balanced offer of goods, and in a clear move to ensure non-competition with the SuperCor store housed in the bottom story of the building.[16] Overall, the project fell in step with the tourism and leisure industries proving themselves resilient in the post-crisis era, and was championed as a lucrative and creative solution to underutilized space.[17] At the same time, the renovated market was an object of discontent for those who found the new focus of the market alienating to locals struggling with social and economic precarity.[18]

The leisure-focused upscaling of San Antón was not an isolated case, but rather the prevailing model for reimagining Madrid's markets during this era, especially for those that were located in the city's most touristed areas. Indeed, one of the most emblematic examples of this type of intervention was the renovation of the Mercado de San Miguel, a glass and iron structure located a stone's throw from the Plaza Mayor. Beginning in 2003, the Gastrónomo de San Miguel restaurant group slowly acquired each of the building's seventy-five stands and reopened the space, now fully privatized, in 2009 as a *mercado gastronómico* (gastronomic market), a designation that emphasized its distinction from the *mercado de abastos* model.[19] Departing entirely from the utilitarian function of markets past, the new space was a culinary playground targeted primarily at the tourists frequenting the area, a role emphasized in promotional materials that described the market as "a monument to Spanish cuisine."[20] The self-proclaimed monument featured a range of remodeled stands and food carts selling "the finest Iberian ham . . . the most exquisite cheeses from Castile, Asturias and the Basque Country" and other small bites to visitors of the attraction.[21] This gastronomic model soon became a rousing success, with immediate access to an array of the peninsula's culinary offerings drawing in local and international consumers alike.[22] At the same time, the explicit molding of this space to the desires and expectations of the spending class drew criticism from those opposed to such developmental priorities. Urban scholar Alejandro Rodríguez Sebastián, for example, discusses the market as a source of inspiration for his work on gentrification in Madrid, explaining, "The moment I decided to take on this project was a night when I was walking around Madrid with some friends. We were stopped in front of San Miguel Market's large windows, watching the people inside sampling excellent wines and consuming tapas designed with the most exquisite taste. It was then that we arrived at a concise but profound conclusion: 'this isn't a market anymore.'"[23]

In this reflection, Rodríguez Sebastián takes issue with the terminology assigned to San Miguel, contending that a space dedicated to upscale, leisure-oriented consumption should not be classified as a market at all. His frustration with the exclusionary nature of the renovated site, inaccessible for those without sufficient spending power, is intertwined with a broader debate regarding the definition of markets themselves. In turn, he draws a clear line in his assessment, expressing nostalgia for a specific commercial model that he feels has been lost in his lamentation of San Miguel's present. In my assessment of Rodríguez Sebastián's sentiments, I draw upon Svetlana Boym's discussion of nostalgia as a "historical emotion" characterized by a longing for a different time. Boym notes, "The nostalgic desires to obliterate history and turn it into private or collective mythology, to revisit time as space," and assigns the term *restorative nostalgia* to perspectives that present themselves as truth and tradition.[24] She further argues that this emotion fuels national and nationalist revivals globally, "which engage in the antimodern myth-making of history by means of a return to national symbols and myths."[25] Rodríguez Sebastián's reflection is certainly imbued with this sense of nostalgia, as he laments the loss of an ostensibly authentic original rooted in a selective memory of *mercados de abastos* prior to globalization. The way this sense of longing hinges on a selective invocation of decades-past is a critical consideration to keep in mind as we delve into the redevelopment of the Mercado de San Fernando, an attempt on the part of local collectives to build an alternative to the gastronomic market trend in the complex identitarian context of Lavapiés.

An Oppositional Model: The Mercado de San Fernando

August in Madrid is a notoriously quiet month. With temperatures regularly grazing 100 degrees fahrenheit and constant sunshine beating down on the city's pavement, there is little respite from the heat. The city tends to slow down during these weeks. Businesses shutter for annual vacations, and workers

FIGURE 4.1. Exterior shot of the Mercado de San Fernando, 2008

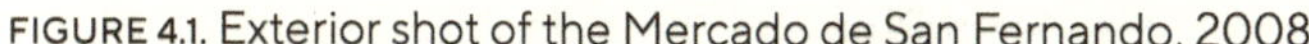

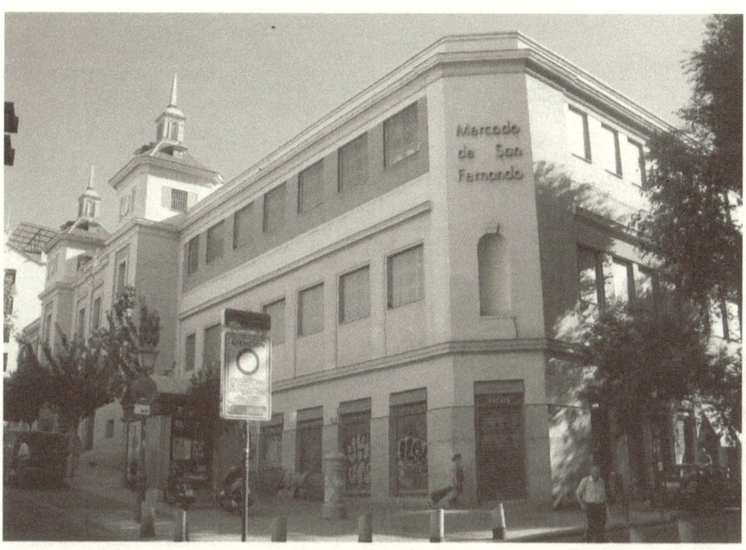

with time off leave for cooler destinations: villages, the coast, and destinations beyond the peninsula. Though many posts in the city's network of markets close during this time, with proprietors opting to take vacations that correspond with the drop in daily shoppers often associated with this month, some remain open for the spike in foot traffic generated by neighborhood festivals like the La Paloma celebrations in La Latina, San Cayetano in the Rastro and Embajadores, and San Lorenzo in Lavapiés. In some of the leisure-focused markets, like San Miguel, many stands do not close at all, continuing to cater to the tourists who still flock to the city during these scorching months.

My afternoon trip to Lavapiés's Mercado de San Fernando in August 2015 proved no exception to these rules. I arrived at the market via Calle Embajadores, a thoroughfare that descends from the Plaza de Cascorro at the northwestern-most limit of Embajadores and continues through Lavapiés in the direction of the city's southern neighborhoods. At the street's intersection with Calle del Sombrerete, I came upon the market. The imposing structure, designed by Castro Fernández-Shaw and inaugurated in 1944, is an homage to the architectural styles of Madrid during the Hapsburg dynasty, known as Madrid de los Austrias, featuring characteristic red facades, prominent corner towers, and pointed roofs.[26] These architectural references, common in constructions dating to the early years of the Franco regime, can be found

FIGURE 4.2. Interior shot of the Mercado de San Fernando, 2015

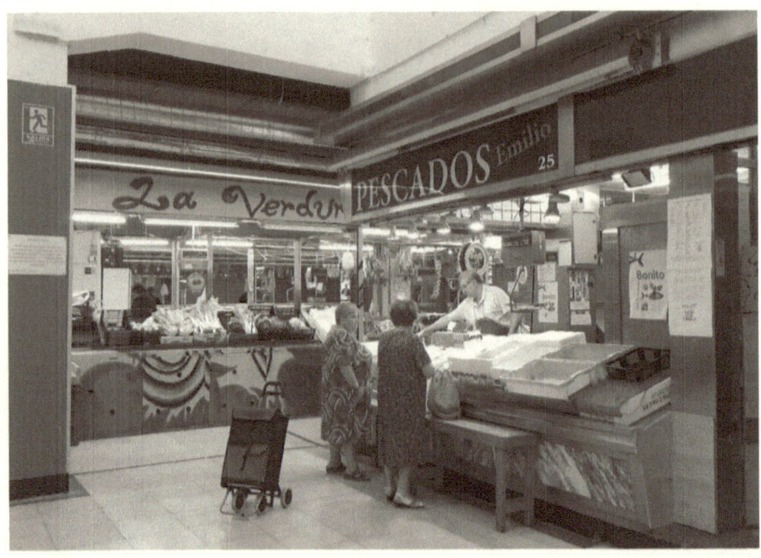

in several corners of the city, including the famed Cuartel General del Ejército del Aire y del Espacio (General Headquarters of the Air and Space Force) in Moncloa and the neighboring compound of buildings on Calle de la Princesa.

Once inside the space it was quiet, given that many proprietors had closed their stands for an extended August vacation. The market echoed in a way that recalled the era before its rehabilitation, when such silence could have been attributed to the number of posts standing vacant behind closed shutters. A short walk around the building's aisles, and a closer peek into different stalls, however, indicated that San Fernando was far from empty, despite the summer lull. Instead, its various posts offered a diverse array of consumer options, with functional *mercado de abastos* stands like butchers, cheese shops, and a locksmith alongside retailers catering toward entertainment and recreation, including a store selling books by the kilo, and a wine shop where customers could stay for a drink or snack.

The Mercado de San Fernando that I explored in 2015 had, like many in the city, changed significantly since its degradation in the late twentieth century, when the evolving lifestyles and commercial practices of consumers had taken a measurable effect on the use and care of the space. In Lavapiés, this downturn was accompanied by the fact that the neighborhood's newest entrepreneurs, in particular those catering to the area's growing immigrant populace, tended to open establishments outside of the more regimented structure of the *mercados de abastos*.[27]

Amid this decline in use, and the city-wide push to redesign its municipal markets, the Mercado de San Fernando became a recurring point of interest for rehabilitation efforts. In 1997, for example, the interior and exterior of the site underwent renovations under the auspices of Lavapiés's designation as an Area de Rehabilitación Preferente.[28] Later, as traffic to the market continued to falter, the space would be targeted for a second round of restorations in 2005 as part of the *Plan de Innovación y Transformación de los Mercados*. Without sufficient funding, these plans would be left unfinished until two years later, in 2007, when the local government converted a portion of the building into a public health center in an effort to rethink the use of underutilized market spaces.[29] Just a year later, in 2008, it appeared that San Fernando would meet a similar fate to the Mercado de San Antón, as it was slated to be sold to the supermarket chain Eroski.[30] Under the pressures of the financial crisis, the sale fell through, and by 2010, in the aftermath of the collapse, San Fernando's remaining vendors advertised the price of each vacant stall, opening up a dialogue among locals regarding their role in defining the market's future.[31]

At this juncture, the trajectory for the Mercado de San Fernando departed significantly that of the Mercado de San Antón and Mercado de San Miguel. Specifically, the Lavapiés market became distinctly intertwined with the 15-M Movement, emerging as a point of concern for activists involved in the protests. The aggressive privatization of public properties was among the myriad issues with which the Indignadxs engaged, and the trajectory of Madrid's municipal markets was no exception to this conversation. Across the city, principals of self-management, collectivity, assembly, and direct democracy were being mobilized in order to put derelict or abandoned public spaces into the hands of the surrounding community. In turn, activists identified the Mercado de San Fernando as an opportunity to design an alternative, grassroots model for reshaping the city's *mercados de abastos*.

During my visit I spoke with Asunción, one of the co-proprietors of a post named La Huerta del Sol (The Sol Garden), who shared the story of collective organizing stemming from the 2011 protests that had shifted the task of rehabilitating the Mercado de San Fernando to local networks. According to Asunción, this push began with a series of community meetings organized as a continuation of the Sol *asambleas*. Activists gathered at the Tabacalera, a once-vacant tobacco factory turned social and cultural center that stands blocks from the then-ailing Mercado de San Fernando. She explained, "There was a two-day meeting between many collectives with common ideas to see what we could do, and there was the market next door that was about to close. We assessed it together and decided that several collectives would enter at the same time to build up the market."[32]

Asunción's description of the initiative underscores the wave of public interest and investment in reordering spaces discarded or abandoned by speculative capital after the 15-M protests. In particular, the movement galvanized new models of direct democratic participation like the neighborhood *asambleas*, providing the infrastructure for community members to identify and repurpose un- or underexploited corners of the city for social welfare rather than capital gain. The Tabacalera, where the idea for the San Fernando project came to fruition, is an early example of one such space, a recognized cultural and social center that began as the Centro Social Okupado Autogestionado El Laboratorio (The Laboratory Self-Managed Squatted Social Center).[33] Throughout this period, corners of city once conceived as "spaces of refuse," as Feinberg and Larson term them, were increasingly reclaimed and reshaped as participatory sites for direct governance and collaborative social production in the spirit of the Indignadxs movement.[34] Notable examples include the Campo de la Cebada (The Barley Field), an unfinished sports complex adjacent to the Mercado de La Cebada in La Latina that was converted into a multiuse social space, and Esta es una plaza (This Is a Plaza), an empty lot turned community garden in Lavapiés.[35] The grassroots intervention in the Mercado de San Fernando was one of the many evolving cultural forms that emerged in this climate of urban possibilities as a spatial alternative to the status quo.

During the meetings held at the Tabacalera, participants designed plans for different posts that would collectively form what Asunción described as a "neighborhood market for everyone." On this detail, she added "In fact, one of the principles that we kept in mind when we entered the market is that the prices needed to be accessible for most people. This is one of the differences between us and the Mercado de San Miguel, which has very good products, but they are very expensive. They are focused on a very specific audience: tourists and people with money, the people with money to burn."[36] While Asunción's reflections do not go as far as to deny Mercado de San Miguel its moniker of market, like Rodríguez Sebastián, they emphasize how the cooperative decision to repopulate the Mercado de San Fernando was an explicit response to the upscaling of these institutions during this period. The Lavapiés market may thus be understood as an oppositional space in that it was redesigned through a horizontal, participatory model, explicitly going against prevailing neoliberal trends in urban development and design.[37]

Within a matter of months all posts in the once-dwindling space were leased without the intervention of a multinational corporation, and the market was officially managed by the Asociación de Comerciantes de San Fernando (Mercado de San Fernando Merchants' Association).[38] In this regard, it seemed that the movement had succeeded in breaking from patterns of renovation reshaping *mercados de abastos* across the city, finding a way to offer both time-honored and trending provisions while also satisfying community expectations for the commercial model. *El País* journalist Marta Fernández Maeso, for example, wrote in early 2012, after several of the new posts had debuted, that the market brought together, "Traditionalists and hipsters in the same space and with the same objective: to foment traditional commerce."[39] Similarly, the blog *La Playa de Madrid*, celebrated the collaborative nature of the market's renovation, noting, "[It] isn't orchestrated for tourists by the city council, nor is it the latest invention of eco-snobbery."[40] Despite its triumphant reception, cracks in the model would appear in time, bringing into question both the representative limits of the endeavor, and the ability for the cooperatives involved in the initiative to remain true to their stated purpose of injecting life into the space while keeping it accessible for the local community.

Here, we may return into the interplay between frequent—and nostalgic—invocations of "tradition," Lavapiés's heterogeneous demographic context, and the notion that a space such as San Fernando could (and should) be equally valued and enjoyed by all neighborhood residents. As previously mentioned, the nostalgia for and lamentations regarding the declining *mercado de abastos* model highlight how these local symbols are imbued with affective attachments, particularly those linked to a specific set of national ideals. In some instances, like Rodríguez Sebastián's declaration that the Mercado de San Miguel is "not a market," these ideals are expressed as a reaction against the way that speculative capital reshapes urban terrains. In others, the moralistic value placed in "traditional" uses of symbolic thresholds such as these markets is a way of delineating one's national character; that those who value and partake in the collective memory of these spaces *as originally used* are presumed to stake a claim to Spanish identity. In the diverse landscape of Lavapiés, where not all community members share the same investment in or nostalgia for these spaces, this becomes a particularly sticky subject.

Asunción's reflections on the economic pressures faced by the vendors in San Fernando make plain several of these tensions. On this subject, she shared,

> We are also living alongside a lot of *banglas*, for example, who come to live here from Bangladesh and all of them set up a shop of some sort. And they sell at very low prices, with very long hours. Meaning . . . here there has always been the timetable that stores close at 8 p.m., but well, the timetable was because of the Community of Madrid. They've been governing us for a long time, they're liberals, ultraliberals, and they legalized all timetables in Madrid so people can keep their shops open for twenty-four hours. People like the *banglas* or the Chinese who are always in their stores, they don't have lives. Their lives just revolve around their stores, they're there from the time they get up until they go to sleep. They're open at 2 a.m. So there's also this competition with the autochthonous shopkeepers from here.[41]

This description of the competition among small business owners in the broader Lavapiés commercial landscape, both inside and outside the market, falls into the trappings of an us-versus them narrative defined along racial lines. While acknowledging the liberal economic policies that pull clients away from the traditional timetable and toward the conveniences of twenty-four-hour shops, Asunción's commentary on the competition stoked by these policy decisions takes on a decidedly identitarian and culturally essentialist dimension. She demarcates the difference in business hours facilitated by free market policies as evidence of deep cultural divides in the district's community. The population with which she identifies—the "We" in her reflection—abide by the former timetables, while she describes racialized newcomers—"the *banglas*" and "the Chinese," as a type of monolithic archetype driven solely by a robotic work ethic. Donovan, in her study of Spanish constructions of Chinese entrepreneurs, argues that the economic concerns expressed regarding immigrant communities like those of Asunción represent the enduring cultural anxiety that the presence and corresponding influence of such populations threatens "the fabric of a community self-defined as authentically Spanish."[42] Indeed, the drive to protect models of commerce tied to a sense of origins can be seen not just as a push against the homogenizing force of capital, but also part of a more pervasive impulse to protect icons and social practices dating to a "simpler," period in the nation's history—a pre-immigrant past. This reaction arises in response to an increasingly racially heterogeneous present, and the accompanying cultural changes bought about by these demographic shifts. Asunción's unsavory feelings toward these specific neighbors are an additional facet to keep in consideration when evaluating conversations regarding the cultural weight and proper preservation of symbolic thresholds like *mercados de abastos*, as they make plain the exclusionary beliefs that endure in purportedly inclusive movements.

To this point, it is useful to distinguish between performing and practicing inclusivity. As Asunción's explanation of the grassroots Mercado de San Fernando project indicates, neighborhood cooperatives had initially intervened with the pretense of building back a market "for everyone." In addition to her commentary on her perceived competitors outside of the market, which contradicts this premise, a closer examination of the revived market landscape reveals additional limitations in this assertion. For example, those who chose to rent a stall in the building faced a barrier in adhering to the institution's more limited hours of operation, a step that effectively eliminated the type of convenience shops critiqued by Asunción.[43] Moreover, while racialized groups were in no way barred from the space, the market failed to attract new proprietors who could cater to the distinct dietary demands of Lavapiés's large immigrant population, such as a Halal butcher or international grocer. As of my 2015 visit, only a handful of non-White vendors held posts in the market, including the barbershop Peluquería de Caballero Salah; Boutique Baobab, a clothing store focused on North American hip-hop and reggae fashions; and La Tienda de Laye, a tailor specializing in Senegalese fabrics.[44] Although community participation was a stated tenant of the renovation initiative, the limited diversity among the stallholders serves as a reminder that inclusivity requires more than mere intention; it necessitates active engagement and structural support to ensure a range of voices and cultures are represented and accommodated.

This disconnect between inclusivity in theory and in action is a shortcoming previously identified in studies of the 15-M Movement. Gracia Trujillo, for example, observes that while the populations fighting against the categorical limits of the established political culture were initially heterogeneous in terms of social class, age, gender, and legal status, the spaces and collectives forged during the protests, "[were] not free of sexist, homophobic, racist violence. They [were] reproductions of the violence beyond these microcosms, in the city, in the media, in social networks, in society in general."[45] Here, Trujillo makes the significant point that spaces and cultural forms forged in the midst of such a multifaceted movement were not immune to cycles of violence prevalent in society at large. In another reflection on 15-M, Amador Fernández-Savater observes that Indignadxs frequently articulated concerns "for the other, the one who is not here, among us," highlighting representational and participatory shortcomings in the social actions associated with the movement.[46] In essence, this is a lesson in intersectionality: although 15-M itself was a progressive social movement, this did not guarantee that the different collectives identifying and addressing societal challenges during the protests and in their wake (like in the case of the Mercado de San Fernando) would be equally aware of, or invested in, diverging issues of identity, including, but not limited to, race, citizenship, and gender. Instead, much of the advocacy stemming from the movement was informed by what Berlant refers to as the "entitlements of their social location," a sense of place in the world and interpretation of necessity informed by one's collage of identarian traits.[47]

Consequently, one could determine that those with more nostalgic motivations for preserving the Mercado de San Fernando and dictating the parameters of its use according to an ideal constructed through restorative memory practices were situated in a similar social location, thus explaining the relatively homogeneous group of proprietors that participated in the wave of renovation spearheaded during meetings at La Tabacalera. And despite the initial success of the grassroots model for repopulating the space, these new proprietors still faced the very real pressures of consumer tastes and lifestyles that had contributed to the degradation of these sites in the first place. Asunción, to this point, noted that weekends, not daily shopping, was a primary source of income for stands such as hers since, in the tradition of the nearby Rastro street fair, people would stop by to drink and eat in the market. Álex, the proprietor of the wine post La Siempre Llena, shared similar observations, explaining that he had originally set out to sell bulk wine, *a granel*, but soon began to offer wines by the glass in order to turn a profit with this more consistent crowd.[48] In both cases, the retailers had aspired to recreate the model of commerce typical of *mercados de abastos* in decades past, but were pushed in a different direction by the realities of consumer demand.

As I continued to return the market in the years that followed, I observed how the space progressed in a leisure-oriented direction. On a trip in 2017, I noted how posts like Ultramarinos H.E.M.O.R., a small grocery stand selling packaged cheese, cured meats, cookies, and canned goods, had increasingly adapted to the culinary crowd, offering a small menu of tapas for immediate consumption on the premises. La Huerta del Sol, too, offered a menu of snacks for those trickling in from weekend activities in the area, and at Alex's post, La Siempre Llena, workers were busy serving wines by the glass. The dedicated food and beverage stalls were humming with customers who sampled culinary offerings ranging from regional Spanish cuisines to European, Latin American, and East-Asian fare. At Yan Ken Pon, a Japanese restaurant and bookstore, sushi and hot meals were available for consumption in their small seating area or to-go. Advertisements posted around the building announced community events taking place in the market including free swing dancing and live music performances, indicating the success of the space as a center of community engagement beyond itinerant foot traffic.

As the initial push to repopulate the market happened without a modernizing facelift like that of San Antón, or a comprehensive restauration like San Miguel, the space maintained some of its grittier attributes, an aesthetic of the "downwardly mobile," that Zukin notes is often considered a meritworthy association with authenticity.[49] In turn, the Mercado de San Fernando was increasingly perceived and thus promoted as a hipper, more bohemian alternative to the city's repositioned network of leisure markets. For others, displeased with the accelerated progression away from the initial attempt to revive the consumer practices of *mercados de abastos* in decades past, this version was also unsatisfactory. Vitally, these qualms, parallel to concerns brought up by Asunción in our earlier interview, are another reminder of the complicated hierarchy of belonging that surfaces in efforts to defend Lavapiés and its populace against the gentrifying force of tourism and leisure, where *castizo* ideals are frequently held up as the desired standard.

A satirical march organized by activist collective Lavapiés ¿dónde vas? in April 2017 further illustrates this oppositional tendency. During the "International Protest for Tourist Rights," members of the group armed with rolling suitcases, sunglasses, fake sunscreen, and straw hats trooped through the neighborhood to draw attention to the role of the growing tourism industry as an accelerating force behind the gentrification processes displacing the area's residents.[50] As a feature of the event, marchers circulated a list of eighteen tongue-in-cheek demands, each a parody of topics including the privatization of public services, the homogeneous nature of global development trends, the prevalence of "grab and go" culture, and the growth of the creative industries in Lavapiés. In this list, an imagined *castizo* resident is a key touchstone, either through references to symbolic thresholds associated with this archetype, or as an explicitly named victim of the sardonic requests.[51] One of the satirical demands, for example, asks for "*castizos* to arrange wild get togethers for tourists," while another calls to shut down establishments run by "ugly bartenders dressed in uniforms, white shirts, or vests," a common outfit for servers at *castizo* establishments. Number fifteen on the list calls to "eliminate the unaesthetic Markets with fresh products and substitute for them cool little vermouth bars," a point that serves both as a critique of the servile status of the Mercado de San Fernando (and other municipal markets) in the city's landscape of spending-class consumption, and a lamentation of the declining *mercado de abastos* model.[52] Notably, while *castizo* archetypes are of upmost concern, the list does not include any reference to Lavapiés's racialized population, either in terms of their precarity, or the way that they are frequently wielded as an aesthetic trait in the neighborhood's production as a tourist site. This is a critical oversight, given that it illustrates the inclination to mourn the impact of gentrification processes in reference to a mythical point of origin situated in a pre-immigration past, effectively disregarding Lavapiés's more complex identitarian landscape and recurring to a racially homogenous notion of authenticity.

Returning to the Mercado de San Fernando, what began as an exercise in collectivity and self-governance for and by the community resulted in a space a shade off from the development model that produced such consumer destinations as the Mercados de San Antón and San Miguel. By 2020, the number of posts in the Lavapiés market catering to daily shopping had significantly declined. Some stands, like Asunción's La Huerta del Sol, had shuttered, either unable or unwilling to adjust to the expectation that San Fernando was now, above all, a gastronomic destination. By this point, the majority of the market's posts offered goods or services oriented toward gastronomy and leisure with an international emphasis, including establishments like La Guatona, a post selling Chilean beverages and snacks, O Luar, a self-described Spanish-Venezuelan fusion establishment, and La Tentación, a vendor offering Mexican snacks and meals to-go or for consumption in the market. In difference to Mouraria's Mercado de Fusão, these posts had not been engineered through a centralized effort to theme San Fernando as a multicultural space, but a more informal shift toward the cosmopolitan. Meanwhile, none of the new grocery, service, or gastronomic additions substantially engaged with the district's most predominant racialized populations, including East Asian, North African, and Sub-Saharan African immigrants and their descendants. Instead, the Halal butchers, spice shops, African and South Asian restaurants, and specialty grocers serving and maintained by these populations remained firmly outside the institution's walls.

Overall, the Mercado de San Fernando project stands out not just an example of participatory urbanism folding to the pressures of capital, but also as an illustration of the identitarian limits of anti-hegemonic activism. Namely, the good life fantasies that circulate regarding the proper use of Madrid's network of *mercados de abastos* are entangled with racially and culturally homogenous ideals regarding urban authenticity, most visible in the nostalgic return to the *castizo* archetype. Frequent recourse to the victimhood of autochthonous figures, discernable in the complaints launched by Asunción, or the sardonic demands of Lavapiés ¿dónde vas? evade more inclusive advocacy for community welfare in an increasingly heterogeneous city, and demand a closer look at other oppositional interventions that speak to the human impact of predominant trends in urban branding and design.

CHAPTER 5

Vision and Opposition

This chapter returns to the realm of visual culture to assess artistic interventions that critique narratives across the ideological spectrum that were shaping the conception, use, and form of the urban landscape of Lavapiés and Mouraria in the post-2008 era. To do so, I revisit Mirzoeff's concept of visuality, that is, a power to dictate what is seen and how it is perceived.[1] Considering how digital tools and networks foment both activist and artistic initiatives, Mirzoeff highlights the mounting number of artist-activists who employ evolving modes of archiving, networking, and mapping not only to criticize and contest dominant visual forms, but also to actively create "new ways to see and be seen, and new ways to see the world."[2] The pieces studied in this chapter embody this politically engaged, digitally engaged direction in visual culture, which Mirzoeff describes as an "interaction of pixels and actions to make change." Specifically, two cases—a map and physical installation by Spanish street artist PorFavor, and illustrations by Portuguese artist José Smith Vargas—demonstrate how contemporary creators leverage digital tools and platforms to create and disseminate distinct perspectives on the urban evolution of Lavapiés and Mouraria, ranging from sardonic visions of alternate realities to didactic reflections on the present, and allegorical invocations of the past.

Beyond these questions of form, my analysis focuses on how each of these artists identify and harness the interplay between affect and urban development in their work; the reciprocal relationship between space and affective expressions that, as examples from previous chapters have shown, shaped the physical and conceptual landscapes of Lavapiés and Mouraria throughout the post-collapse period of unravelling and reorganization. In doing so, I continue to pay special attention to the role of race in these oppositional interventions, from those who recognize and critique how racial heterogeneity was being employed as an aestheticized trope in the service of the brand, to others that dig into the way that myths of origin were cultivated and disseminated in the service of producing an urban ideal. While the following texts from Madrid and Lisbon are, as always, informed by sociohistorical particularities, their parallels in terms of themes and form point to a broader cultural push against the urban and social repercussions of the prevailing developmental model that transcends national borders.

As in the case of the market renovations interrogated in Chapter 4, these visual texts were positioned in direct response to the consumption and leisure-oriented drive in urban development that was rapidly changing the landscape of each of these neighborhoods in the decade following the financial crisis. With this in account, I explore how these works depart from the ideological trappings and exclusionary tropes discernable in conversations surrounding the second life of the Mercado de San Fernando, and the ways they offer alternative perspectives on the subject of demographic heterogeneity and urban change. Moreover, as mentioned in the interlude, I do not seek to evaluate the extent to which these oppositional mediations on urban culture successfully impeded development in either neighborhood. Rather, by keeping the question of visuality at the forefront, and acknowledging the modes of communication that provide a platform for these different ways of seeing, these case studies offer a sample of the range of contestations probing systems of power both intersecting with and extending beyond the influence of capital.

Mapping Lavapiés

> The map is open and connectable in all of its dimensions; it is detachable, reversible, susceptible to constant modification. It can be torn, reversed, adapted to any kind of mounting, reworked by an individual, group, or social formation. It can be drawn on a wall, conceived of as a work of art, constructed as a political action or as a mediation.
>
> —DELEUZE AND GUATTARI, *New Mappings in Politics, Philosophy, and Culture*

In 2016 Madrilenian urban artist PorFavor harnessed the critical power of mapping to envision Lavapiés as a satirical theme park in his entry for the C.A.L.L.E., Convocatoria# Artística# Libre#Lavapiés#Emergente (Open

Submission#Artistic#Free#Lavapiés#Emerging) street art festival, an annual event spearheaded by the neighborhood's small business association in 2013.[3] For the 2016 edition of C.A.L.L.E., themed "The Future: Lavapiés 2029," the artist designed a cartographic depiction of the neighborhood titled *Parque Temático Barrio de Lavapiés* (Lavapiés Neighborhood Theme Park) that directly indicted the way that the tourist industry attempts to manage the "real world" by casting lived space as an attraction.[4] Largely, the piece is an exercise in counter cartography, that is, a mapping practice that questions, subverts, and reframes hegemonic representations of space.[5] Furthermore, in a notable departure from origins-focused critiques of tourism and gentrification encapsulated in interventions like that of the activist group Lavapiés ¿dónde vas?, reviewed in the last chapter, PorFavor's map pays particular attention to the spatial dimensions of race, alterity, and counterculture that shape the district in the public imaginary. Overall, the artist's parody of the explicit production of Lavapiés as an attraction *because of* its association with Otherness offers a more nuanced indictment of developmental trends driven by affective expressions and their spatial and human impact, with criticisms levied against surveillance, racial stereotyping, and the commercialization inherent to these processes.

PorFavor's work as an artist-activist is firmly situated within the broader cultural legacy of the 15-M protests at Madrid's Puerta del Sol in 2011. After joining the movement as one of the Indignadxs, the artist became involved in the encampments by lending his expertise in audiovisual production, one of the uses of technology that set the protests apart as a networked, digitally driven initiative. Soon, PorFavor began to explore other avenues for advocacy beyond the plaza.[6] It was through this path that he began to collaborate with other protestors in painting satirical advertisements throughout the Madrid's center, that launched critiques regarding corporate interests and neoliberal governance on the part of the the Indignadxs.[7] Once the encampments had dismantled and organizing efforts shifted to community working groups, PorFavor continued to participate actively in Madrid's urban art community by covertly painting and installing pieces that engage with pillars of the movement including collective action, social justice, and anti-hegemonic perspectives.[8]

The Lavapiés Commercial Association's C.A.L.L.E. festival was a noteworthy departure from the nature of PorFavor's previous interventions, which were largely informal, unsanctioned pieces that the artist installed in public spaces throughout the city. In difference, this annual event is officially regulated and commercially sponsored, with participating neighborhood businesses inviting artists to exhibit their work on their facades for a designated period. As part of the opportunity, artists are offered payment for fees and production costs, in addition to the chance for a cash prize furnished by a corporate sponsor (in 2016 this was the Spanish multinational beer corporation Mahou). While C.A.L.L.E. is described by the Commercial Association as an effort to foster artistic creation in the neighborhood in an open and participatory manner, it explicitly does so in the service of corresponding economic interests, like many initiatives dating to this period.[9] During the timeframe of the festival, the street is mobilized as an open-air museum, including a week during which the public is invited to watch artists install their pieces on storefronts, and another two weeks dedicated to exhibition. Though some establishments in different iterations of C.A.L.L.E. have left pieces up beyond the time constraints of the festival, their generally ephemeral display boosts foot traffic to the neighborhood during the event, and, consequently, to local businesses where the art is featured, highlighting the utility of the arts in the commercialization and branding of the district. Moreover, the parameters of the festival allow for participating businesses to approve or deny artists' proposals, thereby shaping the image projected of the neighborhood and its commercial offerings.

Both activists and scholars have employed the term "artwashing" to describe how initiatives like C.A.L.L.E. mobilize artistic production in the service of consumption and consumer-oriented development. In this process, local authorities, corporate interests, investors and organizations turn to art under the pretense of what Stephen Pritchard describes as "narrow notions of the civic," a veneer of social welfare that, in actuality, shrouds a drive for urban renewal directed at the spending class.[10] Art-based attractions, while framed as serving the community by improving the aesthetic qualities of the lived environment, often open new terrains for capital accumulation. Consequently, they commonly play a role in the upscaling of districts which, in the absence of social protections, often leads to an exodus of community members. Moreover, while painting urban spaces without permission is a manner of asserting one's right to the city, as artists question notions of appropriate and inappropriate use of the urban environment through their work, sanctioned street art, like those facilitated by the C.A.L.L.E. festival, subvert this aspect of the genre and even have the potential to reinforce the systems of authority otherwise questioned through this medium.[11] These factors, along with the explicitly countercultural nature of PorFavor's work, generate several tensions in the artist's design and display of his vision of Lavapiés in the year 2029 for this specific event.

Artists applying to C.A.L.L.E. in 2016 were invited to submit proposals according to the theme *The Future: Lavapiés 2029*. The year's call for submissions, wherein the neighborhood is discussed according to its "unique personality," brings together many recurring tropes, explored in previous chapters, in both the branding and defense of this district,

> Lavapiés is a Madrilenian neighborhood with a unique personality. In it, more than fifty distinct nationalities coexist with generations of people born in the neighborhood from the beginning of the twentieth century to today. Its bustling, colorful streets exude art and culture from all sides, from its theaters and concert venues to the most free and cutting-edge expressions. All of this mixed with bars and shops, some hundreds of years old and *castizo* and others extremely modern and underground. Far from chains and franchises, this combination of genuine and authentic places creates the particular, intimate atmosphere that is Lavapiés. With this edition's leit motiv of Lavapiés 2029, we at C.A.L.L.E. 2016 want to use our open, detail-oriented natures to think, reflect, and create based on the FUTURE.[12]

This announcement perpetuates the happy multiculturalism discourse, weaving a narrative of colorful conviviality, pairing adjectives charged with positive feelings like *bustling*, *artistic*, and *cultural* with references to the heterogeneous population of the neighborhood. The description of Lavapiés's demographic makeup draws a clear distinction between autochthonous populations "born in the neighborhood" and the "more than fifty different nationalities" with whom they coexist, reinforcing differentiated standards of belonging within this smiling melting pot. As a means by which to emphasize the purported authenticity of the district, the announcement calls attention to both "hundred-year-old and *castizo*" bars and shops—the gradual buildup of life experience that is correlated with a type of moral right to the city—and "hip and underground" establishments—a push against homogeneous urban experiences in an appeal to anti-tourism sensibilities. Overall, the call for submissions captures the greatest hits of talking points invoked in the emotionally charged branding and promotion of Lavapiés, providing productive fodder for those who might critique these tendencies rather than add to these narratives. PorFavor, interested in the topic of gentrification, opted to respond to the call by designing an intervention in which he presented Lavapiés as an open-air multi-ethnic theme park for paying visitors, building on the urban trends of the moment to envision the district in a dystopian future.[13]

In the *Parque Temático Barrio de Lavapiés*, PorFavor turns the trending discourses brought together in the C.A.L.L.E. 2016 call for submissions against themselves, mapping the neighborhood as a militarized zone where paying visitors are invited to partake in a racial and ideological safari sponsored (in his words, *gentrificado por*, gentrified by) credit card companies. The scene, recognizable as a simplified version of the government projection of Embajadores wherein official symbols are replaced with satirical alternatives, subverts expectations of the typical icons that mediate the comprehension and use of this type of space, forming a sardonic display of the district out of the municipal government's own cartographic product. By invoking these authoritative binaries inherent to the mapping process, PorFavor plays with the oppositional possibilities of counter-cartography, creating new layers of meaning through his alternate rendering of a familiar text-type.[14] Subsequently, the mapping medium serves as an expression of the production of Lavapiés, both a template for creation and a guide for navigation, given that the form is traditionally wielded to order and create territories. Through additional icons and text, including a list of rules and regulations for visitors, and an accompanying legend that highlights key attractions throughout the district, the artist constructs the type of signage that one would encounter when entering a themed attraction, living up to the park moniker in the title, and satirizing how designated precincts are primed for tourist consumption.[15]

Using these formal features to his advantage, PorFavor presents viewers with a display of the district that parodies common positions regarding appropriate uses and users of urban space. Mitchell, on this subject, points out how the unhoused, loiterers, racial Others, and protestors are the actors in the built environment most frequently engaged in a fight for their right to the city.[16] These tendencies are clear in PorFavor's depiction of the theme park, where visitors are granted access, by way of a paid attraction, to a controlled set of objectified human subjects including squatters, protestors, and members of different racialized African, Asian, and Iberian groups divided into reservations, and cordoned off within the bounds of an electrified fence. Further stoking the way that this alternate universe mimics racial hierarchies and relationships within and beyond this neighborhood, PorFavor refers to the imagined inhabitants as *indígenas* (indigenous), making rule number five on the list "Do not help the indigenous groups escape the park under any circumstances."[17] By accentuating their stated purpose as a showcase for a curious spectator, the artists draws attention to the tendency to cast the "real world" of Lavapiés as an attractive landscape of consumption—*because of* the Otherness of its inhabitants—a type of viewing that follows the logic of the racial axis established during the colonial period.

Indeed, as he draws parallels between Lavapiés's social and spatial realities

FIGURE 5.1. *Parque Temático Barrio de Lavapiés* created by PorFavor for C.A.L.L.E. festival, 2016

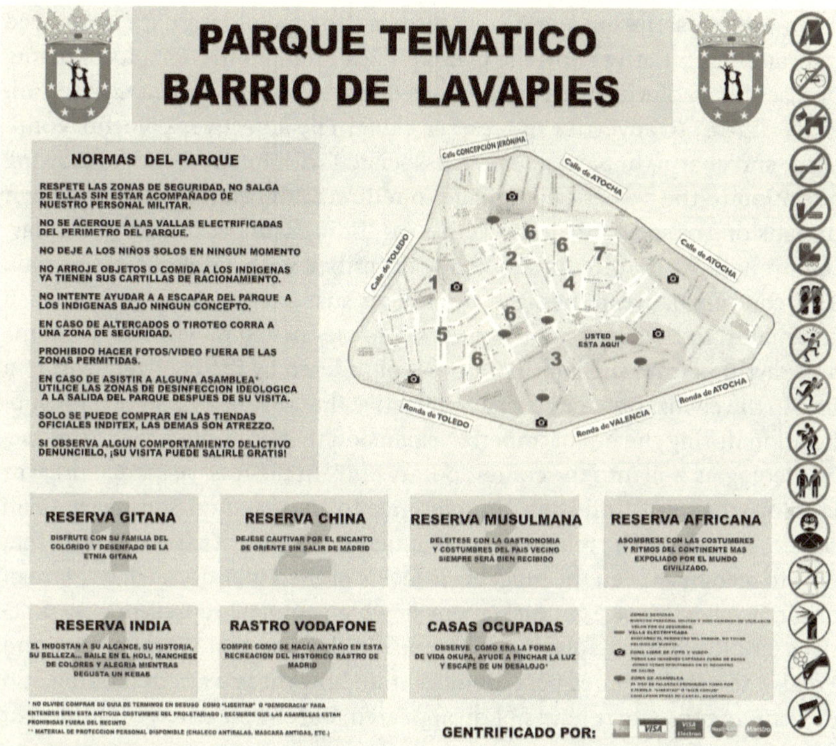

and a dystopic future in 2029, PorFavor shares a critique that, instead of shying away from the question of racial categories as they relate to the legacy of colonial power structures, expressly invokes the xenophobic, Orientalist, and class-based discourses that impact the perception and corresponding development of the district. For example, the artist assigns names to each of the map's *reservas* (reservations) based on their intersecting identitarian and spatial associations, mimicking the impulse to organize perceptions of the Other according to dominant material and conceptual frameworks.[18] Accordingly, the neighborhood's identity-based precincts include *Gitana* (Gypsy), *China* (Chinese), *Musulmana* (Muslim), *India* (India), and *Africana* (African), a wide range of multidimensional collectives that find common ground through their frequent treatment as decorative monoliths in urban development initiatives. These divisions also draw attention to how, in the process of using the Other as a token, race, ethnicity, religion, and point of origin are often employed interchangeably: an entire continent on display in the *reserva africana* and diverse practitioners of a religion in the *reserva musulmana.*

In each description PorFavor imitates the type of language employed in branding initiatives and the C.A.L.L.E. call for submissions itself, using phrases like "colorful and confident" to describe the *reserva gitana*, and "oriental charm" to advertise the *reserva china*. The adjectives colorful, confident, and charm, in particular, are associated with happy feelings, drawing attention to the power of language to redirect attention from the bleaker dimensions of social realities. In this sardonic example, the act of displaying humans as if animals at a zoo is described with a delighted flourish. This contrast between message and tone is sustained with each outlandish statement. In the *reserva africana*, visitors are invited to witness "customs and rhythms from the continent most plundered by the civilized world," a nod to the civilization and barbary narrative that served as a pretext for subjugation during the era of imperial expansion that continues to inform racist ideologies well into the contemporary era.[19] In the *reserva india*, PorFavor employs the term "indostan" in reference to an imagined Southeast Asian nation, parodying the tendency to treat racialized groups as a monolith, that fails to recognize even the most basic facets of their identity such as place of origin. Each of these examples, many of which emulate representative practices employed for displaying difference in the very real World's Fairs and Freak Shows of decades past, demonstrate how these ways of looking and objectifying the Other have not disappeared, but simply emerge in different forms as society evolves.

In addition to satirizing how Otherness is employed as a marketable aesthetic, PorFavor's map riffs on trends in neoliberal governance and public surveillance, from the prioritization of corporate interests in urban design, to how the experience of the street is shaped by systems of vigilance and control. While hyperbolic, these references are grounded in the wealth of urban trends that privilege private over public interests and policing over reform. The *Rastro Vodafone*, for example, is a nod to when the same company became the official sponsor of the Puerta del Sol metro stop from 2013 to 2016, driving a proverbial knife into the spaces' symbolic importance as the point of origin of the 15-M protests.[20] Rules outlining unwelcome uses and users within the bounds of the park draw from two polemic pieces of legislation: the *Ley 5/2002, de 27 de junio, sobre Drogodependencias y otros Trastornos Adictivos* (Law for the Prevention of Drug Addiction) and the *Ley Orgánica de protección de la seguridad ciudadana* (Law for The Protection of Citizen Security), known colloquially as the *Ley antibotellón* and *Ley mordaza*, the former which deemed the consumption of alcohol in public spaces illegal and subject to fine, and the latter of which policed exercises of civil disobedience by prohibiting participation in unauthorized protests, resisting or filming authority, interfering in evictions, and squatting.[21] The park's 2000 security cameras, likewise, are an exaggerated depiction of the camera network first installed in Lavapiés in 2009, a watershed moment for policing public space in Madrid's city center that would continue to expand after its inception.[22] Together, these details envision the spatial consequences of a society stripped of the balancing power of public and civil disobedience, and demonstrates how the public rationale for hypervigilance and monitoring practices is fomented by expressions of fear and the corresponding desire for protection. Furthermore, these details emphasize the ways that the state emboldens itself to mediate the use of the city, establishing the parameters of legal and illegal activity, and the role of private enterprise in this process.

This magnification of reality calls attention to what Mirzoeff identifies as visuality's ability to present authority as self-evident. To this end, he states,

> First, visuality classifies by naming, categorizing, and defining, a process defined by Foucault as "the nomination of the visible." . . . Second, visuality separates the groups so classified as a means of social organization. Such visuality separates and segregates those it visualizes to prevent them from cohering as political subjects, such as the workers, the people, or the (decolonized) nation. Third, it makes this separated classification seem right and hence aesthetic. As the decolonial critic Frantz Fanon had it, such repeated experience generates an "aesthetic of respect for the status quo," the aesthetics of the proper, of duty, of what is felt to be right and hence pleasing, ultimately even beautiful.[23]

This process of classifying, separating, and aestheticizing is successful because of its ability to influence perception. In PorFavor's Lavapiés, the artist maneuvers in a fissure between reality and farce, and in doing so calls attention to physical and psychic operations that foment the reciprocal relationship between authority and power. Typically innocuous details, such as the designated photo spots throughout the map, take on new meaning in this alternate reality where terms like *liberty* and *common good* are subject to imprisonment, underscoring the power inherent to rendering space, people, and practices visible, and dictating the parameters of their perception. The *Casas Ocupadas* attraction, too, captures how ways of seeing drive historical formations, with visitors are invited to, "observe what the life of an Okupa was like, hack into the electric grid and escape an eviction." Here, the specific form of antispeculative squatting that took off in Lavapiés in the late twentieth century is reduced to a misspelled title (using a "c" instead of the movement's symbolic "k," which is an intentional transgression of orthographic norms) and set of prescribed activities, emulating the type of reductive interpretation that is often cemented as history.

Indeed, these critical layers were fomented by the fact that, even though the *Parque Temático* is situated in a dystopian future, one could hypothetically experience a version of the world captured in the map by using it as a guide to walk the streets of Lavapiés. Indeed, PorFavor shared that he had originally envisioned the piece as part of a large parodical display for which he would act as a tour guide for the week of the festival, handing out informational pamphlets and providing advice to passersby.[24] Yet, these plans came to a halt when the artist was told by the owners of the restaurant La Buga del Lobo, where he was meant to complete the installation, that they were not comfortable with the polemic nature of his proposal. Namely, PorFavor reported, the retailers were worried that the public would not understand that the piece was satirical, and would take offense. This decision to censure what the artist had envisioned for his exhibition reveals the structural limits of contestatory artistic practices that attempt to work within the framework of consumer-centric events like C.A.L.L.E. Though these parameters of display could facilitate a broad audience for the artist's critique, and protect the piece from immediate removal, this reach was contingent on the amenability of the business set to host the intervention. Confronted with unwilling collaborators, PorFavor designed an alternate piece for the festival, and waited until the next year to try again.

The artist had better luck exhibiting his piece during the 2017 edition of C.A.L.L.E. with the consent of the owners of Taberna Alabanda. For this iteration of the event, PorFavor installed his original piece and an additional two posters, a simplified version of the map, and a blown-up version of a pamphlet advertising the theme park. In addition, he printed copies of the sardonic pamphlet to disseminate to passersby and place on car windshields throughout the neighborhood. During the festival period, PorFavor reported that he passed out around one thousand brochures and posted an additional five hundred satirical advertisements on empty storefronts throughout the district announcing that Burger King, Zara, and Starbucks were coming soon. The artist was deliberate in placing several of these signs in spaces symbolic to processes of indignation and contestation in the neighborhood. In one such case, PorFavor posted an advertisement adjacent to a shuttered storefront that had already been tagged by artist-activist El Rey de la Ruina. There, El Rey de la Ruina had painted the building's gate with an anatomical heart and the phrase "Enjoy the crisis," one of several pieces that he had placed

FIGURE 5.2. PorFavor's C.A.L.L.E. 2017 installation on the façade of Taberna Alabanda, image courtesy of artist

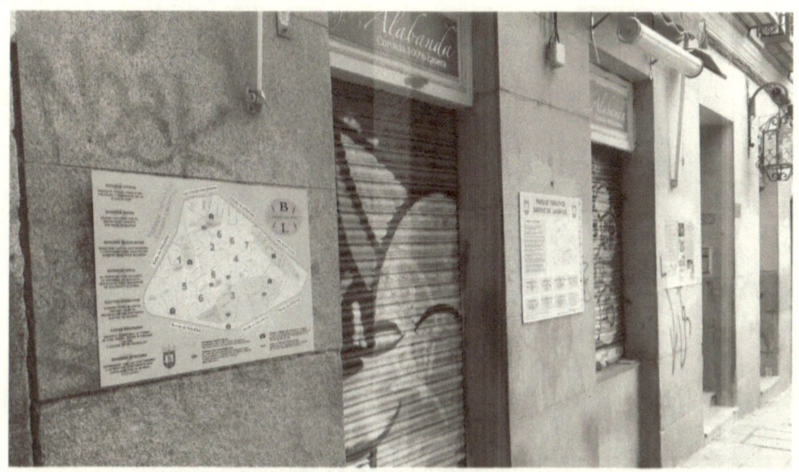

in Madrid neighborhoods grappling with gentrification. PorFavor erected another sign announcing a new Zara store on the front door of La Quimera, a once-abandoned building on the neighborhood's Plaza Nelson Mandela that, since 2013, had been re-appropriated as a squatted social center.[25] Through these juxtapositions, PorFavor called attention to concrete ways that the neighborhood's built environment could be re-signified through spatial practices—ranging from the hegemonic to the oppositional—where the same sterile environs of consumption could swiftly become a space of social possibility, and vice versa.

The affective response to these provocative additions beyond the façade of Taberna Alabanda was further stoked by the closing gap between PorFavor's satirical display and Lavapiés's realities. Just a few months prior, the supermarket chain Carrefour had opened on the Plaza Lavapiés. Nearby, Calle de Valencia 8–10 was in the throes of its conversion to an Ibis hotel, and on Calle Argumosa the clothing chain Kling had opened just a couple of doors down from PorFavor's original exposition space at La Buga del Lobo. In turn, the artist reported that several of his fake advertisements had been vandalized, spray-painted over with the words "Fuera de Lavapiés" (Get out of Lavapiés). Evidently, some of the details of the dystopian future that the artist had imagined for the neighborhood were not perceived outside of the realm of possibility for some community members.

FIGURE 5.3. Satirical advertisement on the door of La Quimera, image courtesy of PorFavor

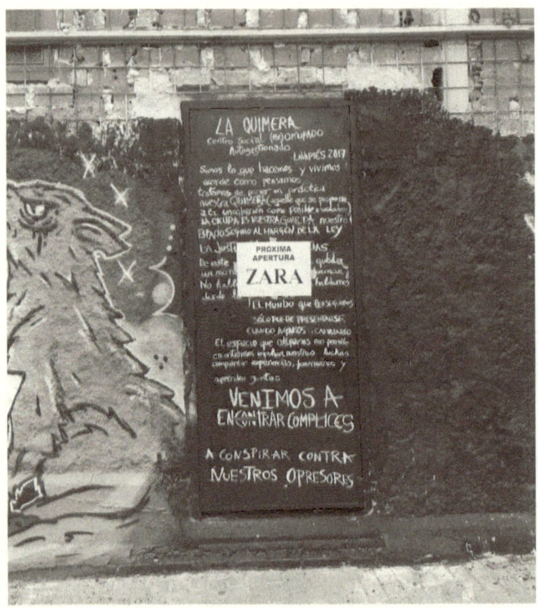

Through this distinct combination of digitally designed art, spatial installation, and performance, Por Favor brought to the public a distinct way of seeing Lavapiés that cultivated its affective impact through discrete parallels with the present. Rather than dwell on the neighborhood's relationships to an imagined *castizo* form, a leading trope in cultural representations both fomenting and contesting the neighborhood's evolution, PorFavor elected to focus on how the aestheticization of alterity conceals the sanitization of the Other (racial, political, and so on) in a rhetoric of celebration. In doing so, his intervention rendered visible the multidimensional networks of physical and psychic identity, power, and interest that played a role in shaping the neighborhood in the years following the financial crisis.

Drawing Mouraria

Cartoonist José Smith Vargas's comic strips provide another example of oppositional visual culture that, while speaking specifically to the Portuguese national context, finds common ground with PorFavor in his inversion of the most common discourses both driving and contesting change in Mouraria. The artist's body of work, the majority of which circulates online through his personal website, Instagram, and the activist publication *Jornal Mapa*, touches upon topics including environmental justice, politics, urbanity, and social justice. Here, I focus on two specific illustrations that fall under the umbrella of oppositional culture. The first, published in 2012, critiques the nostalgic production of patrimony in Mouraria's cultivation and consumption as a tourist site, and the second, published in 2018, explores how contempt for the Other has informed the district's development throughout its historical trajectory. The intersections between Vargas's critical assessment of urban trends and those articulated by PorFavor further illuminate the proximity between Mouraria and Lavapiés, and these two nations more broadly, in both the experience of and responses to the urban change catalyzed by the crisis.

BOUDRILHAR NA MOURARIA

> There is no real and no imaginary except at a certain distance. What happens when this distance, even the one separating the real from the imaginary, begins to disappear and to be absorbed by the model alone?
>
> —JEAN BAUDRILLARD, "Two Essays"

Vargas's comic strip "Boudrilhar na Mouraria," published in 2012, follows Jean Baudrillard on a walk through Mouraria in the era of its rebranding.[26] Just as *boudrilhar* indicates, a punny version of the theorist's name recast as a verb, this act of physically navigating Mouraria through Baudrillard's theoretical lens is a nameable action in and of itself. Throughout the piece, Vargas juxtaposes translated quotations from Baudrillard's assessment of the postmodern in "The Precession of Simulacra" with sketches of the author observing his surroundings, applying the idea that images precede reality to represent the physical and psychic experience of exploring the Mouraria district.[27] These scenes of praxis serve as a plot device that pushes readers to see different hierarchies of power and access that shape Mouraria in the tourist imaginary. In this same vein, "Boudrilhar na Mouraria" mobilizes Baudrillard's commentary to deconstruct the collective mythologizing of the neighborhood, from the expediency of *fado* to the nostalgic invocations of origins that foment consumption, advancing the position that these priorities have rendered the district a symbol of itself. With the idea of simulacra at the forefront, Vargas's critique demonstrates how visuality, which dictates what is seen and how it is perceived, is not limited to the realm of the real.

This idea is established from the outset. In the first panel of the strip Vargas summarizes Baudrillard's argumentation regarding the hyper-real, that is, a "real without origin" in a text box laid over an illustration of a map.[28] To the right of this text Vargas includes a sketch of the guitar-shaped monument to Mouraria located on the Rua do Capelão, a few meters from the building where famed singer Maria Severa passed in the mid-19th century. The marble statue, erected in 2006 at the behest of then-mayor of Lisbon António Pedro Nobre Carmona Rodrigues is engraved with the phrase "Mouraria, berço do fado" (Mouraria: the cradle of *fado*).[29] References to the deliberate cultivation of a relationship between the district and *fado* continue throughout the piece. As Sánchez Fuarros explains in his comprehensive study of the music genre as an avenue for urban development, this way of perceiving Mouraria was stoked by the launch of the 2011 QREN-Mouraria "As cidades dentro da cidade" municipal renewal program, which drew from the legitimacy of institutions and figures located within the bounds of the district to foment its image as a "*living* fado neighborhood."[30] Vargas's piece engages with the wave of tours, exhibitions, festivals that flooded the district during this period, using Baudrillard's conclusions to emphasize the fabricated nature of both the *fado* revival and the positioning of Mouraria as a form of living museum vis-à-vis its relationship to cultural heritage.

Vargas takes a didactic approach as he articulates these positions, using illustrations to provide readers with a concrete application of Baudrillard's arguments, which he adapts and translates throughout the piece. Consider as an example, the second page of the series, in which Baudrillard appears in a doorway, his gaze directed toward the panel to his right. In the accompanying text box laid over two frames, Vargas includes Baudrillard's phrase, "When the real no longer exists, nostalgia assumes its full meaning." In the bottom left quadrant of the page, a woman sings to a crowd of spectators, music notes emerge from a speaker mounted on a building, and a man plays a Portuguese guitar in another balcony below. These details are juxtaposed with additional citations from Baudrillard that critique the weight attributed to myths of origin, providing a scene that embodies the deliberate investment in and cultivation of cultural practices revered for their authenticity. Vargas follows this analytical strand throughout the sequence, next turning to Baudrillard's commentary on life-as-museum. In *Simulacra and Simulation* he writes, "The museum, instead of being circumscribed as a geometric site, is everywhere now, like a dimension of life." As an illustration, Vargas includes a scene in which a group of women washing clothes in a public bath are photographed by onlookers, their quotidian activities serving as both an

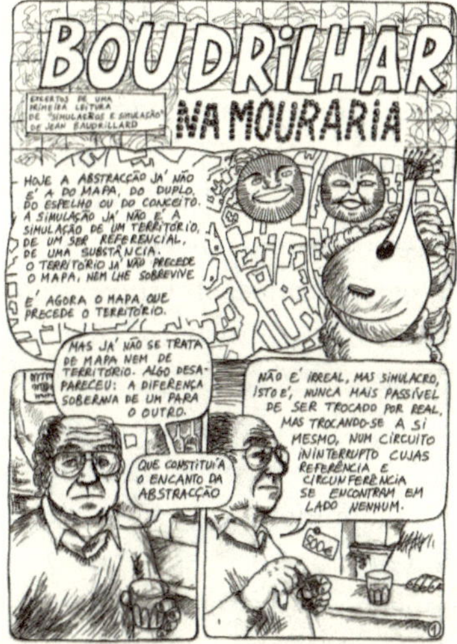

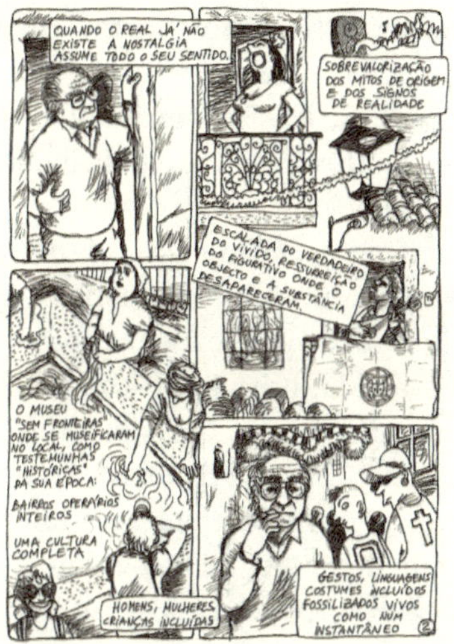

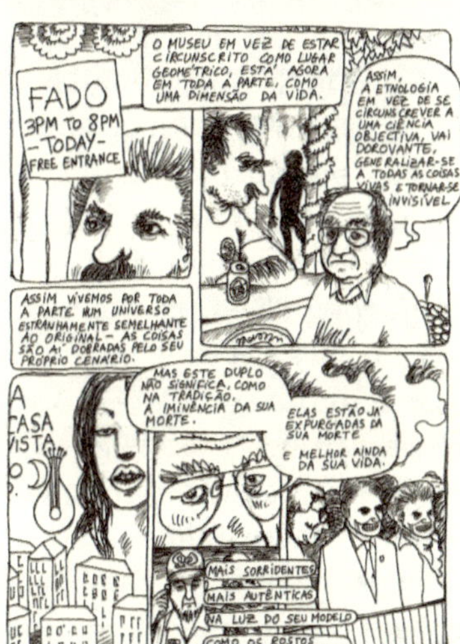

FIGURES 5.4, 5.5, and 5.6. José Smith Vargas's "Boudrilhar na Mouraria," 2012. Published in *Vale dos vencidos* (Chili com carne, 2023)

attraction and backdrop for a visiting public. On the next page, Vargas alludes once more to the international audience for whom this version of authenticity is most expressly performed, his first panel depicting a close-up of an advertisement for a *fado* show published in English.

The movement in Vargas's comic is produced by individuals perceiving one another, the production of meaning and perception that Mirzoeff terms visuality. In each sequence, it is a visiting public according to whose presumed expectations for authenticity that meaning is ordered in the neighborhood. The public watches the singer and guitarist on their balconies, the tourist photographs the washerwomen, and two men look at Baudrillard as he passes them on the street, the district and those who inhabit it signified through acts of looking. These details, too, point to a juxtaposition between those who actively perform myths of origin and authenticity, like the singer on the balcony and the advertisement for a *fado* performance, and those who are folded into the hyper-realistic display of Mouraria-as-museum, such as the figures doing laundry in a public bath. As these relationships are presented in the same urban ecosystem, the comic highlights how the manner that the district is cast and perceived stems from a complex network of public institutions, private investors, community stakeholders, and the visitors whose sustained interest fuels the reproduction of the real.

Consequently, the social and spatial consequences of hyper-realistic displays are a frequent touchstone throughout the strip. In the first sequence, in which Baudrillard is pictured at a bar with a drink and a cigarette, a conspicuous five-hundred-euro price tag is positioned in the foreground of a panel. This depiction of the type of price inflation associated with precincts of consumption is an apprehensive prediction of the potential monetary consequences of casting life as an exhibit. Here, Vargas's piece finds common ground with PorFavor as the artist presents a hyperbolic possibility in an alternate reality based on his perceptions of the rising cost of living in Mouraria, maneuvering in a rapidly closing fissure between reality and imagination.

This sense is driven home in the final panel of the strip, where Vargas paraphrases and illustrates Baudrillard's assertion "Everywhere we live in a universe strangely similar to the original. . . . But this doubling does not signify, as it did traditionally, the imminence of their death—they are already purged of their death, and better than when they were alive; more cheerful, more authentic, in the light of their model, like the faces in funeral homes."[31] His depiction of these ideas is quite literal, as the artist draws a pair of ominous figures with blacked-out eyes facing in the direction of an undisclosed scene, a likely allusion to the hollow quality of fabricated displays of authenticity. It is also curious to consider other ways in which Mouraria's "death," is distanced from neighborhood realities in Vargas's strip. While largely focusing on the opportunistic engagement with the history of *fado* in the public-facing positioning and promotion of the district, the piece does not refer at all to the neighborhood's racially diverse populace. This demonstratively selective engagement with different neighborhood populations and tropes, too, points to the extent to which perception is guided by the discursive—and, consequently, spatial—production of the real.

RENOVAR A MOURARIA 1496

Vargas approaches from a different thematic angle in his didactic critique of the development and design of Mouraria in his strip "Renovar a Mouraria 1496," which first appeared in the publication *Jornal Mapa* in 2018.[32] At this point, several years had passed since the debut of the QREN-Mouraria action plan and subsequent development initiatives aimed at bolstering interest and investment in the district by leveraging its reputation as a site of cultural heritage and creative activity. Some tangible outcomes of this agenda included the installation of signposts marking a tourist trail throughout the neighborhood, as well as the construction of a government-subsidized creative incubator, the Centro de Inovação da Mouraria / Mouraria Creative Hub, on Rua dos Lagares 23. By this year, some rehabilitation initiatives had also changed course, such as the shuttered Mercado de Fusão in the Praça do Martim Moniz, studied in Chapter 2, and Casa da Severa, a *fado*-focused cultural center that was ultimately converted into a restaurant.

In "Renovar a Mouraria 1496," Vargas's critical focus shifts from the expediency of *fado* and historical patrimony in the production of Mouraria as a tourist landscape to a pointed representation of how stigmatized populations factor into these processes of urban development. Namely, he turns to the district's origins as a Muslim quarter to illustrate how cleansing discourses driven by prejudice have and continue to shape the neighborhood from the medieval to the contemporary era. In the service of this critique, the artist employs a historically situated parallel, the expulsion of religious minorities from the Portuguese kingdom, to demonstrate the social and spatial effects of reinforcing correlations between stigmatized collectives and negative categories like filth and danger. These narrative patterns, as Ahmed argues, are the way that certain "objects," like those who diverge from Whiteness or another category positioned as standard, neutral, or the norm, take on negative affective meaning.[33] It is through such discursive processes that the eradication or sanitization of the Other, a "sticky" object, is present as subtext in discussions regarding hygiene, safety, and the rehabilitation of urban environments.

In the comic, Vargas depicts the eradication of Lisbon's Muslim population at the end of the fifteenth century as a type of "renovation" of Mouraria, borrowing from contemporary discourse regarding the neighborhood's rehabilitation to reflect on the past. The sequence begins with Damião de Góis, a Portuguese philosopher once persecuted by the Portuguese Inquisition, commenting on recent changes to the city of Lisbon. Like in "Boudrilhar na Mouraria," these introductory statements establish the thematic lens according to which the reader is to interpret the purported "renovations" depicted in the sequence. Góis as narrator states, "We arrive at this happy and fertile valley where the Muslims live until, as the city grows, their vocations and businesses begin to attract greed."[34] As the figure of Góis on horseback blends into the frame below, another comments "Dom Manuel did well to dismantle the Moorish commune and open it to the city," referencing Manuel I's decree of expulsion of the Kingdom of Portugal's religious minorities.[35] The grim reaper, with a cross in hand, stands between this character and another, who responds "so many people in Lisbon that never passed through these streets," implying a connection between the now-eradicated population and the area's reputation as an undesirable space.[36] To his right, two men carry a crescent moon affixed to stone, a Muslim symbol removed from the built environment, and in another speech bubble the figure proclaims, "And their traditions are purified," emphasizing this erasure as necessary step for this cleansing process.[37]

These celebratory declarations, which satirically frame the expulsion of this religious group as an act of urban purification, recall Mary Douglas's seminal commentary on the construction of the category of dirt itself. She states, "As we know it, dirt is essentially disorder. There is no such thing as absolute dirt: it exists in the eye of the beholder. If we shun dirt, it is not because of craven fear, still less dread of holy terror. Nor do our ideas about disease account for the range of our behavior in cleaning or avoiding dirt. Dirt offends against order."[38] Several scholars have applied this theorization of the category of dirt to explore how different collectives, objects, and practices are viewed as filthy or impure in cultural production and practice. In Iberian Studies, for example, Diana Burkhart mobilizes the concept to investigate the correlation between immigrant populations and waste in the Spanish film *Las Cartas de Alou* as indicative of the perception of racialized foreign populations as the root of disorder within the nation.[39] Anne McClintock, in her study of how gender, race, and class shaped British imperialism, employs Douglas's ideas to conclude that dirt "is the counterpoint of the commodity," given that it transgresses the acceptable values of the commercial market.[40] Each of these observations serve to illuminate the sanitizing discourses that frequently accompany perceptions of dirt: from the desire to restore what is accepted as "order," to the push for purification as a value-adding enterprise.

In Vargas's strip, the Muslim religious minority is depicted as having been

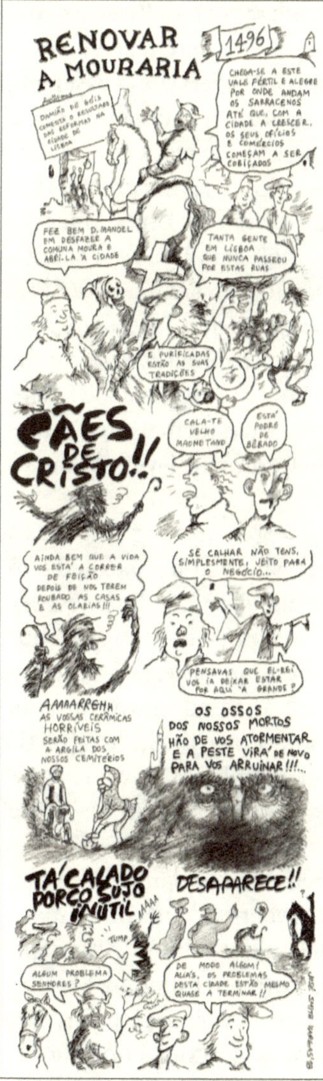

FIGURE 5.7. José Smith Vargas's "Renovar a Mouraria 1496," 2018 (*Jornal Mapa*). An updated version of this comic appears in his *Vale dos vencidos* (Chili com carne, 2023)

made synonymous with dirt and disorder, their eradication from Mouraria articulated by those in support of their expulsion as a solution to the city's ills.[41] Góis's narration, meanwhile, articulates how fear and even jealousy of the Other stokes these sticky associations. This network of feelings and motives is further explored in the next scene in the sequence, where a new character emerges: a figure drawn as a mass of black scratches and scribbles who represents one of the neighborhood's exiled Muslim inhabitants. This character confronts the men who celebrate changes to the city, condemning their joy over the cleansing of Mouraria, and asserting that they have robbed his community of their homes and professions. The characterization of this figure as Other is heightened by the stark contrast between his appearance and the other figures in the strip, as Vargas draws him as a barely human mass of unrefined lines. The man scorns the Christians for having taken over their brickyards and warns that their ceramics will be made of clay sources from Muslim's cemeteries, asserting that the bones of the deceased will haunt those who exiled them, bringing back the plague and leading the remaining populace to ruin. Although these remarks are presented as hyperbolic exclamations, they emphasize how the city may be understood as a palimpsest shaped by social and spatial transformations. While meaning is inscribed and reinscribed on the environment, layers of the past remain perceptible in its future iterations.

The men, in response, disregard the angry figure's accusations, suggesting that perhaps he and others who had been exiled had lost their professions simply because they were not adequate businesspeople.[42] These patronizing remarks, which equate religious identity with business acumen, further underscore how the treatment of this exiled figure—and the collective that he represents—is considered justified, and a consequence of their presumed inferiority. The perceived solution to the ills the religious minority has ostensibly caused is represented quite literally in the panel, with one of the characters kicking the dissenting figure, whom he calls a "dirty useless pig," as he wills him to disappear.

The title of the strip alludes to the parallel between the historic discourse represented in Vargas's intervention, and contemporary narratives regarding the renovation of the same neighborhood. Although Góis, in the last panel, is told by the two men supportive of expelling Muslims from the district that "this city's problems are almost over," their claim is contradicted by the long legacy of interventions in Mouraria that continue into the twenty-first century.[43] In the present, however, the expulsion of stigmatized communities from Mouraria is less overt. Instead, the perception of the Other (racial, religious, or otherwise) as a disruptive, and therefore impure force is often mitigated by their utility as a marketable aesthetic. This approach is evident in previously discussed interventions including the Mercado de Fusão and the Renovar a Mouraria's themed tours. As argued previously, these strategies for molding perceptions of the local Other serve not to erase, but to recast these communities in the public imaginary, another example of the hyper-realistic practice in presenting life-as-museum that Vargas explores in the first comic studied in this chapter. Meanwhile, although the working-class immigrant populations for which Mouraria garnered its multiracial reputation are not obligated leave, they face the new challenge of living in a neighborhood increasingly inaccessible to those of their social and economic standing.

The work of both PorFavor and Vargas, which is situated at the intersection of activism and artistic production, captures two distinct creative and narrative possibilities for contesting prevailing ways of conceiving of Lavapiés and Mouraria in the era of their post-crisis development. In both cases, the artists articulate their critiques by presenting alternate realities that build on recurring patterns of adjustment within each district. Moreover, their exploration of the interplay between affect and urban development probes systems of power in ways that evade, and in Vargas's case, explicitly critiques, the nostalgic recourse to authenticity seen in other oppositional efforts, such as the redevelopment of the Mercado de San Fernando. In terms of my ongoing comparison between the two neighborhoods, Vargas's and PorFavor's pieces reflect similar concerns regarding both the commercialization of the everyday and the hierarchies of belonging dictating one's right to the city. These commonalities can be attributed to the mounting pressures of global capital in the region, as well as the converging ways the Iberian nations have defined and debated race, power, and identity from the era of imperial expansion and into the twenty-first century. Meanwhile, these nations would soon confront another acute affective event that would catalyze a renewed period of transnational crisis and adjustment: the onset of a global pandemic in early 2020.

CONCLUSION

The Continuity of Crisis

Crisis is not exceptional to history or to consciousness, but a process embedded in the ordinary that unfolds in stories about navigating what's overwhelming.

—LAUREN BERLANT, *Cruel Optimism*

The 2008 financial collapse catalyzed a protracted period of unraveling and reorganizing, through storytelling, of the existing paradigms that mediated everyday life across the Iberian region. For the Spanish and Portuguese, who had been maneuvering toward the prosperity of their European neighbors since the decades prior, this economic downturn was felt as an especially acute affective event. As different institutions and collectives navigated toward a post-crisis urban future, their affective expressions, visible in such mediums as text, visual culture, and the built environment itself, would drive the corresponding evolution of the spatial and psychic terrain of cities like Madrid and Lisbon. The complex ways that this moment was lived, perceived, and discussed came to a head in historically marginalized districts like Lavapiés and Mouraria, axes of increasing political, economic, and social interest due to their central location and heterogeneous populace. In turn, the question of race was often at the forefront of these cultural negotiations, the perception and expression of which was informed by a long legacy of colonial thinking in each Iberian nation. The narratives that emerged in this climate, from nativist affirmations of self and the nation to the unexploited social and economic value of each of these cities, made newly relevant the enduring question of who, exactly, urban centers would serve.

By and large, the texts that I have analyzed in *Cities Beyond Crisis* demonstrate how promise of urban growth as a path to prosperity—and therefore, beyond the crisis—propelled the evolution of Lavapiés and Mouraria in the wake of the 2008 crisis. Throughout this period, stakeholders ranging from public and private institutions to local actors demonstrated a renewed interest and investment in these districts in terms of their unexploited exchange-value, leading to a wave of consumer-facing development that positioned these sites as new terrains for capital accumulation. The discursive patterns that accompanied this development, which circulated in digital and physical spheres, from the pages of Airbnb, to art installations and opportunities to walk each neighborhood according to a specific thematic lens, demonstrated how the districts' most stigmatized attributes, from their histories as hubs of the urban poor to their contemporary evolution into centers of racial heterogeneity, were recast as aestheticized tropes in the service of consumption. Likewise, as explored in the final chapters of study, this push occurred in tandem with an upsurge in politically engaged urban activism, as individuals enraged by the impunity of public and private institutions following the financial collapse imagined and enacted possibilities beyond the status quo. Corresponding initiatives, from the rise of municipalist political movements, to grassroots interventions in the built environment further demonstrated the influence of oppositional discourse in the making and mediation of the urban.

My review of the "good life" fantasies expressed by social actors across the ideological spectrum has revealed a range of unexpected commonalities in tropes and aspirations. For example, both those driving and contesting the consumer-oriented production of each neighborhood often turned to nostalgic invocations of myths of origin when expressing their respective visions for the city, evident in the recurring use of the *castizo* moniker in Lavapiés, and in the cultivation of Mouraria's relationship with the *fado* genre. The treatment of the racial Other in these increasingly heterogeneous districts, too, demonstrated the measured acceptance of such collectives in terms of their value as a commodity, or, alternatively, on the condition of their affinity for national ideals. These cycles of expression were apparent in both the Spanish and Portuguese contexts, while informed by the historic, geographic, and economic specificities of each of these Iberian regions. Although these were by no means identical cases, the similar norms, forms, and institutions into which cycles of expression settled in the post-crisis era pointed to a shared experience of urban living, aspirations, and exasperations in an increasingly intersecting world.

The role of visuality in shaping both the perception and form of these urban spaces, too, is a primary takeaway from this study. This manner of shaping what is seen and how it is perceived was often quite literal, such as in Juan Valbuena's *Nosotros* and Gonçalo Gaioso's *All Around Us*, two photographic interventions that showcase the tendency to cast the racial Other as useful to a themed depiction of the neighborhood while simultaneously distinguishing them from standards of national belonging framed in proximity to Whiteness. In other cases, the "visualization of history" in Lavapiés and Mouraria was the product of local actors and institutions who mobilized their authority to name, categorize, and define each space according to their unique interests, working within and beyond the image-world, from the resignification of the Praça do Martim Moniz by NCS Produções, to the Tapapiés food festival in Lavapiés.

With time, the narrative rhythms triggered by the affective response to the financial collapse on the Iberian Peninsula began to recede into the ordinary. The push-and-pull between the authority of public and private institutions and the will of the public, loudest in the years immediately following the 2008 crisis, settled in as a dimension of the everyday. Yet, just as these heightened senses and responses stoked by this global affective event began to taper, a new calamity emerged. In early 2020, the onset of the COVID-19 pandemic brought these prevailing modes of everyday life to an abrupt halt, ushering in a new stage of affective responses to the threats of the present.

The era of the virus officially arrived on the Iberian Peninsula on February 25, 2020, when Spanish authorities announced their first confirmed case in Cataluña. Days later, another infected patient was declared by Portuguese media outlets.[1] With the number of infections growing at an unprecedented rate, the spread of the disease bolstered by the accelerated pace and globalized infrastructures of the modern era, COVID-19 was officially declared a pandemic by the World Health Organization on March 11 of the same year. Public health mandates including mandatory quarantines and closures of both public and private spaces quickly followed, and once-bustling cities across the globe fell quiet, save for the chorus of ambulance sirens that ushered the rising number

FIGURE 6.1. "Distanciamiento Social" series by Dos Jotas, 2020

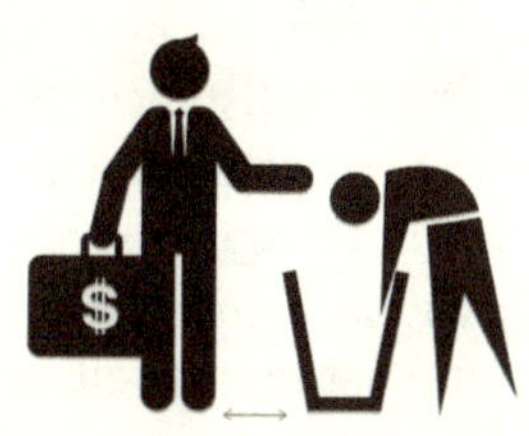

of patients to hospitals. As the pandemic continued, and the initial weeks of restrictions extended into months, governing bodies across the globe scrambled to balance a total financial collapse with the health of the population. In countries like Spain and Portugal, the travel and leisure industry that had played a central role in helping each nation's economy claw its way beyond the 2008 financial collapse was no contender for this deadly and rapidly evolving disease, paralyzed by ongoing measures to mitigate its impact.

Amid this renewed sense of crisis, the urban emerged once more as a central arena for thinking through the intersecting social and spatial effects of this viral threat. As much of the population was confined at home, watching the situation unfold with fear and apprehension, cultural producers began to use the lens of the pandemic to interrogate the relationship between space and society. Take, as an example, the work of Spanish urban artist DosJotas, whose interventions prior to COVID-19 were largely public installations addressing hot-button issues including real-estate speculation, surveillance, and income inequality. During state-mandated quarantines, DosJotas published a set of images titled "Social Distancing" on his Instagram, employing the phrase used to encourage separating physically from one another in order to limit contagion as an avenue to comment on persisting forms of inequality.[2] This series, along with other Instagram posts the artist published at the height of the pandemic, were later shared on his website as a broader COVID-19 series, in which he uses the vocabulary associated with the control and spread of the virus to explore different social dilemmas.

In the three pictures published on Instagram, DosJotas depicts examples of "social distance" that hinge on social and material welfare. His message comes across through juxtaposition: in the first image, a figure in the foreground sleeps next to a shallow dish, and uses newspapers as a blanket while a couple enjoys a glass of wine on a terrace behind him. In the next, a character dressed in a suit and tie holds a briefcase with a large dollar sign emblazoned on its front. They gesture to the figure at their side, who is hunched over a garbage can, and an arrow at the base of the image signals the distance between the characters. The widening expanse between the have and have-nots of society is applied most concretely to the context of the pandemic in the final image of the series, where a character performs stretches on a balcony while another sleeps on a bench below.

This scene builds on the images that circulated across media and social platforms of apartment-dwellers in dense urban centers exercising and connecting with one another from their balconies, roofs, and patios in the peak of the pandemic. In one highly publicized instance, a fitness instructor in

Seville led his neighbors in a series of exercises from the roof of his apartment complex, celebrated as an icon of health and solidarity in the midst of the crisis.[3] In another, a man in Madrid ran the equivalent of a marathon in the space of his seven-meter terrace, celebrated for his ingenuity in light of ongoing restrictions on movement through public spaces.[4] In this depiction, however, DosJotas contrasts an icon representative of these public acts of resilience with the plight of the unhoused, drawing attention to the ways that COVID-19 made more acute, and thus more visible, the inequalities engrained in the rhythms of everyday life.

Several commenters on Instagram noted how these critiques laid bare societal challenges relevant beyond the ongoing health crisis. In one such case, a user named @daniellavillan wrote "That is the true pandemic, permanent and criminal."[5] In another, @aly.calle stated "Separating things that were together or make them even more distant than they were before = social distancing" to which the artist responded "Everything continues with the same distance, in fact more."[6] According to this view, the pandemic was not simply the beginning of a "new normal," as frequently stated, but the latest catalyst for a more heightened experience of the ordinary, a visible and visceral calamity that made more palpable the enduring cracks in social, governmental, and monetary structures that shaped the quotidian in and beyond the Iberian Peninsula. DosJotas's critique, thus, is a broader condemnation of the human casualties of a highly individualistic social and economic system that, though aggravated by the latest crisis, are positioned to continue regardless of a viral threat.

Evidently, the nature of the event provoking affective responses had changed, yet many of the fundamental issues that had shaped discourse since the financial collapse endured. With this in mind, it is useful to return to Berlant's notion of crisis ordinariness, defining the present as an impasse shaped by a series of crises to which people respond by finding "new modes of living on."[7] They explain, "across diverse geopolitical and biopolitical locations, the present moment increasingly imposes itself on consciousness as a moment in extended crisis, with one happening piling on another."[8] In the contemporary era, it seems we are feeling our way through periods of shock and reorganization at an accelerated pace, a rhythm fomented by the temporal structures of modern living. Meanwhile, the social and structural dilemmas of which we take stock during these frequent and compounding moments of reckoning—the heightened ordinary—are often left unresolved, settling in as imperceptible systems and power structures when we return to the sense of a steady every day, and reemerging in a new light from event to affective event.

As *Cities Beyond Crisis* has shown through the analysis of a wide range of cultural texts produced in the heightened affective climate of the post-2008 era, emotionally charged reactions to such moments of calamity shape the urban. With each affective event, the tensions of the present rise and recede, leaving in their wake an evolved version of the ordinary. In the case of the financial collapse, the network of expressions that emerged in districts like Lavapiés and Mouraria actively navigated each neighborhood toward an evolved version of the quotidian, for better or for worse (depending, of course, on one's notion of what "better" or "worse" entails). COVID-19, then, would pick up where this latest crisis left off, a new guiding force for debating both the right to and the purpose of the city that would settle into the impasse until the advent of the next.

All signs point to a complicated road ahead. As the pandemic demonstrated, pending environmental crises will continue to close the artificial gaps between human and nonhuman life forms and agents, and corresponding affective responses such as fear, anxiety, and existential dread will play a central role in shaping the built environment. Madrid and Lisbon, identified as the most vulnerable European capitals to extreme heat, are already at the front lines of the climate crisis, and a central arena for debating visions for a path forward.[9] Luis Prádanos, in this regard, has issued the necessary call for scholars discussing urban cultural processes to pay more attention to "how urban cultural processes interact with the socioecological intricacies of cities."[10] This is a necessary future direction for studying the relationship between affect and urban development, as climate events including rising temperatures, water scarcity, drought, and wildfires, increasingly rear their head on the peninsula. These moments of heightened affect, met with responses ranging from optimistic attachments to growth, to more radical visions for a break with the status quo, will be a primary compass going forward in the shaping of urban futures. Likewise, these conversations are certain to be shaped by the xenophobic, exclusionary, and nativist sentiments that are increasingly visible in the rhythms of the everyday, exemplified in the rise of right-wing populist political parties like Spain's Vox and Portugal's Chega, whose electoral platforms are built on biases against collectives including undocumented immigrants, the LGBTQ+ community, and racial and religious minorities.[11] Another crisis is certain, yet it remains to be seen the shape these cities will take, and according to whose vision, in these moments fueled by feeling.

NOTES

INTRODUCTION

1. Many studies detail the genesis, effects, and mediation of the 2008 financial crisis in Spain and Portugal. See, for example, Jõao César das Neves, *As 10 Questões da Crise* (Dom Quixote, 2011); Observatorio sobre Crises e Alternativas, "A anatomia da crise: Identificar os problemas para construir as alternativas" (Centro de Estudos Sociais Laboratório Associado, Universidade de Coimbra, 2013); Observatorio Metropolitano, *Paisajes devastados: Después del ciclo inmobiliario: Impactos regionales y urbanos de la crisis*, Útiles 14 (Traficantes de Sueños, 2013); José Castro Caldas, "O impacto das medidas 'anti-crise' e a situação social e de emprego" (Comité Económico e Social Europeu, 2013); Carlos Encinas-Ferrer and Juan Tugores Ques, eds., *La crisis del euro y su impacto en la economía y la sociedad*, Economía UB 02 (Universitat de Barcelona, Publicacions i Edicions, 2015); Juan Pablo Colmenarejo, "Crónica de la Crisis del Euro en España ¿Qué podemos aprender?," *Actualidad Económica* 30, no. 102 (2020): 35–49; Donato Fernández Navarrete, "La crisis económica española: Una gran operación especulativa con graves consecuencias," *Estudios internacionales* (Santiago) 48, no. 183 (January 2016): 119–51.
2. Canonical examples of this narrative trope may be found in the work of José Cadalso, Miguel de Unamuno, Camilo José Cela, Eça de Queirós, Fernando Pessoa, and Camilo Castelo Branco. Later in this introduction, I discuss the disparaging construction of the Iberian region specifically as it relates to the social construction of race and how it has informed both Spain's and Portugal's complex relationship to the category of Whiteness.
3. Several reports delve into the precursors to and details of these demographic shifts. See, for example, Mário Leston Bandeira, "Dinâmicas demográficas e envelhecimento da população portuguesa," *Fundação Francisco Manuel dos Santos*, March 4, 2015; and Ministerio para la Transición Ecológica y el Reto Demográfico, "¿Qué es el Reto Demográfico?," accessed November 28, 2022, https://www.miteco.gob.es/es/reto-demografico/temas/que-es/. According to

data collected by Mikolaj Stanek and Jean-Michel Lafleur, the primary destination of Spanish emigrants from 2007 to 2017 was the United Kingdom, followed by France, Germany, and the United States; see Mikolaj Stanek and Jean-Michel Lafleur, "Emigración de españoles en la UE: Pautas, implicaciones y retos futuros," *Anuario CIDOB de la Inmigración*, 2017, 187. While Spain was a principal destination country for emigrants from Portugal leading up to the global financial crisis, 2008 marked an abrupt shift in Portuguese inflows; see Filipa Pinho and Rui Pena Pires, "Espanha" (Observatório da Emigração, 2013), 6. Main destinations for Portuguese emigrants following the economic recession included the United Kingdom, Switzerland, France, Germany, and Brazil; see David Justino, "Emigration from Portugal: Old Wine in New Bottles?" (Migration Policy Institute, February 2016), 2, http://www.migrationpolicy.org/research/emigration-portugal-old-wine-new-bottles. This topic is also extensively explored in news media, including *Público*'s "Número de licenciados a emigrar aumentou 49,5% entre 2009 e 2011," *Público*, March 1, 2012 and *El País'* "El Plan B: 700 millones desean emigrar," *El País*, February 21, 2010.

4. This is detailed, for example, in the series of annual reports put out by the Observatorio Español del Racismo y la Xenofobia, functioning under the auspices of Spain's Ministerio de Inclusión, Seguridad Social and Migraciones. See, also, María Ángeles Cea D'Ancona and Miguel S. Valles Martínez, *Evolución del racismo y la xenofobia en España: Informe 2009* (Ministerio de Trabajo e Inmigración, 2009). An additional series of studies, titled the Informe Raxen, were published by the group Movimiento contra la Intolerancia; "Informe Raxen: Racismo, Xenofobia, Antisemitismo, Islamofobia, Neofascismo, Homofobia y otras manifestaciones relacionadas de Intolerancia a través de los hechos" (Movimiento contra la Intolerancia, 2010), http://www.movimientocontralaintolerancia.com/html/raxen/raxen.asp. Studies specific to Portugal regarding this period include Jorge Malheiros and Alina Esteves, "Diagnóstico da população imigrante em Portugal: Desafios e potencialidades" (Alto Comissariado para a Imigração e Diálogo Intercultural, 2013), and the European Commission Against Racism and Tolerance's "ECRI Report on Portugal" (Council of Europe, 2013), https://www.refworld.org/docid/51dd50db4.html.
5. Take, as an example, Spain's sale of assets from the national utility company Endesa and Portugal's transferral of EDP (Energias de Portugal) to the private sector.
6. There is an extensive bibliography on both the anti-austerity protests of 2011 and the municipalist movement in Europe. Some examples include Carles Feixa and Jordi Nofre, eds., *#GeneraciónIndignada: Topías y utopías del 15M*, Primera edición, Ensayo Milenio 55 (Milenio, 2013); Britta Baumgarten, "Geração

à Rasca and Beyond: Mobilizations in Portugal after 12 March 2011," *Current Sociology* 61, no. 4 (July 1, 2013): 457–73; the *Journal of Spanish Cultural Studies* special issue on 15-M (vol. 15, no. 1–2, 2014); Barcelona en Comú, Debbie Bookchin, and Ada Colau, *Fearless Cities: A Guide to the Global Municipalist Movement* (New Internationalist, 2019); Salomé Sola Morales, "Precários nos querem, rebeldes nos terão! Tecnopolítica e indignación, de la Geração à Rasca a Que se lixe a Troika!," *Electrónico de Estudios en Comunicación Social "Disertaciones"* 13, no. 2 (May 13, 2020); Observatorio Metropolitano, *La apuesta municipalista: La democracia empieza por lo cercano* (Traficantes de Sueños, 2023), https://traficantes.net/libros/la-apuesta-municipalista.

7. Manuel Castells, *Networks of Outrage and Hope: Social Movements in the Internet Age* (John Wiley & Sons, 2015); Luis Moreno-Caballud, *Cultures of Anyone: Studies on Cultural Democratization in the Spanish Neoliberal Crisis* (Liverpool University Press, 2015).
8. Stephen Luis Vilaseca, "The 15-M Movement: Formed by and Formative of Counter-Mapping and Spatial Activism," *Journal of Spanish Cultural Studies* 15, no. 1–2 (April 3, 2014): 119–39; Jonathan Snyder, *Poetics of Opposition in Contemporary Spain: Politics and the Work of Urban Culture* (Palgrave Macmillan, 2015).
9. Snyder, *Poetics of Opposition in Contemporary Spain: Politics and the Work of Urban Culture*, xv.
10. Lauren Berlant, *Cruel Optimism* (Duke University Press, 2011).
11. Berlant, *Cruel Optimism*, 4
12. Raymond Williams, *Marxism and Literature* (Oxford University Press, 1977), 133–34.
13. Berlant, *Cruel Optimism*, 5.
14. Berlant refers to the notion of a good life when defining their concept "cruel optimism." They write "A relation of cruel optimism exists when something you desire is actually an obstacle to your flourishing. It might involve food, or a kind of love; it might be a fantasy of the good life, or a political project. It might rest on something simpler, too, like a new habit that promises to induce in you an improved way of being. These kinds of optimistic relation are not inherently cruel. They become cruel only when the object that draws your attachment actively impedes the aim that brought you to it initially," 1.
15. Berlant, *Cruel Optimism*, 69.
16. Don Mitchell, *The Right to the City: Social Justice and the Fight for Public Space* (Guilford Press, 2003), 42.
17. Berlant, *Cruel Optimism*, 9
18. This theoretical framework, Benjamin Fraser aptly summarizes, accounts for space, "not merely as external to the human mind as a static landscape, but

also as a method of division, or carving up reality which in itself produces not only physical space, mental space, and social space but also their conceptual division from one another." See *Henri Lefebvre and the Spanish Urban Experience: Reading the Mobile City* (Bucknell University Press, 2011), 10.

19. A range of scholars have sought to establish definitions and differentiations between the conceptual categories of space and place through analysis of human experience and the creation of meaning. Relevant references include Yi-Fu Tuan, *Topofilia: A Study of Environmental Perception, Attitudes and Values* (Prentice Hall, 1974), *Space and Place: The Perspective of Experience* (University of Minnesota Press, 1977); Edward Relph, *Place and Placelessness* (Pion, 1976); Anne Buttimer and David Seamon, eds., *The Human Experience of Space and Place*, Routledge Revivals (Routledge, 2015).
20. Here, Lefebvre proposes a triadic model for analyzing spatial production, that is, an understanding of space (conceptually and concretely) as reciprocal exchanges between spatial practices, representations of space, and representational spaces. See Henri Lefebvre, *The Production of Space*, trans. Donald Nicholson-Smith (Blackwell Publishing, 1991).
21. Doreen Massey, *Space, Place, and Gender* (University of Minnesota Press, 1994), 2.
22. Brooke Neely and Michelle Samura, for example, offer the "theory of racial space" to link scholarly interventions situated under the umbrella of both space and race, identifying four main characteristics regarding space "contested, fluid and historical, interactional and relational, and defined by inequality and difference," as useful vocabulary to discuss its relationship to racial inequality. Camilla Hawthorne also offers an overview of prominent thematic areas in the study of Black Geographies, including "space-making and the Black geographic imagination; racial capitalism; cities, policing and carceral geographies; and racism and plantation futures." See Brooke Neely and Michelle Samura, "Social Geographies of Race: Connecting Race and Space," *Ethnic and Racial Studies* 34, no. 11 (November 2011): 1933–52; Camilla Hawthorne, "Black Matters Are Spatial Matters: Black Geographies for the Twenty-first Century," *Geography Compass* 13, no. 11 (November 2019).
23. Benjamin Fraser, *Toward an Urban Cultural Studies* (New York: Palgrave Macmillan, 2015).
24. Matthew Feinberg, *From the Theater to the Plaza: Spectacle, Protest, and Urban Space in Twenty-First-Century Madrid* (McGill-Queen's University Press, 2022), 24.
25. They write, "We understand race as an unstable and 'decentered' complex of social meanings constantly being transformed by political struggle. With this in mind, we advance the following definition: Race is a concept that signifies

and symbolizes social conflicts and interests by referring to different types of human bodies. Although the concept of race invokes seemingly biologically based human characteristics (so-called phenotypes), selection of these particular human features for purposes of racial signification is always and necessarily a social and historical process. Indeed, the categories employed to differentiate among human beings along racial lines reveal themselves upon serious examination, to be at best imprecise, and at worst completely arbitrary. They may be arbitrary, but they are not meaningless. Race is strategic; race does ideological and political work." Michael Omi and Howard Winant, *Racial Formation in the United States*, 3rd ed. (Routledge, 2015), 110–11.

26. Achille Mbembe, *Necropolitics* (Duke University Press, 2019); Kimberlé Crenshaw, "Demarginalizing the Intersection of Race and Sex: A Black Feminist Critique of Antidiscrimination Doctrine, Feminist Theory, and Antiracist Politics," *University of Chicago Legal Forum* 1989, no. Article 8 (1989); Kimberlé Crenshaw, "Mapping the Margins: Intersectionality, Identity Politics, and Violence against Women of Color," *Stanford Law Review* 43, no. 6 (July 1991): 1241; Gloria Anzaldúa, *Borderlands / La Frontera: The New Mestiza*, 4th ed. (San Francisco: Aunt Lute Books, 2012).
27. Quijano, as an example, delineates differences in colonial/racial relationships as expressed in North America, "the space of Anglo-American colonial dominion" and the Southern Cone. See Quijano, "Coloniality of Power and Eurocentrism in Latin America," 560.
28. Goldberg writes that the contours of racist thought, "are often interactive historically, overlapping landscapes. But it remains nevertheless revealing to delineate them, to distinguish one kind and style from another in terms of differences in their conditions of possibility, expression, effects, and implication." In response to the undeniably networked present and its influence on such social configurations he adds that a regionally specific focus on racial formations, "is not to limit the (partial) influence of their logics and effects on other places, spaces, and regions that might not be readily identified with their coordinates of origination. Racisms have a history of travelling and transforming in their circulation. What I register here as more or less discrete in order to identify its socio-material and intellectual conditions of emergence, logics, social manifestations, effects, and implications is in practice interactive with other regional variants at different times and places on the ground and across borders and oceans." David Theo Goldberg, "Racial Europeanization," *Ethnic and Racial Studies* 29, no. 2 (March 2006): 333.
29. Some seminal texts on this topic include Frantz Fanon, *Black Skin, White Masks*, trans. Richard Philcox (Grove Press, 2008) and W. E. B. Du Bois, *Black*

Reconstruction in America: Toward a History of the Part Which Black Folk Played in the Attempt to Reconstruct Democracy in America, 1860–1880 (Transaction Publishers, 2013).

30. Aníbal Quijano, "Coloniality of Power and Eurocentrism in Latin America," *International Sociology* 15, no. 2 (June 1, 2000): 534.
31. Julia H. Chang, *Blood Novels: Gender, Caste, and Race in Spanish Realism* (University of Toronto Press, 2022); Joshua Goode, *Impurity of Blood: Defining Race in Spain, 1870–1930* (Louisiana State University Press, 2009); Max S. Hering Torres, "La limpieza de sangre. Problemas de interpretación: acercamientos históricos y metodológicos.," *Historia Crítica* 45 (2011): 32–55.
32. Stoler writes, "Race as a concept performs in a mobile field. It animates vacillating discourses with dynamic motility. Racial lexicons accumulate recursively, producing new racial truths as they requisition and reassemble old ones." *Duress: Imperial Durabilities in Our Times* (Duke University Press, 2016), 250.
33. See, for example, Ramiro de Maeztu, *Defensa de la Hispanidad* (ePubLibre, 1934), https://archive.org/details/de-maeztu-ramiro.-defensa-de-la-hispanidad-1934-2014; Juan Valera, "Cartas americanas," 1958, https://www.cervantesvirtual.com/obra-visor/cartas americanas--o/html. For a critical text on the topic see Ángel Loureiro, "Spanish Nationalism and the Ghost of Empire," *Journal of Spanish Cultural Studies* 4, no. 1 (2003): 65–76.
34. Texts on this topic include Eduardo González Calleja and Fredesvinta Limón Nevado, *La hispanidad como instrumento de combate: Raza e imperio en la prensa franquista durante la Guerra Civil española* (Madrid: Consejo Superior de Investigaciones Científicas, 1988); David Marcilhacy, "La Hispanidad bajo el franquismo: El americanismo al servicio de un proyecto nacionalista," in *Imaginarios y representaciones de España durante el franquismo*, ed. Stéphane Michonneau and Xosé M. Núñez Seixas (Casa de Velázquez, 2014), 73–102.
35. For further information on *Portugalidade* and its cultural manifestations during the Salazar regime see, for example, Ellen Sapega, *Consensus and Debate in Salazar's Portugal: Visual and Literary Negotiations of the National Text 1933–1948* (Pennsylvania State University Press, 2008); David Corkill and José Carlos Pina Almeida, "Commemoration and Propaganda in Salazar's Portugal: The 'Mundo Português' Exposition of 1940," *Journal of Contemporary History* 44, no. 3 (July 2009): 381–99.
36. The crux of Freyre's argument is found in *Casa-grande e senzala* (1933) and *O mundo que o português criou* (1940). See *Casa-grande & Senzala*, 43. ed (Record, 2001); *O mundo que o português criou: aspectos das relações sociais e de cultura do Brasil com Portugal e as colônias portuguesas* (É Realizações Editora, 2010).

37. For further inquiry into this term see, for example, Vítor de Sousa, "Da 'Portugalidade à Lusofonia" (Braga, Universidade do Minho Instituto de Ciências Sociais, 2015); António Pinto Ribeiro, "Para acabar de vez com a lusofonia," *Lusotopie* 17, no. 2 (2018): 220–26.
38. See Goode, *Impurity of Blood.* Jo Labanyi speaks to similar points in when discussing the racial discourse employed by the Franco regime. She writes, "Like fascism elsewhere, Francoist rhetoric made abundant use of racial terminology, but Spain's different imperial trajectory gave this racial emphasis a very different inflection from the Nazi model—or indeed from British imperial discourse. Contrary to the British colonial model of commerce and exploitation, presupposing racial segregation, Spain's imperial expansion from 1492 had been based on conquest, settlement and conversion: that is, on enforced assimilation. The violence of the assimilation process bordered on, and in some places led to, genocide—but in the name of incorporation rather than exclusion. . . . Spanish colonial discourse was no less racist than its British counterpart but its belief in white superiority was articulated differently, in a way that allowed Spaniards—and post-independence Latin Americans—to convince themselves that they were not guilty of the racism that so visibly characterized the segregated societies of Britain's past or present empire," "Miscegenation, Nation Formation and Cross-Racial Identifications in the Early Francoist Folkloric Film Musical," in *Hybridity and Its Discontents: Politics, Science, Culture*, ed. Avtar Brah and Annie Coombes (Taylor and Francis, 2000), 58.
39. Miguel Vale de Almeida, *An Earth-Colored Sea: "Race," Culture, and the Politics of Identity in the Postcolonial Portuguese-Speaking World* (Berghahn Books, 2004), 65.
40. Daniel Silva, *Empire Found: Racial Identities and Coloniality in Twenty-First-Century Portuguese Popular Cultures* (Liverpool UP, 2022).
41. Throughout this text, I capitalize both Whiteness and Blackness to affirm how both terms refer to socially created categories that signify race.
42. "Coloniality and Modernity/Rationality," *Cultural Studies* 21, no. 2–3 (2007): 168–69.
43. Some examples of scholarship discussing the expression of these beliefs in different time periods include Boaventura de Sousa Santos, "Between Prospero and Caliban: Colonialism, Postcolonialism, and Inter Identity," *Luso-Brazilian Review* 39, no. 2 (2002): 9–43; Daniela Flesler, *The Return of the Moor: Spanish Responses to Contemporary Moroccan Immigration* (Purdue University Press, 2008); Roberto M. Dainotto, *Europe (in Theory)* (Duke University Press, 2006).
44. Some notable monographs on this subject include Cacilda Rêgo and Marcus Brasileiro, *Migration in Lusophone Cinema* (Springer, 2014).; N. Michelle Murray, *Home Away from Home: Immigrant Narratives, Domesticity, and Coloniality in Contemporary Spanish Culture* (University of North Carolina Press, 2018); Silvia

Bermúdez, *Rocking the Boat in Contemporary Spanish Music* (University of Toronto Press, 2018); Jeffrey K. Coleman, *The Necropolitical Theater: Race and Immigration on the Contemporary Spanish Stage* (Northwestern University Press, 2020); Daniel Silva, *Empire Found: Racial Identities and Coloniality in Twenty-First Century Portuguese Popular Cultures* (Liverpool University Press, 2022).

45. See Lou Charnon-Deutsch, *The Spanish Gypsy* (Pennsylvania State University Press, 2004); Susan Martin-Márquez, *Disorientations: Spanish Colonialism in Africa and the Performance of Identity* (Yale University Press 2008); Baltasar Fra-Molinero, "The Suspect Whiteness of Spain," in *At Home and Abroad: Historicizing Twentieth-Century Whiteness in Literature and Performance*, ed. La Vinia Delois Jennings (University of Tennessee Press, 2009), Eva Woods Peiró, *White Gypsies: Race and Stardom in Spanish Musical Films* (University of Minnesota Press, 2012), 147–69; Martin Repinecz *Volatile Whiteness: Race, Cinema, and Europeanization in Spain* (University of Toronto Press, 2025).

46. After Equatorial Guinea gained independence from Spain in 1968, Francisco Macías Nguema seized power through a coup d'état. Subsequently, a 1979 coup brought Teodoro Obiang Nguema Mbasogo to the presidency. Yolanda Aixelà-Cabré notes that the rise of both the Macías and Obiang regimes led to significant waves of migration from the region to Spain in "Entre las dictaduras y el petróleo: Las migraciones trasnacionales de Guinea Ecuatorial." *Revista Andaluza de Antropología*, vol. 3 (Jan. 2012): 89–103. In similar manner, the growth of Spain's Argentine populace during this same era could be related to the resettlement of those fleeing the Videla dictatorship. Laura Pérez López explores this in "Exiliados argentinos en la España de la transición: la imagen de un diario español (*El País*)," in *Actas del IV Simposio de Historia Actual: Logroño, 17–19 de octubre de 2002*, vol. 2, 2004, 893–914. For more on the *retornado* phenomenon in Portugal see Morgane Delaunay, "Portugal e o regresso dos colonos de Angola e Moçambique," *Cidades: Comunidades e territórios*, no. 44 (June 15, 2022); Christoph Kalter, *Postcolonial People: The Return from Africa and the Remaking of Portugal* (Cambridge University Press, 2022).

47. Coleman, *The Necropolitical Theater*, 4. This same push was happening in Portugal, which entered the European Economic Community the same year.

48. As of the writing of this publication, Portugal requires that the parents of an individual born in the country must have lived and worked there with legal documentation for a minimum of six consecutive years in order to obtain citizenship.

49. Kesha Fikes, *Managing African Portugal: The Citizen-Migrant Distinction* (Duke University Press, 2009), 43–44.

50. Jefatura de Estado, "Ley 51/1982, de 13 de julio, de modificación de los artículos 17 al 26 de Código Civil" (BOE, July 1982).
51. An additional article in the law created an accelerated path to citizenship for migrants hailing from former colonial territories including all Iberoamerican nations, the Philippines, and Equatorial Guinea. At the same time, these parameters still required two years of legal residence for members of the aforementioned groups seeking citizenship, adding another legal hurdle for those in a more privileged position on the migrant hierarchy.
52. See Diego López de Lera, "La inmigración a España a fines del siglo XX: Los que vienen a trabajar y los que vienen a descansar," *Reis*, no. 71/72 (1995): 225–45.
53. See Maria Ioannis Baganha, José Carlos Marques, and Pedro Góis, "Imigrantes em Portugal: Uma síntese histórica," *Ler História*, no. 56 (May 1, 2009): 123–33; Pedro Góis and José Carlos Marques, "Retrato de um Portugal migrante: A evolução da emigração, da imigração e do seu estudo nos últimos 40 anos," *E-Cadernos CES*, no. 29 (June 15, 2018).
54. Matt St. John, "Remembering Spain's First Official Hate Crime," *El País English*, June 23, 2017; "Alcindo Monteiro morreu há 25 anos. Uma vítima do racismo," *Diário de Notícias*, June 10, 2020; "Más de 11 de años de prisión por el crimen que desencadenó los incidentes racistas en El Ejido," *La Vanguardia*, October 21, 2003.
55. In a more recent turn, scholars are pushing to consider race beyond the scope of migration, and the ways that Spanish and Portuguese cultural producers embrace or reject racial plurality as a dimension of life in twenty-first century Iberia.
56. Portugal's "Golden Visa" was introduced as a residence permit program in 2011 with the objective of attracting investment from non-EU citizens. This visa type was granted in return for investments including the creation of ten jobs or more, the purchase of real estate at an amount of at least 500,000 euros, and differing forms of capital transfer at a minimum of 250,000 euros. See Sofia Gaspar and Fernando Ampudia de Haro, "Buying Citizenship? Chinese Golden Visa Migrants in Portugal," *International Migration* 58, no. 3 (June 1, 2020): 58–72. Spain introduced a similar program in 2013 under the Residency Visa for Property Acquisition Law. For an analysis of social and geopolitical impacts of this law in Spain see, for example, Max Holleran, "Buying Up the Semi-Periphery: Spain's Economy of 'Golden Visas,'" *Ethnos: Journal of Anthropology* 86, no. 4 (October 2021): 730–49.
57. Lefebvre, *The Production of Space*, 44.
58. Lavapiés is bound by the larger district of Embajadores and, Mouraria, as of Lisbon's 2012 administrative reorganization of the Portuguese capital, is

housed within the parish of Santa Maria Maior. Prior to this most recent reorganization of Lisbon's municipal districts, the neighborhood was still only recognized colloquially, spanning across two of Lisbon's parishes: Socorro and São Cristóvão e São Lourenço.

59. For further discussion of these topics see Pedro de Répide, *Las calles de Madrid*, 4th ed. (Afrodisio Aguado, 1981); Santos Juliá, David R. Ringrose, and Cristina Segura, *Madrid: Historia de una capital* (Alianza Editorial y Fundación Caja de Madrid, 1994); Ángel López López, "Historia de Lavapiés. El latido de Madrid que resiste a lo largo del tiempo," *El Salto Diario*, accessed July 28, 2023.
60. Feinberg, *From the Theater to the Plaza*, 9–10.
61. Marluci Menezes, *Mouraria, retalhos de um imaginário: Significados urbanos de um bairro de Lisboa* (Celta, 2004).
62. Menezes cites the work of Vitor Ribeiro and Pedro de Azevedo in her discussion of the origins of the neighborhood following the Catholic conquest of the city.
63. "Los barrios bajos. A estas nuevas barriadas, apartadas y humildes, debieron naturalmente refluir las clases más desvalidas de la población cuando, creciendo ésta en número e importancia, rebasó las antiguas cercas y cubrió de edificios costosos las calles y términos de la villa." Romano, *El antiguo Madrid, 1861*, 29.
64. Benito Pérez Galdós, *Misericordia*, 19th ed., ed. Luciano García Lorenzo (Catedra, 2016).
65. "Un tipo original y especialísimo, aunque compuesto de la gracia y de la jactancia andaluzas, de la viveza valenciana y de la seriedad y entonamiento castellanos," *El antiguo Madrid*, 29.
66. Teresa Rodrigues discusses the impact of Portuguese internal migrations on the city's landscape at length in *Nascer e morrer na Lisboa oitocentista: Migrações, mortalidade e desenvolvimento*, Cosmos história 10 (Edições Cosmos, 1995) and *Cinco séculos de quotidiano: A vida em Lisboa do século XV aos nossos dias*, Cosmos história 20 (Edições Cosmos, 1997).
67. Teresa Rodrigues synthesizes archival information from this period to illustrate this point. For example, documents describe Mouraria as having six hundred inhabitants per square meter by the end of the eighteenth century. See *Cinco séculos de quotidiano*, 45.
68. For a rigorous study on how *fado* has been employed as a form of national self-understanding in Portugal see Lila Ellen Gray, *Fado Resounding: Affective Politics and Urban Life* (Duke UP, 2014).
69. Fernando Maurício, "O meu bairro," n.d.
70. José Luis de Arrese, "No queremos una España de proletarios, sino de propietarios," ABC, May 2, 1959, 41. For a discussion of Franco-era urban plans see, as an example, Carlos Sambricio, "La vivienda en Madrid, de 1939 al Plan de

Vivienda Social en 1959," in *La vivienda en Madrid en la década de los cincuenta: El Plan de Urgencia Social* (Electa, 1999), 14.

71. Daniel Sorando and Álvaro Ardura, *First We Take Manhattan: La destrucción creativa de las ciudades* (Catarata, 2016), 38. Sorando and Ardura also note that another approach to getting rid of long-time renters in rent stabilized units was to scare them off by intentionally renting to stigmatized groups, such as the racialized Roma and newer immigrant populations. Proprietors, then, could further exploit those residents by demanding higher rents.
72. These plans are described in both Francisco Keil Amaral's *Lisboa: Uma cidade em transformação* (Publicações Europa-América, 1969) and Michael Colvin's "Gabriel de Oliveira's 'Há Festa Na Mouraria' and the 'Fado Novo's' Criticism of the Estado Novo's Demolition of the Baixa Mouraria," *Portuguese Studies* 20 (2004): 134–51.
73. "bairro de construções antigas desajeitadas e inestéticas já não tinha razão de existir no coração da cidade," cited in Menezes, *Mouraria, retalhos de um imaginário*, 56.
74. Between the 1930s and 1960s the entire lower portion of the neighborhood was demolished. Other notable demolitions dating to the Estado Novo period include the razing of the Marquês de Alegrete palace in 1946, the Igreja do Socorro and Praça da Figueira in 1949, the Teatro Apolo in 1957 and the Arco do Marquês do Alegrete in 1961, the remaining gate of the fourteenth century Fernandine Wall.
75. Colvin, "Gabriel de Oliveira's 'Há Festa Na Mouraria,'" 137.
76. For a discussion of the way *castizo* heritage was produced in Madrid's collective imaginary during the early twentieth century see Deborah Parsons, *A Cultural History of Madrid: Modernism and the Urban Spectacle* (Berg, 2003).
77. The *manolo/a* is the name attributed specifically to residents of Lavapiés. Other *castizo* archetypes include *chulapos/as*, *chisperos/as*, *isidros/as*, and *majos/as*, each associated with a specific neighborhood. One article on the subject explains, "Con el paso de los años los términos 'chulapo,' 'chulapa,' 'chulo' y 'chulapona' se han convertido en formas genéricos [*sic*] de aludir al madrileñismo castizo, aunque en origen convivieron en el Madrid de la época con otros identificativos locales, como los de 'manolos' y 'manolas,' 'chisperos,' 'isidros' o 'majos' y 'majas,' que se diferenciaban entre sí por los colores y cortes de sus trajes y en las formas de las patillas y tupés." See "El origen popular del traje de chulapo, una indumentaria con gran recorrido histórico," *Diario ABC*, May 14, 2014.
78. "Hombre atracado y apuñalado, presuntamente, por un súbdito marroquí," *El País*, July 22, 1981; "Imigração preocupa o bairro da Mouraria," *Jornal de Notícias*, April 11, 1999.

79. Malcolm Compitello, Susan Larson and Fernando Díaz Orueta are some of the foremost voices on the cultural significance of urban design and Madrid's modernization project during this time period. See, as a point of entry, Compitello's "Designing Madrid, 1985–1997," *Cities* 20, no. 6 (2003): 403–11; Larson's "Shifting Modern Identities in Madrid's Recent Urban Planning, Architecture and Narrative," *Cities* 20, no. 6 (2003): 395–402; and Díaz Orueta's "Madrid: Urban Regeneration Projects and Social Mobilization," *Cities* 24, no. 3 (2007). In the Portuguese context, Jean-Paul Carrière and Christophe Demazière's "Urban Planning and Flagship Development Projects: Lessons from EXPO 98, Lisbon," *Planning, Practice and Research* 17, no. 1 (2002): 70–71, outlines the role of Expo '98 in catalyzing urban interventions throughout the city. Additional interventions on this topic include Vítor Matias Ferreira and Francesco Indovina, *A Cidade da Expo'98* (Bizancia, 1999); Jõao Cabral and Berta Rato, "Urban Development for Competitiveness and Cohesion: The Expo '98 Urban Project in Lisbon," in *The Globalized City: Economic Restructuring and Social Polarization in European Cities*, ed. Arantxa Rodriguez, Frank Moulaert, and Erik Swyngedouw (Oxford University Press, 2002): 217. Sansão Pereira Branco Clemente identifies the debut of the EPUL, the Public Urbanization Company of Lisbon, as part of what he deems a paradigm shift in Portuguese urban development in "EPUL—Empresa Pública de Urbanização de Lisboa: Da reabilitação à regeneração urbana," Master's Thesis, Universidade Lusíada de Lisboa, 2013, 72.
80. Carrière and Demazière, "Urban Planning and Flagship Development Projects."
81. David Harvey discusses the shift to entrepreneurialism in urban governance in "From Managerialism to Entrepreneurialism: The Transformation in Urban Governance in Late Capitalism," *Geografiska Annaler: Series B, Human Geography* 71, no. 1 (April 1989): 3–17.
82. Some texts covering this include Ellen Sapega, "Remembering Empire/Forgetting the Colonies: Accretions of Memory and the Limits of Commemoration in a Lisbon Neighborhood," *History and Memory* 20, no. 2 (2008): 18–38 and Asociación Legado Expo Sevilla, "¿Qué fue Expo'92?," accessed July 30, 2023.
83. Compitello explores at length both the stated objectives and unforeseen urban and social repercussions in "Designing Madrid, 1985–1997"; "From Planning to Design: The Culture of Flexible Accumulation in Post-Cambio Madrid," *Arizona Journal of Hispanic Cultural Studies* 3, no. 1 (1999): 199–219; and "A Good Plan Gone Bad, From Operation Atocha to the Gentrification of Lavapiés," *International Journal of the Constructed Environment* 2, no. 2 (2012): 75–93. Studies discussing resident responses and social mobilization against the 1997 plan include Díaz Orueta, "Madrid: Urban Regeneration Projects and Social Mobilization," and Montserrat Cañedo Rodríguez, "Discursos vecinales sobre la

inseguridad ciudadana y políticas de rehabilitación urbanística: El caso de los 'antiguos vecinos' y la ARI-Lavapiés (Madrid) desde una perspectiva antropológica," *Scripta Nova: revista electrónica de geografía y ciencias sociales*, 201.

84. Díaz Orueta, "Madrid: Urban Regeneration Projects and Social Mobilization," 188.

85. While the AiMouraria action program included initiatives related to public health and cultivating community through the arts, a significant portion of the planned projects focused on recasting public spaces for consumption. Urban image, patrimonial value, and the creation of appealing leisure spaces came to the forefront of these efforts. For example, plans were made for a multicultural festival aptly named "Há Mundos na Mouraria," guided tours of the neighborhood run by the Renovar a Mouraria association (studied in Chapter 1 of this book), and the conversion of the building in which *fado* singer Maria Severa purportedly lived as a museum. See Câmara Municipal de Lisboa, "aiMouraria - Programa QREN Mouraria: Plano de Intervenção," accessed July 30, 2023.

86. "objeto de recalificaciones masivas al servicio de los intereses de las grandes corporaciones multinacionales; todas ellas víctimas de la codicia de un sistema de mundo al que no le importa deformarlas hasta convertirlas en su propia caricatura o su parodia; todas ellas convertidas en grandes máquinas de excluir y expulsar a cualquier habitante o forastero considerado insolvente," Manuel Delgado Ruíz, *La ciudad mentirosa: Fraude y miseria del "modelo Barcelona"* (Madrid: Catarata, 2009), 9–10.

87. This treatment of race-as-commodity has been studied at length outside of the Iberian Peninsula, particularly in regard to the consumption of Black women's bodies. For example, bell hooks argues that the detached way the gaze is called to the Black female body in popular culture is a manner through which to "mutilate black female bodies yet again" and "does not successfully subvert sexist/racist representations." See "Selling Hot Pussy," in *Black Looks: Race and Representation* (South End Press, 1992), 64. Similar observations have been made in studies of public figures including Josephine Baker, Saartje Baartman, and Carmen Miranda. For more on this topic see María Isabel Romero Ruiz, "Black States of Desire: Josephine Baker, Identity and the Sexual Black Body," *Revista de Estudios Norteamericanos* 16 (2012): 125–39; Janell Hobson, *Venus in the Dark: Blackness and Beauty in Popular Culture* (Routledge, 2018).

88. Ahmed discusses the hatred of certain groups articulated as protecting an object of love in her chapter "The Organisation of Hate," in *The Cultural Politics of Emotion* (Edinburgh University Press, 2014), 42–61. Her discussion of happiness as an emotion used to obscure injustice is found in *The Promise of Happiness* (Duke University Press, 2010).

89. In previous publications I have referred to this process as "invented difference." In my analysis here, I have adjusted the term to "manufactured" to more precisely capture the blending of real and imagined cultural attributes. Catalina Iannone, "Invented Difference: On Inter-Culturality in Mouraria's Mercado de Fusão," *Journal of Lusophone Studies*, September 2017, 101–21.

CHAPTER 1

Epigraphs. "Time Out Travel on Instagram," Instagram, September 19, 2018, https://www.instagram.com/p/Bn5uF--j6Me/, "Lisbon's Hippest Neighborhood: A Pocket Guide to Mouraria," Suitcase Magazine, July 18, 2018, https://suitcasemag.com/a-pocket-guide-to-mouraria.

1. Ahmed, *The Promise of Happiness*, 50.
2. Ahmed, *The Promise of Happiness*, 50.
3. Glass employs the term to describe the influx of middle-class people displacing lower-class residents in neighborhoods in London during the 1960s in *London: Aspects of Change* (MacGibbon and Kee, 1964).
4. The study of gentrification in Spain and Portugal became especially prevalent in the 2010s. Examples of interventions that have informed my approach to the subject in *Cities Beyond Crisis* include Simone Tulumello and Giovanni Allegretti, "Articulating Urban Change in Southern Europe: Gentrification, Touristification and Financialisation in Mouraria, Lisbon," *European Urban and Regional Studies* 28, no. 2 (April 2021): 111–32; Luís Mendes, "Gentrification and the New Urban Social Movements in Times of Post-Capitalist Crisis and Austerity Urbanism in Portugal." *Arizona Journal of Hispanic Cultural Studies* 22 (2018): 199–215, "Bye Bye Lisbon: Tourism Gentrification Impacts on Lisbon's Inner-City Housing Market," in *Advances in Hospitality, Tourism, and the Services Industry*, ed. Cláudia Ribeiro de Almeida et al. (IGI Global, 2020), 136–55; and Sorando and Ardura, *First We Take Manhattan*.
5. Sharon Zukin, *Naked City: The Death and Life of Authentic Urban Places* (Oxford University Press, 2010).
6. Harvey writes, "The basic idea of the spatio-temporal fix is simple enough. Overaccumulation within a given territorial system means a condition of surpluses of labour (rising unemployment) and surpluses of capital (registered as a glut of commodities on the market that cannot be disposed of without a loss, as idle productive capacity, and/or as surpluses of money capital lacking outlets for productive and profitable investment). Such surpluses may be absorbed by: (a) temporal displacement through investment in long-term capital projects or social expenditures (such as education and research) that

defer the re-entry of current excess capital values into circulation well into the future, (b) spatial displacements through opening up new markets, new production capacities and new resource, social and labour possibilities elsewhere, or (c) some combination of (a) and (b)." *The New Imperialism* (Oxford University Press, 2003), 64.

7. State-sponsored initiatives are outlined in Spain's *Plan Turismo Español Horizonte 2020* (2008) and *Plan Nacional Integral Turismo 2012–2015* (2012). See "Planes Nacionales de Turismo," SEGITTUR, accessed March 29, 2023. In Portugal, the country's approach to tourism was detailed in the *Plano Estratégico Nacional do Turismo*. The strategic plan incorporated quantitative benchmarks, such as the number of overnight stays in urban centers as a means to measure growth of the tourism sector. See Ministério da Economia e da Inovação, *Plano Estratégico Nacional do Turismo: Para o desenvolvimento do turismo em Portugal*, 2007.
8. Fernando Almeida García compares tourism policy in Spain and Portugal throughout the twentieth century and into the aughts in "La política turística en España y Portugal," *Cuadernos de turismo*, no. 30 (2012): 9–34.
9. My discussion of tourism trends and practices is informed by John Urry and Jonas Larsen's *The Tourist Gaze 3.0* (SAGE Publications, 2011). For more critical studies on contemporary tourism see George Ritzer and Allan Liska, "'McDisneyization' and Post-Tourism': Complementary Perspectives on Contemporary Tourism," in *Touring Cultures: Transformations of Travel and Theory*, ed. Chris Rojek and John Urry (New York: Routledge, 1997): 96–112; Alan Quaglieri Domínguez and Antonio Paolo Russo, "Paisajes urbanos en la época posturística. Propuesta de un marco analítico," *Scripta Nova* 14, no. 323 (May 2010); and Antonio Paolo Russo and Greg Richards, *Reinventing the Local in Tourism: Producing, Consuming and Negotiating Place* (Channel View Publications, 2016).
10. Zukin, *Naked City*, 3.
11. Zukin, *Naked City*, 3. This argument builds on work of scholars including Walter Benjamin, Jean Baudrillard, and Umberto Eco who have interrogated the departure of contemporary models of reality (and thus, authenticity) from a mythical original in distinct contexts. See Walter Benjamin, "The Work of Art in the Age of Mechanical Reproduction," trans. Harry Zohn, *The Norton Anthology of Theory and Criticism*, ed. Vincent Leitch (Norton & Company 2001), 1166–86; Jean Baudrillard, "Two Essays," trans. Arthur B. Evans, *Science Fiction Studies* 55, vol. 18, no. 3 (November 1991); Umberto Eco, *Travels in Hyperreality* (Mariner Books, 1990).
12. George Ritzer and Allan Liska expand on this point in "'McDisneyization' and 'Post-Tourism,'" 99.

13. I employ the term *hyperreality* according to Baudrillard's definition. See *Simulacra and Simulation*, trans. Sheila Glaser (University of Michigan Press, 1995).
14. George Yúdice, *The Expediency of Culture: Uses of Culture in the Global Era* (Duke University Press, 2003), 9.
15. David Harvey, "The Art of Rent: Globalisation, Monopoly and the Commodification of Culture," *Socialist Register* 38 (2002): 93–110.
16. For more on the topic of place branding see Robert Govers and Frank Go, *Place Branding: Glocal, Virtual and Physical Identities, Constructed, Imagined and Experienced* (Palgrave Macmillan, 2009).
17. Joseph S. Nye, "Soft Power," *Foreign Policy*, no. 80 (1990): 166.
18. "Se crea el Alto Comisionado del Gobierno para la Marca España al que corresponde proponer al Gobierno las medidas para la mejora de la imagen exterior de España, así como la planificación, y el impulso, coordinación y seguimiento de la acción exterior española, pública y privada, en los ámbitos económico, cultural, social, científico y tecnológico." See Presidencia del Gobierno, "Real Decreto 998/2012, de 28 de junio, por el que se crea el Alto Comisionado del Gobierno para la Marca España y se modifica el Real Decreto 1412/2000, de 21 de julio, de creación del Consejo de Política Exterior," Pub. L. No. Real Decreto 998/2012, § 1, BOE-A-2012-8672 46129 (2012).
19. See Pedro Ramiro, *Marca España: ¿A quién beneficia?* (Icaria, 2014); Joaquim Rius Ulldemolins and Mariano Martín Zamorano, "Spain's Nation Branding Project Marca España and Its Cultural Policy: The Economic and Political Instrumentalization of a Homogeneous and Simplified Cultural Image," *International Journal of Cultural Policy* 21, no. 1 (2015): 20–40.
20. There are a wealth of studies on Airbnb from different disciplinary perspectives including sociology, tourism studies, geography, and economics, many of which include case studies from the Iberian Peninsula. See, for example, Maartje Roelofsen and Claudio Minca, "The Superhost: Biopolitics, Home and Community in the Airbnb Dream-World of Global Hospitality," *Geoforum* 91 (2018): 170–81; Pedro Palos-Sánchez and Marisol Correia, "The Collaborative Economy Based Analysis of Demand: Study of Airbnb Case in Spain and Portugal," *Journal of Theoretical and Applied Electronic Commerce Research* 13, no. 3 (September 2018): 85–98; Czeslaw Adamiak, "Mapping Airbnb Supply in European Cities," *Annals of Tourism Research* 71 (2018): 67–71; Salvador García-Ayllón, "Urban Transformations as an Indicator of Unsustainability in the P2P Mass Tourism Phenomenon: The Airbnb Case in Spain through Three Case Studies," *Sustainability* 10 (2018): 1–21.
21. Studies documenting the impact of sharing-economy tourist rentals on the housing market within and beyond Europe include Agustín Cócola Gant,

"Holiday Rentals: The New Gentrification Battlefront," *Sociological Research Online* 21 (2016): 1–9; Dayne Lee, "How Airbnb Short-Term Rentals Exacerbate Los Angeles' Affordable Housing Crisis: Analysis and Policy Recommendations," *Harvard Law and Policy Review* 10, no. 1 (2016): 229–53; Natalie Stors and Andreas Kagermeier, "The Sharing Economy and Its Role in Metropolitan Tourism," in *Tourism and Gentrification in Contemporary Metropolises: International Perspectives*, ed. Maria Gravari-Barbas and Sandra Guinand (New York: Routledge, 2017), 181–206.

22. Leonardo Rodrigues, Francisco Silva, and Tiago Lopes, "Alojamento local no centro histórico da cidade de Lisboa," *Finisterra*, May 19, 2022, 65–86.

23. Jõao Pereira dos Santos, Duarte Gonçalves, and Susana Peralta, "Short-Term Rental Bans and Housing Prices: Quasi-Experimental Evidence from Lisbon," Discussion Paper Series (ISEG- University of Lisbon: IZA Institute of Labor Economics, 2022).

24. Some texts on this topic include Renato Miguel do Carmo, Rita Cachado, and Daniela Ferreira, "Desigualdades em tempos de crise: Vulnerabilidades habitacionais e socioeconómicas na Área Metropolitana de Lisboa," *Revista Portuguesa de Estudos Regionais* 40 (2015): 5–22; Iago Lestegás, "Lisbon after the Crisis: From Credit-Fuelled Suburbanization to Tourist-Driven Gentrification," *International Journal of Urban and Regional Research* 43, no. 4 (July 1, 2019): 705–23; and Alberto Amore, Cecilia de Bernardi, and Pavlos Arvanitis, "The Impacts of Airbnb in Athens, Lisbon and Milan: A Rent Gap Theory Perspective," *Current Issues in Tourism* 25, no. 20 (October 15, 2022): 3329–42.

25. Castells, *Networks of Outrage and Hope*, 6.

26. José, "Buardilla con encanto en Lavapiés," accessed September 15, 2020, https://www.airbnb.com/rooms/11731488/location?location=Madrid%2C%20Spain&check_in=2020-09-15&check_out=2020-09-26&source_impression_id=p3_1598366518_sgIQWmPvaRRZij8y. As of this writing the listing is no longer on Airbnb, indicating that the host has taken the property off the marketplace.

27. "Situado en el corazón de Madrid, Lavapiés es uno de los barrios más multiculturales de la capital, con una oferta de ocio muy amplia que apuesta por lo alternativo. En sus calles, puedes encontrar restaurantes de varias partes del mundo donde podrás degustar gastronomía india, libanesa, griega, senegalesa, etc., y, por supuesto, española. Además, el barrio está repleto de teatros, como el Centro Dramático Nacional Valle-Inclán, el Teatro del Barrio, Pavón, y un sin fin de bares que se transforman para acoger cualquier tipo de expresión artística (música en directo, recital de poesía, microteatro, etc.). Y, por si fuera poco, Lavapiés cuenta también con el Mercado de San Fernando, uno de los mercados con más encanto de Madrid."

28. "Embajadores and Euljiro Are on the List of Time Out's Coolest Neighbourhoods Right Now – Hackney and Williamsburg Are Not." TimeOut, September 20, 2018, https://www.timeout.com/about/latest-news/embajadores-and-euljiro-are-on-the-list-of-time-outs-coolest-neighbourhoods-right-now-hackney-and-williamsburg-are-not-092018.
29. Nuno, "Capelão 15 - 20," n.d., https://www.airbnb.com/rooms/28556083?check_in=2022-11-18&check_out=2022-11-20&guests=1&adults=1&s=67&unique_share_id=ad95a68c-883e-4d0a-9207-a5525c2f4196. As of 2024 this listing is still active on the Airbnb marketplace.
30. Marco, "Charming and Traditional Lisbon Apartment," n.d., https://www.airbnb.com/rooms/19671102?check_in=2020-10-15&check_out=2020-10-22&source_impression_id=p3_1599749435_NVfmCxneyPW%2BZgKT. As of 2024 this listing is no longer active on Airbnb.
31. Andreia, "Lisbon - Rose Apartment," 1881, https://www.airbnb.com/rooms/16228038?check_in=2020-10-15&check_out=2020-10-22&source_impression_id=p3_1599750741_f%2FGoG8VSucoj2OJ3. As of 2024 this listing is still active on the Airbnb marketplace.
32. Zukin, *Naked City*, 21.
33. Montse, "Sunny & Spacious room in Central Madrid," n.d., https://www.airbnb.com/rooms/2254525?check_in=2022-01-07&check_out=2022-01-09&guests=1&adults=1&s=67&unique_share_id=8d0bd437-e3b4-4980-bb5c-0d7df9a46d67. As of 2024 this listing is still active on Airbnb.
34. Ulrik, "Mouraria I, Eco-Duplex&french Balcony&smart Access," n.d., https://www.airbnb.com/rooms/449080?location=Lisbon%2C%20Portugal&check_in=2020-10-13&check_out=2020-10-15&source_impression_id=p3_1599580257_rFWkcl%2F4ODiBwDSw&guests=1&adults=1. As of 2024 this listing is no longer active on Airbnb.
35. John Hannigan, *Fantasy City Pleasure and Profit in the Postmodern Metropolis* (Routledge, 1998).
36. "A associação tem como fim o desenvolvimento de acções que promovam a revitalização urbanística, social, cultural e turística do bairro da Mouraria." Associação Renovar a Mouraria, "Objectivos," 2009, http://web.archive.org/web/20090615133942/http://www.renovaramouraria.pt/a-associacao/objectivos.
37. Em fevereiro de 2008 fizemos um desfile com música pelas ruas que chamou muita atenção da população, e apresenta-se . . . foi uma forma de apresentar a associação e dizer às pessoas do bairro que estamos aqui, estamos a lutar, juntem-se a nós. E depois, em março, formalizamos a associação, portanto fizemos uma formalização legal, constituímos legalmente a associação. Depois em junho de 2008 fizemos o nosso primeiro arraial. O arraial para nós não é

só festa, foi um momento muito importante de dizermos às pessoas: estamos aqui, e estamos aqui para lutar, dizer que queremos defender o direito a ter um parque infantil, que já temos agora; direito a ter um jardim onde as pessoas possam passear, e levar os filhos para brincar, e namorar, ou seja um espaço verde que não havia já obtemos agora; direito a ter as ruas direitas, e arranjadas, bonitas, temos as ruas bonitas com bancos de jardim, com árvores, com fontes. Portanto, tudo isso não existia, e acho que foi muito fruto da nossa luta, mas também fruto do querer da câmara. Se a Câmara Municipal não tivesse acompanhado a nossa luta, nada disto se tinha feito e possivelmente a associação já teria morrido por cansaço nosso. Nuno Franco, personal interview with Nuno Franco, July 2015.

38. In Portugal, a Câmara Municipal (Municipal Council) is the executive body of a municipality (*município*) responsible for the administration of a specific territorial division, and led by a president (Presidente da Câmara Municipal) who is elected during local elections. The Câmara Municipal is charged with a range of local services and decisions, including urban planning, infrastructure maintenance, waste management, education, cultural initiatives, and public transportation. It also manages municipal budgets and enforces regulations within its jurisdiction. The Câmara works alongside the Assembleia Municipal (Municipal Assembly), which serves as the municipal district's legislative branch.
39. In *The Great Good Place*, Ray Oldenburg discusses third spaces as surroundings separate from two primary social environments: the home and the workplace. Third spaces are other sites of community life such as churches, cafés, and even public parks. See *The Great Good Place: Cafes, Coffee Shops, Bookstores, Bars, Hair Salons, and Other Hangouts at the Heart of a Community* (Da Capo Press, 1999). This term differs from Edward Soja's theory of thirdspace, which is meant to describe "fully lived spaces" that are simultaneously real-and-imagined loci of collective experience and agency. See Edward Soja, *Thirdspace: Journeys to Los Angeles and Other Real-and-Imagined Places* (Wiley-Blackwell, 1996).
40. Compitello, "A Good Plan Gone Bad," 75.
41. Compitello, 77.
42. Since Glass's pioneering study in 1964, scholars have debated the relationship between global capital and the multiple, often regionally specific forces, that shape redevelopment and displacement in urban centers. Some titles from this extensive bibliography include Shirley Bradway Laska and Daphne Spain, eds., *Back to the City: Issues in Neighborhood Renovation*, Pergamon Policy Studies on Urban Affairs (Pergamon Press, 1980); Neil Smith, "Gentrification and the Rent Gap," *Annals of the Association of American Geographers* 77, no. 3 (1987):

462; Rowland Atkinson and Gary Bridge, eds., *Gentrification in a Global Context: The New Urban Colonialism*, Housing and Society Series (Routledge, 2005). Authors Loretta Lees, Hyun Bang Shin, and Ernesto López Morales discuss some limitations to the concept of gentrification and other approaches to understanding urban change in *Global Gentrifications: Uneven Development and Displacement* (Policy Press, 2015).

43. P. E. Moskowitz proposes the following in his effort to imagine the steps toward a future without gentrification: 1. Public land must be increased, protected, and made accessible. 2. Citizens must be given the right to decide on the processes in the city. 3. The housing market must be strictly regulated. Rent increases must be prevented and real estate speculation must be taxed. *How to Kill a City: Gentrification, Inequality, and the Fight for the Neighborhood* (Nation Books, 2017).

44. "História e estórias com gente dentro" Associação Renovar a Mouraria and Nuno Saraiva, *Visita a Mouraria*, 2015.

45. Later, these tours were discontinued and replaced with Migrantour, an initiative co-funded by the European Union that seeks to engage tourists with the lived experience of migrants through urban walking tours led by migrant-residents in cities like Lisbon, Paris, Bologna, and Rome. "Migrantour Sustainable Routes," n.d., http://www.migrantour.org/en/migrantour-sustainable-routes.

46. Some of Saraiva's commissioned pieces include: *Cavaleiros do Correio-Mor*, Travessa da Mata, 2015, commissioned by the Associação Renovar a Mouraria and Junta de Freguesia de Santa Maria Maior; *Porta 21*, 2020, Rua de São Cristóvão, commissioned by the Casa de Fados; *Filigrana*, 2018, Largo São Carlos, commissioned by the Museu da Filigrana; *Nelson Mandela centenário—e nunca esquecer onde Portugal esteve em 1987 e 1989*, 2018, Rua Dr Jõao Soares, commissioned by CML and GAU (Galeria de Arte Urbana).

47. This project was completed in 2012 with permission from the EPUL (Empresa Pública de Urbanização de Lisboa), who owned but did not have the funds to rehabilitate the structure at the time, and disbanded that same year. The organization had been founded in 1971 by the Câmara Municipal de Lisboa with the stated objective of functioning as an auxiliary service for the local authorities in the design and implementation of urban projects. See getLISBON, "Fado in the Urban Art of Lisbon," June 2, 2021, and Clemente, "EPUL."

48. Scott A. Lukas, *The Themed Space: Locating Culture, Nation, and Self* (Rowman & Littlefield, 2007), 296.

49. Barbara Kirshenblatt-Gimblett, *Destination Culture: Tourism, Museums, and Heritage* (University of California Press, 1998), 7; Scott A. Lukas, *The Themed Space*, 1.

50. Kirshenblatt-Gimblett, *Destination Culture*, 7.
51. Harvey, "The Art of Rent," 2002.
52. Urry and Larsen, *The Tourist Gaze*, 1.
53. "Na diversidade dos topónimos são evocados santos padroeiros, ofícios desaparecidos, famílias aristocratas e caminhos antigos."
54. Iñigo Sánchez Fuarros, "'Ai, Mouraria!' Music, Tourism, and Urban Renewal in a Historic Lisbon Neighbourhood," *MUSICultures* 43, no. 2 (2016): 67.
55. Sánchez Fuarros, "'Ai, Mouraria!'" 68.
56. Sánchez Fuarros, "'Ai, Mouraria!'" 70.
57. "Conhecer a riqueza e diversidade das comunidades que vivem e trabalham neste bairro é o objectivo desta visita;" "vindas do extremo oriente."
58. Steve Nelson, "Walt Disney's EPCOT and the World's Fair Performance Tradition," *The Drama Review: TDR* 30, no. 4 (1986): 106–46.
59. Baartman's life and legacy is widely discussed in scholarly as well as public-facing texts. A few monographs with a biographical emphasis include Rachel Holmes, *African Queen: The Real Life of the Hottentot Venus* (Random House, 2006), *The Hottentot Venus: The Life and Death of Saartjie Baartman: Born 1789–Buried 2002* (Bloomsbury, 2008); and Clifton C. Crais and Pamela Scully, *Sara Baartman and the Hottentot Venus: A Ghost Story and a Biography* (Princeton University Press, 2009).
60. João Vasconcelos, "Custom and Costume at a Late 1950s Marian Shrine in Northwest Portugal," *Etnográfica* 9, no. 1 (2005): 20. As Vasconcelos explains, this costume is also laden with religious meaning. This is attributed to the Marian cult of Our Lady of Minho, which took prominence beginning in the mid 1950's, worshipping a virgin dressed in the *vianesa*. Processions related to Our Lady of Minho are one of several folkloric events during which the *vianesa* dress might be donned.
61. Berlant writes, "The fantasies that are fraying include, particularly, upward mobility, job security, political and social equality, and lively, durable intimacy. The set of dissolving assurances also includes meritocracy, the sense that liberal-capitalist society will reliably provide opportunities for individuals to carve out relations of reciprocity that seem fair and that foster life as a project of adding up to something and constructing cushions for enjoyment," *Cruel Optimism*, 3.
62. "De tapas por el mundo sin salir de Lavapiés."
63. John Hannigan, *Fantasy City*.
64. Sara Ahmed, *The Promise of Happiness*, 138.
65. "Bienvenido al mágico barrio de Lavapiés, soy un hervidero de un sinfín de tapas intrépidas esperando tu buen mordisco. Un año más, y van nueve, nuestras hosteleras y hosteleros se unen para soñar un increíble tapamundi de

Pekín a Quito, de Jaén a Bombay, de Roma a la Cochabamba, de Nueva York a Badajoz." Asociación de Comerciantes de Lavapiés, "Guía Tapapiés," 2019, 3.

66. Edward W. Said, *Orientalism* (Vintage Books, 1979), 2.
67. Said, *Orientalism*, 2.
68. Linda Tuhiwai Smith, *Decolonizing Methodologies: Research and Indigenous Peoples*, 2nd ed. (Zed Books, 2012), 2–3.
69. Zilkia Janer, "(IN)EDIBLE NATURE: New World Food and Coloniality," *Cultural Studies* 21, no. 2–3 (March 2007): 385.
70. My reasoning follows Yúdice's argument that "the notion of culture as a resource entails its management." *The Expediency of Culture*, 4
71. Zukin, *Naked City*, 3.
72. The concept of intersectionality is most commonly attributed to legal scholar Kimberlé Crenshaw, who first presented these ideas in "Demarginalizing the Intersection of Race and Sex: A Black Feminist Critique of Antidiscrimination Doctrine, Feminist Theory, and Antiracist Politics," *University of Chicago Legal Forum* 1989, no. Article 8 (1989). In this text, she argues that the oppression faced by Black women was not sufficiently addressed by either feminist or anti-racist movements, given that different aspects of a person's identity shape their experiences of oppression and privilege. She expands further on these ideas in "Mapping the Margins: Intersectionality, Identity Politics, and Violence against Women of Color," *Stanford Law Review* 43, no. 6 (July 1991): 1241, and later work. A 1977 statement by the Combahee River Collective is widely viewed as a precursor to this work, in which they discussed (but did not specifically assign a term) interlocking oppressions of race, gender, class, and sexuality. See "(1977) The Combahee River Collective Statement," November 16, 2012, https://www.blackpast.org/african-american-history/combahee-river-collective-statement-1977/. To date, many scholars have taken up intersectionality as a theoretical framework to study systems of oppression in a range of national contexts. One may consult, as a brief introduction to the field, Patricia Hill Collins, *Intersectionality as Critical Social Theory* (Duke University Press, 2019).
73. For an example of how this position was covered in the media see "El mantero Mame Mbaye no murió por la persecución policial en Lavapiés," *La Vanguardia*, April 22, 2019, https://www.lavanguardia.com/local/madrid/20190422/461782142437/mantero-mbaye-lavapies-no-murio-persecucion-policial.html.
74. Some of the most vocal groups discussing the Mbaye case include Sindicato Manteros, Regularización Ya, and SOS Racismo. See, as an example, the statement published on March 16, 2018 by SOS Racismo "Comunicado tras la muerte

de Mame Mbaye Ndiaye," March 16, 2018, https://sosracismo.eu/muerte-de-mame-mbaye-ndiaye/.

CHAPTER 2

1. Virginia Gómez, "La Policía detiene a seis personas en el desalojo de cuatro vecinas de Argumosa tras un año sin pagar," *El Mundo*, February 22, 2019, sec. Madrid, https://www.elmundo.es/madrid/2019/02/22/5c6fcodbfdddff00628b4619.html; Carlota Barcala, "Ejecutado el desahucio de cuatro familias en Argumosa con seis detenidos," *Diario ABC*, February 22, 2019, https://www.abc.es/espana/madrid/abci-tension-y-fuerte-presencia-policial-argumosa-antes-ejecuten-cuatro-desahucios-201902220959_noticia.html.
2. Marta Ley, "Así se vacía un barrio por culpa de la gentrificación: el caso de Lavapiés," *El Mundo*, June 8, 2017, https://www.elmundo.es/grafico/madrid/2017/08/06/596cdf3ee2704e07148b45eb.html.
3. In 2009, Madrid's city hall declared a building located on Calle Valencia 8–10 as uninhabitable, evicted the remaining renters, and tore it down. In 2012, the lot was converted into a community space called Solarpiés, hosting activities open to the public including book fairs, film nights, community meals, and workshops. Two years later, Solarpiés was closed by the Instituto de la Vivienda de Madrid under the auspices of creating social housing, before changing hands to Nadego S.L. The site was later turned into an Ibis Budget Hotel.
4. "Estudo sobre novas dinâmicas residenciais económicas e urbanísticas no centro histórico de Lisboa," *Quaternaire Portugal*, June 2017, https://www.jf-santamariamaior.pt/wp-content/uploads/2018/04/Enquadramento-e-diagnostico.pdf. Later reports state that between 2013 and 2017, the number of short-term apartments in the broader district of Santa Maria Maior had risen an astronomical 92 percent. These specific numbers are cited in Carmen Guilherme and Daniela Soares Ferreira, "Junta de Freguesia de Santa Maria Maior anuncia número de alerta para denunciar alojamento local ilegal," *Sol*, April 5, 2019, https://sol.sapo.pt/artigo/652675/junta-de-freguesia-de-santa-maria-maior-anuncia-n-mero-de-alerta-para-denunciar-alojamento-local-ilegal.
5. Jõao Pedro Pincha, "Há 17 famílias num prédio da Mouraria que vão ficar sem casa," *Público*, February 22, 2017, https://www.publico.pt/2017/02/22/local/noticia/ha-17-familias-que-vao-ficar-sem-casa-num-predio-da-mouraria-1762862. In 2016, residents of this building received eviction notices after the structure was acquired by a developer. While they were not told how this would impact the building, inquiries conducted by journalists revealed that the plot was being

evaluated for conversion to tourist rentals. After appealing to the municipal government in a highly publicized case, their contracts were extended by five years, halting but not entirely erasing the potential for eviction. Other buildings on that same street, abandoned or in ruin, continued to be remodeled as tourist apartments and luxury condominiums.

6. Discussed in Lefebvre, *The Production of Space*; Harvey, *Social Justice and the City*, 2nd ed. (University of Georgia Press, 2009), *Rebel Cities: From the Right to the City to the Urban Revolution* (Verso, 2012).
7. For more on *lusofonia* in tourist contexts see, for example, "Identidades transnacionais e transculturais. Pós-colonialidade, lusofonias e interculturalidade. O caso do Museu Virtual da Lusofonia," *Chasqui*, no. 147 (August 2021): 105–21; Ye Xu, "Impact of Cultural Proximity on Destination Image and Tourists' Perceptions: The Case of the Portuguese Cultural Festival Lusofonia in Macao," *Journal of Vacation Marketing* 30, no. 1 (January 1, 2024): 45–57.
8. Silva, *Empire Found*, 2. The invocation of such narratives can also be discussed according to the affective strategies studied in Chapter 1 wherein injustice (colonial conquest and oppression) is obscured as the origin of a good feeling (imperial nostalgia).
9. Baudrillard, *Simulacra and Simulation*.
10. Berlant, *Cruel Optimism*, 9.
11. While the local government had held a public competition for the opportunity to develop the plot of land, the production company later confirmed that they had approached the Câmara prior to this opportunity with their idea for reimagining the space. Nuno Miguel Duarte Rodrigues details the genesis of the Mercado project under the auspices of the publicly funded AiMouraria program, including the central role of NCS Produções in its developmental stages in "Intervenções, espacialidades e relações de poder: O caso da praça do Martim Moniz" (Lisbon, Instituto Universitário de Lisboa and Universidade Nova de Lisboa, 2014). See also Pedro Gomes, "The Birth of Public Space Privatization: How Entrepreneurialism, Convivial Urbanism and Stakeholder Interactions Made the Martim Moniz Square, in Lisbon, 'Privatization-Ready,'" *European Urban and Regional Studies* 27, no. 1 (2020): 86–100.
12. Rodrigues, "Intervenções, espacialidades e relações de poder," 99.
13. "Martim Moniz com 'nova vida,'" *Jornal Expresso*, June 8, 2012, https://www.cmjornal.pt/cultura/detalhe/martim-moniz-com-nova-vida/.
14. "Martim Moniz com 'nova vida.'"
15. Menezes writes, "Entre os anos 1930 e 1960, a Mouraria torna-se foco de uma política urbana promulgadora de um 'urbanismo civilizador' e difusor de uma perspectiva de 'higienização e embelezamento' que pretendeu renovar aquela zona da cidade numa óptica de modernização, alterando radicalmente

as suas dinâmicas sociais, culturais e urbanas." For a detailed review of these social dynamics during the twentieth century see Menezes, *Mouraria, retalhos de um imaginário,* 53–58, and "A praça do Martim Moniz: Etnografando lógicas socioculturais de inscrição da praça no mapa social de Lisboa," *Horizontes Antropológicos* 15, no. 32 (2009): 306.

16. Ignasi de Solà-Morales, "Terrain Vague," in *Anyplace*, ed. Cynthia Davidson (MIT Press, 1995), 120. Emphasis added.
17. As discussed in the introduction, this group was founded by official decree in 1971 for the express purpose of urban intervention and revitalization, and continued in this role following the 1974 Carnation Revolution and until the Câmara Municipal approved its dissolution in 2012.
18. Menezes, *Mouraria, retalhos de um imaginário*, 59.
19. Menezes, *Mouraria, retalhos de um imaginário*, 59.
20. Menezes, "A Praça do Martim Moniz," 308.
21. Menezes, "A Praça do Martim Moniz," 309.
22. Timothy Sieber, "Composing Lusophonia: Multiculturalism and National Identity in Lisbon's 1998 Musical Scene," *Diaspora* 11, no. 2 (2002): 163.
23. Menezes, "A Praça do Martim Moniz," 311.
24. Menezes, "A Praça do Martim Moniz," 312.
25. Ahmed, *The Cultural Politics of Emotion*, 11.
26. Ricardo Dias Felner, "Cerco ao Martim Moniz," *Público*, June 19, 1999, https://www.publico.pt/1999/06/19/jornal/cerco-ao-martim-moniz-135077.
27. Menezes, "A Praça do Martim Moniz," 313.
28. Irene de Assunção Rodrigues, "Flows of Fortune: The Economy of Chinese Migration to Portugal" (Phd diss., Universidade de Lisboa, 2012).
29. Menezes, *Mouraria, retalhos de um imaginário*, 181.
30. Menezes, 181; Rodrigues, "Intervenções, espacialidades e relações de poder," 89
31. Menezes, "A Praça do Martim Moniz," 314–15.
32. António Brito Guiterres, "Interações reflexivas sobre o novo plano MARTIM MONIZ," *Buala*, 2012, https://www.buala.org/pt/cidade/interacoes-reflexivas-sobre-o-novo-plano-martim-moniz.
33. According to Rebelo Pinto, the purpose of this concert series was to "bring the city outdoors," encouraging people to explore less touristed areas of the city by holding shows in various parks and gardens. These quotes appear in "José Filipe, o nome por trás da nova cena cultural de Lisboa," *Lux/Good*, 2012, http://luxgood.blogspot.com/2012/09/jose-filipe-o-nome-por-tras-da-nova.html. For more on the LX Factory see "A fábrica das artes," *Time Out Lisboa*, May 27, 2009, https://web.archive.org/web/20130810021742/https://lxfactory.com/ficheiros/noticias/TimeOUT27Maio.pdf.

34. "A crise é excelente pra agarrar oportunidades. Quando conseguiria trabalhar uma praça deste tamanho (Martim Moniz) numa capital européia? Não havia essa possibilidade. A crise está levando gente jovem e bem formada como advogados e engenheiros a abrirem e inovarem hostels e restaurantes com uma cara nova para a cidade, sem deixar o que tem de genuíno para trás." "José Filipe."
35. "A Praça do Martim Moniz aparece numa altura em que estava a pensar fazer voluntariado. Tendo em conta que a praça estava abandonada e tinha uma séria de comunidades imigrantes que estavam esquecidas pela nossa cidade, decidi que o Mercado de Fusão era o meu projeto humanitário. A ideia seria devolver a praça do Martim Moniz à cidade num projeto de reintegração social das comunidades locais." "À conversa com José Filipe Rebelo Pinto," *LOOKmag*, September 13, 2016, https://lookmag.pt/blog/conversa-jose-filipe-rebelo-pinto.
36. *Cinema piolho* is a colloquial phrase used to refer to neighborhood theaters that were popular with the working classes in early twentieth century Lisbon. "Essa praça estava no lixo. Ninguém queria. Como estou sempre à procura, agarrei. Quero devolver à população de Lisboa o que lhe pertence. Quero tornar esse lugar genuíno. Me dói ver um antigo cinema piolho transformado em chinês, o Antigo Império . . . o salão de Lisboa. . . . Não faz sentido! Isso tudo é nosso, faz parte da nossa história e precisa ser reintegrado à cidade," "José Filipe, o nome por tras da nova cena cultural de Lisboa."
37. "Na Praça do Martim Moniz provam-se sabores do Mundo e respira-se cultura. A premissa de partida é que este seja um espaço dinâmico, ponto e ponte de contacto através da gastronomia, intervenções artísticas, instalações, cinema, exposições, workshops, música, feira e muita animação. Todo o projecto se desenrola à volta dos 10 quiosques de comida do mundo: podemos encher a alma e aliviar o espírito com as mais tentadoras iguarias daqui e d'além mar. Cores e cheiros que nos fazem viajar desde a China à Argentina, do Japão ao Brasil com paragem obrigatória por África e Bangladesh. Os petiscos portugueses também tem [*sic*] lugar marcado nesta espiral de sabores." NCS Produção, Som e Video, "Mercado de Fusão," 2013, https://web.archive.org/web/20130611060202/http://www.ncs.pt/mercadodefusao.php.
38. Paula Mota Santos studies the role of these events for young and post-colonial countries as nation-building endeavors in "The Imagined Nation: The Mystery of the Endurance of the Colonial Imaginary in Postcolonial Times," in *Tourism Imaginaries: Anthropological Approaches*, ed. Noel Salazar and Nelson Graburn (Berghahn, 2014), 199.
39. Imagineers, *Walt Disney Imagineering: A Behind the Dreams Look at Making the Magic Real* (Hyperion, 1996).

40. "Quero transformar a praça num pólo criativo. Trazer chefs, restaurantes, hostels, escritórios criativos. . . . Quero trazer gente jovem criativa da moda, do design, para abrir escritórios nos centros comerciais daqui. . . . Quero receber essa malta jovem e urbana, sangue novo, trazer quem está no Bairro Alto, no Chiado, no Cais Sodré." "José Filipe, o nome por tras da nova cena cultural de Lisboa."
41. Sorando and Ardura, for example, call gentrification the "creative destruction" of cities in their study of Lavapiés. This dynamic is also the focus of Estevens et al., "Arts and Culture in Lisbon's Recent Revitalization: Observing Mouraria and Intendente Square through Alternative Local Initiatives as Drivers of Marginal Gentrification," *Interventions Économiques*, no. 63 (March 1, 2020).
42. Zukin, *Naked City*, 31.
43. Rodrigues, "Intervenções, espacialidades e relações de poder," 101.
44. Rodrigues, "Intervenções, espacialidades e relações de poder," 101.
45. "Comida e cocktails de fusão, uma verdadeira miscelânea de sabores do mundo." "Um quiosque tropical com cheirinho a África" "As famosas chamuças do Ali são irresistíveis" "No BBQMM podemos deliciar-nos com sabores raros na cidade de Lisboa como 'Korean Pancakes' de marisco!" "A Ásia está mesmo Martim Moniz!" "Inspirado nos 'postos' de praia do Rio de Janeiro" "um ponto de interesse dos amantes das iguarias do país do Sol Nascente" "Comida saudável" "petiscos portugueses" "Sabores sul-americanos...tenha cuidado, não venha armado!"
46. Rodrigues, "Intervenções, espacialidades e relações de poder," 101.
47. David Roh, Betsy Huang, and Greta Niu, "Technologizing Orientalism," in *Techno-Orientalism: Imagining Asia in Speculative Fiction, History, and Media*, ed. David Roh, Betsy Huang, and Greta Niu (Rutgers University Press, 2015), 1.
48. Anne Anlin Cheng, *Ornamentalism* (Oxford University Press, 2019), 19–21. Emphasis added.
49. Roh, Huang, and Niu term such "hypo- or hypertechnological" representations of Asia and Asians as "techno-Orientalism," which capitalizes on a spectrum of images derived from both East and West that privilege "the project of modernity," "Technologizing Orientalism," 3.
50. Rodrigues, "Intervenções, Espacialidades e Relações de Poder," 105.
51. Lu's restaurant was so successful that he eventually expanded beyond his second-floor kitchen on Benformoso to a space in Arroios, a neighborhood to the north of Mouraria.
52. This view of the Chinese community is encapsulated in statements made by Inês Andrade, director of the Renovar a Mouraria association. In an article

written in 2018 regarding the latest stage in the Martim Moniz renovations, she described the neighborhood's Chinese population in the following way, "São comunidades que estão vocacionadas para o trabalho intenso, vivem para o trabalho. Aí têm muito menos disponibilidade para trabalhos extra aquilo que é o seu dia-a-dia laboral. De segunda a segunda, 24 horas por dia. . . . Normalmente, os miúdos chineses não vão porque os pais estão a trabalhar e não os podem levar. São este tipo de detalhes que demonstram a falta de participação deles numa vida social mais normal segundo os nossos padrões." Dias Coelho, Beatriz, and Rita Pereira Carvalho, "Vida e polémicas do Martim Moniz," *Jornal i*, n.d., https://ionline.sapo.pt/especiais/vida-e-polemicas-do-martim-moniz.

53. Only a few years later, in 2016, artist Joana Vasconcelos erected another Rooster of Barcelos in a different part of Lisbon, the Avenida Ribeira das Naus, which runs along the Tejo River, perpendicular to the city's tourist center. The installation, known as the "Pop galo," was composed of 1700 tiles and 1600 LED lights, and served as a traveling exhibition to promote tourism to Portugal. The next stop for this embodied display of Portugal as a site of globalized modernity was in Beijing, coinciding with the Year of the Rooster celebrations.
54. The group spearheading the initiative made a video summarizing this work on the plaza. See *WRITERS DELIGHT Lisbon 2015 Martim Moniz GRAFFITI*, 2018, https://www.youtube.com/watch?v=b2nHITZbMt8.
55. Mercado de Fusão, "OPEN AIR CINEMA - MARTIM MONIZ," Facebook, 2013, https://www.facebook.com/events/mercado-fus%C3%A3o-martim-moniz/open-air-cinema-martim-moniz-lan%C3%A7amento-4-de-setembro/581968781841377/; "This Saturday You Will Turn All Colours: It's Bollywood Holly in Martim Moniz," Taste of Lisboa, 2015, https://www.tasteoflisboa.com/blog/bollywood-holly-in-martim-moniz/.
56. "Eu gosto de como está estruturada a praça do Martim Moniz. O que eu não gosto é que as coisas na praça Martim Moniz são caras. E isso influencia muito quem vai ao Martim Moniz. Se tornou uma coisa mais elitista. É chique, podemos dizer assim. Mas ao lado do Martim Moniz, ao lado do largo de Martim Moniz, do Mercado de Fusão, há outras coisas também." Augusto, personal interview, 2015.
57. "Agora tem um quiosque no Martim Moniz que se chama Market 7, onde o dono é o Tom, acho que ele é...não sei, ele é imigrante, ele é de um país que agora não consigo lembrar. Era do sul de Europa. Mas tem uma mente muito aberta. E está a haver muitos concertos, muitas aberturas que é uma misturada de coisas alí no Martim Moniz, muito vendo da parte dele." Augusto, personal interview, 2015.
58. Carole, personal interview, 2015.

59. Solà-Morales, "Terrain Vague," 122–23.
60. Nós queríamos sentir de facto Martim Moniz era parte da Mouraria. Mas na realidade quando lá chegamos já não sentimos isso. Porque ela é frequentada por tantos imigrantes de facto, que lá se encontram, somos nós que acabamos por sentir que não estamos lá bem. Ninguém nos faz mal, ninguém nos trata mal, só que chegamos lá, todas aquelas casinhas que lá foram abertas, acho que nenhuma é de um português. E porque, pelos preços que foram postos, portanto chegas lá e e vês tudo menos um português. Amália, personal interview, 2015.
61. João Pedro Pincha, "Casa cheia disse 'não' aos contentores no Martim Moniz," *Público*, November 21, 2018, https://www.publico.pt/2018/11/21/local/noticia/casa-cheia-nao-contentores-martim-moniz-1851848.
62. The process of transferring ownership was not transparent. *Público* reports, citing city councelor Manuel Salgado, "a solução do mercado de contentores foi apresentada pela primeira vez à câmara em 2016, quando município e concessionário do espaço se sentaram à mesa para resolver as dívidas que este tinha para com a autarquia. 'Já em 2017, depois de uma longa negociação, houve uma transferência de concessão e apresentado um estudo mais detalhado. Em setembro de 2018 foi finalmente fechada uma adenda ao contrato e este passou a ter um prazo mais longo,' explicou o vereador. Vários munícipes quiseram saber qual a duração agora prevista mas ninguém respondeu. De acordo com informações recolhidas pelo PÚBLICO, a concessão está em vigor por mais 14 anos." "The container market solution was first presented to the *câmara* in 2016, when the municipality and the space's contract holder sat down to resolve debts owed to the local government. 'By 2017, after a long negotiation, the contract was transferred, and a more detailed study presented. In September 2018, an addendum to the contract was finally signed, and it now has a longer term,' explained the councilor. Several residents wanted to know how long the new contract would be for, but no one answered them. According to information gathered by PÚBLICO, the concession is now valid for another 14 years." João Pedro Pincha, "Casa cheia disse 'não.'"
63. Coverage of this protest includes such articles as Lusa, "Cordão humano pede suspensão imediata de obras no Martim Moniz," *Diário de Notícias*, February 2, 2019, https://www.dn.pt/pais/cordao-humano-pede-suspensao-imediata-de-obras-no-martim-moniz-10527989.html; João Pedro Pincha, "'Queremos um jardim,' gritou-se no Martim Moniz," *Público*, February 2, 2019, https://www.publico.pt/2019/02/02/local/noticia/queremos-jardim-gritouse-martim-moniz-1860498.

64. "A CML tem o dever e obrigação de respeitar a democracia e a vontade dos lisboetas. Queremos um jardim público. Lisboa não está à venda. Lisboa é de todos" João Pedro Pincha, "Queremos um jardim."
65. Jõao Pedro Pincha, "Queremos um jardim."

CHAPTER 3

1. Roland Barthes, *Image-Music-Text*, trans. Stephen Heath (Macmillan, 1977), 19–20.
2. Tina Campt, *Image Matters: Archive, Photography, and the African Diaspora in Europe* (Duke University Press, 2012), 6.
3. Juan Valbuena, *Nosotros, un álbum colectivo del barrio de Lavapiés* (Casa Árabe, 2009), 13.
4. Gonçalo Gaioso, *All Around Us*.
5. Nicholas Mirzoeff, *The Right to Look: A Counterhistory of Visuality* (Duke University Press, 2011), 2.
6. See, as an example of the extensive bibliography on this subject, Magali Marie Carrera, *Imagining Identity in New Spain: Race, Lineage, and the Colonial Body in Portraiture and Casta Paintings* (University of Texas Press, 2003); Ilona Katzew, *Casta Painting: Images of Race in Eighteenth-Century Mexico* (Yale University Press, 2004); Pamela Patton, ed., *Envisioning Others: Race, Color, and the Visual in Iberia and Latin America* (Brill, 2015); Rebecca Earle, "The Pleasures of Taxonomy: Casta Paintings, Classification, and Colonialism," *William and Mary Quarterly* 73, no. 3 (2016): 428.
7. José Conrado Roza, *The Bridal Masquerade*, 1788. For more on Portuguese artistic works that could be considered under the umbrella of racialized viewing see, for example, Leann G. Schneider, "Capturing Otherness on Canvas: 16th–18th Century European Representation of Amerindians and Africans" (MA thesis, Kent State University, 2015); Darlene J. Sadlier, *The Portuguese-Speaking Diaspora: Seven Centuries of Literature and the Arts* (University of Texas Press, 2016).
8. There is also a sizeable bibliography related to cultural producers from different geographic regions who have used visual modes of production to push against hegemonic representations of race established during and in relation to the colonial era. Some texts include Deborah Poole, *Vision, Race, and Modernity* (Princeton University Press, 1997); Jorge Coronado, *Portraits in the Andes: Photography and Agency, 1900–1950* (University of Pittsburgh Press, 2018); Campt, *Image Matters*; Jennifer Bajorek, *Unfixed: Photography and Decolonial Imagination in West Africa* (Duke University Press, 2020).
9. Quijano, "Coloniality of Power," 533.

10. Some manuscript-length texts that discuss different forms of racialized viewing in the contemporary era, with special emphasis on representations of race related to immigration, include Isabel Santaolalla, *Los "otros": Etnicidad y "raza" en el cine español contemporáneo* (Prensas Universitarias de Zaragoza, 2005); Isolina Ballesteros, *Immigration Cinema in the New Europe* (Intellect Books, 2015); Murray, *Home Away from Home*; Coleman, *The Necropolitical Theater*; Silva, *Empire Found.*
11. Luis Martín-Cabrera, "Postcolonial Memories and Racial Violence in *Flores de otro mundo*," *Journal of Spanish Cultural Studies* 3, no. 1 (January 1, 2002): 43–56.
12. Du Bois, *Black Reconstruction in America.*
13. Mary Kate Donovan explores this in detail in "Memory and Migrant Solidarity in Icíar Bollaín's *En tierra extraña*," *Journal of Spanish Cultural Studies* 21, no. 4 (October 1, 2020): 547–64.
14. Casa Árabe, "Quiénes somos," n.d., https://www.casaarabe.es/p/quienes-somos.
15. Juan Valbuena, *Noray: Libro de viajes por la ancha frontera* (Phree, 2012).
16. NoPhoto, "Nosotros, un álbum colectivo del barrio de Lavapiés," n.d., http://nophoto.org/nosotros-un-album-colectivo-del-barrio-de-lavapies.
17. While beyond the scope of this analysis, the fact that this initiative came from the Casa Árabe, specifically, is of note. One could certainly interpret this as part of a push against Islamophobia in the years following the 2004 bombing of Madrid's Atocha station, which was perpetrated by Islamist extremists. Jill Robbins investigates forms of expression surrounding this event in *Poetry and Crisis: Cultural Politics and Citizenship in the Wake of the Madrid Bombings* (University of Toronto Press, 2019).
18. "resulta imposible poner fronteras cuando se trata de abrirnos al conocimiento mutuo y la convivencia en una sociedad, la nuestra, la de *Nosotros*, cada vez más intercultural." Valbuena, *Nosotros*, 5.
19. "Valbuena indaga en la sutil frontera que separa identidad común y diversidad, y apuesta por la especial relación entre el ser humano y la fotografía. Para ello, está dispuesto a conseguir que el alma del álbum familiar transmigre a la gran familia del barrio entero." Valbuena, *Nosotros*, 7.
20. Yeon-Soo Kim, *The Family Album: Histories, Subjectivities, and Immigration in Contemporary Spanish Culture* (Bucknell University Press, 2005), 21.
21. Kim, *The Family Album*, 21.
22. "El proyecto *Nosotros* consiste en la construcción—mediante la recopilación de fotografías y pequeñas historias asociadas a ellas- de un álbum colectivo de los habitantes del barrio de Lavapiés. Dado que la identidad de una comunidad queda marcada en el mundo de hoy por las imágenes de que ella se muestran, parece oportuno no dejar siempre la creación, selección y difusión de estas

imágenes a otra comunidad y apostar, de entre todas las opciones posibles, por la de nosotros vistos por nosotros." Valbuena, *Nosotros*, 13.

23. "sólo había que buscar fotos e historias y ponerlas todas juntas. La suma de singulares siempre tiene como resultado un plural, no falla," Valbuena, *Nosotros*, 13.

24. "El mapa resultante no es perfecto, está hecho a escala humana, a escala 1: *Nosotros*, concretamente," Valbuena, *Nosotros*, 14.

25. Coco Fusco, "Racial Time, Racial Marks, Racial Metaphors," in *Only Skin Deep: Changing Visions of the American Self*, ed. Coco Fusco and Brian Wallis (International Center of Photography in association with Harry N. Abrams, 2003), 24.

26. Fusco, "Racial Time," 24.

27. For example, until the buildings were reformed in later centuries, the *corrala* typically included a single community bathroom on each floor, shared by several households.

28. "Parece que ahora se va a volver a hacer" Archivo Asociación de Vecinos La Corrala, in Valbuena, *Nosotros*, 98.

29. This problematic division between self and Other is frequent in Spanish cultural interventions touching upon the subject of multiculturalism. For further discussion of this narrative tendency see, for example, Kim's chapter "The Family Album and the Promotion of Multiculturalism: Icíar Bollaín's *Flores de otro mundo* and Rick Dávila's *Portraits of Migrant Workers in El Ejido*," in Yeon-Soo Kim, *The Family Album: Histories, Subjectivities and Immigration in Contemporary Spanish Culture* (Bucknell University Press, 2005).

30. For more on how artistic representations of the model family, like in *Nosotros*, are wielded to adapt different cultures' notions of kinship to Western ideals see Marianne Hirsch, *Family Frames: Photography, Narrative, and Postmemory* (Harvard University Press, 1997), 52.

31. "Las Mayas," Villa de Orgaz, June 12, 2013, https://web.archive.org/web/20130612224958/http://villadeorgaz.es/orgaz-folklore-mayas.html; "Origen de la fiesta de la Maya," *Muévome*, April 11, 2011, https://web.archive.org/web/20140118045228/http://www.muevome.com/2011/04/origen-de-la-fiesta-de-la-maya.html; "Fiesta de las Mayas de la Comunidad de Madrid," Comunidad de Madrid, April 28, 2023, https://www.comunidad.madrid/cultura/patrimonio-cultural/fiesta-mayas-comunidad-madrid.

32. "Madrid es el sitio donde por primera vez me di cuenta de la gran suerte que tenía, por haber nacido en Gran Bretaña, de poder viajar libremente con un pasaporte fácilmente conseguido. Fotografiando a mi vecino Maxime durante días, sentía que nuestras situaciones, por un lado tan distintas, se parecían:

recién llegado a Madrid los dos, con un idioma en común que era el francés, y sin conocer a casi nadie," Valbuena, *Nosotros*, 97.

33. Deborah Poole, "An Excess of Description: Ethnography, Race, and Visual Technologies," *Annual Review of Anthropology* 34 (2005): 160.
34. Nicole R. Fleetwood, *Troubling Vision: Performance, Visuality, and Blackness* (University of Chicago Press, 2011).
35. Fleetwood, *Troubling Vision*, 34.
36. Fleetwood, *Troubling Vision*, 9.
37. Mirzoeff, *The Right to Look*, 474.
38. "Exposição de fotografia 'All Around Us' de Gonçalo Gaioso," *The Gentleman*, May 18, 2013, https://thegentleman.pt/2013/05/exposicao-de-fotografia-all-around-us-de-goncalo-gaioso.
39. "Aquilo que se passa à nossa volta"; "Exposição de fotografia 'All Around Us' de Gonçalo Gaioso." Gaioso's personal website notes that his photographs have appeared in *Neo2*, *La Barna*, and *Tendencias*, which are fashion and design publications. "About Gaioso," Gonçalo Gaioso Photography, accessed May 10, 2023, https://cargocollective.com/gaioso/about-gaioso.
40. "*All Around Us* espelha a multiculturidade e simpatia do comércio nesta zona da cidade, ao qual aconselho a visita com um olhar bem atento!" Elsa Furtado and Tânia Fernandes, "Mercado de Fusão do Martim Moniz recebe a exposição de Gonçalo Gaioso *All Around Us*," *CH - Magazine de Cultura, Lazer e Viagens*, May 17, 2013, https://chmagazine.pt/mercado-de-fusao-do-martim-moniz-recebe-a-exposicao-de-goncalo-gaioso-all-around-us.
41. "*All Around Us* é uma detonação de cor, sorrisos e multiculturalidade." Furtado and Fernandes, "Mercado de Fusão do Martim Moniz recebe a exposição de Gonçalo Gaioso *All Around Us*." "trás [*sic*] o comércio local para dentro da Praça: várias fotografias dos comerciantes da Mouraria que nos mostram a multiculturalidade da envolvente," "Verão na cidade é no Mercado de Fusão Martim Moniz," *Cultura de Borla*, August 9, 2013, http://culturadeborla.blogs.sapo.pt/1407294.html.
42. For more on this subject see Les Back and Vibeke Quaade, "Dream Utopias, Nightmare Realities: Imaging Race and Culture within the World of Benetton Advertising," *Third Text* 7, no. 22 (1993): 65–80; Serra A. Tinic, "United Colors and Untied Meanings: Benetton and the Commodification of Social Issues," *Journal of Communication* 47, no. 3 (September 1, 1997): 3–25.
43. Fusco, "Racial Time," 21.
44. Marc Augé, *Non-Places: An Introduction to Supermodernity*, trans. John Howe (Verso, 1995).

45. Augé, *Non-Places*, 78.
46. Cheng, *Ornamentalism*, 19.
47. Cheng, *Ornamentalism*, 19.
48. Cheng, *Ornamentalism*, 17, 22.
49. Ana Matias discusses the stereotypes specifically associated with Portugal's Chinese population in "Imagens e estereótipos da sociedade portuguesa sobre a comunidade chinesa. Interacção multissecular via Macau" (2007), https://repositorio.iscte-iul.pt/handle/10071/1270.
50. Ralph Grillo, "Cultural Essentialism and Cultural Anxiety," *Anthropological Theory* 3 (2003): 165.
51. Mirzoeff, *The Right to Look*, 27.
52. Between just 2010 and 2017, Embajadores' resident population shrank by around four thousand inhabitants, a 9 percent drop in the district's total populace. Likewise, in central Lisbon the resident population dropped by twenty percent between 2013 and 2019. See Ley, "Así se vacía un barrio por culpa de la gentrificación," and Guilherme and Soares Ferreira, "Junta de Freguesia de Santa Maria Maior anuncia número de alerta para denunciar alojamento local illegal."
53. While initial reports indicated that seventeen families were affected by the evictions, later coverage refers to only sixteen. The same year as Watson's exhibit was erected, activist associations Habita and Left Hand Rotation produced a short documentary related to the event, accessible on the Left Hand Rotation platform. "Rua dos Lagares," Museo de los desplazados, accessed May 25, 2023, https://www.lefthandrotation.com/museodelosdesplazados/colaboraciones/habita-rua-dos-lagares.
54. Camilla Watson, "Canto do Sol," Camila Watson, accessed May 25, 2023, https://www.camillawatson.com/canto-do-sol.

INTERLUDE

1. Harvey, *Rebel Cities*, 4.
2. Manuel Delgado Ruíz, "La ciudad levantada. La barricada y otras transformaciones radicales del espacio urbano," *Arquitectonics: Mind, Land and Society*, Hacia un urbanismo alternativo, no. 19–20 (2010): 137–53.
3. Baumgarten describes the Portuguese protests in May 2011 as emerging in solidarity with the Spanish occupations and framed by the Spanish context. She notes that the demonstrations in Lisbon's Rossio Square originated from a mobilization of primarily Spanish protestors in front of the Spanish consulate, in support of the Indignadxs. Additionally, as Baumgarden observes, the Facebook call to occupy sites in Lisbon, Porto, Coimbra, and Faro was named

"Portuguese Revolution," a direct reference to the "Spanish Revolution" of the Indignadxs. See Baumgarten, "Geração à Rasca and Beyond."

4. Acknowledging that a summary of the desires expressed during the Sol encampments by participants in the movement risks reductionism, Snyder categorizes the wide range of proposals related to the 15-M protests into four broad categories: state and partisan politics, education and social rights, regulations for the banking and financial sector, and strategies for environmental sustainability, the defense of free culture, and animal rights. Snyder, *Poetics of Opposition*, 100.
5. Snyder writes, "The generic structure for local working groups and commissions would be reproduced with growing complexity as the movement in Madrid expanded beyond Sol, which intended to 'export' a form of deliberative democracy to Madrid's neighborhoods. . . . When in contact with the nascent local assemblies and decision-making practices in activist groups and organizations—or, other bodies and habits of doing together—these channels developed in plural ways into the deliberative procedures employed by the 15M neighborhood assemblies in Madrid, which would become an extensive operative network by June 2011." *Poetics of Opposition*, 97.
6. The exact number of local assemblies and working groups in Madrid continued to evolve following the initial encampments. As of May 2023, the number listed on 15Mpedia, a public, crowd-sourced internet archive of both 15M and related social movements was 148. 15Mpedia, "Lista de asambleas de la Comunidad de Madrid," 15Mpedia, accessed May 31, 2023, http://15mpedia.org/wiki/Lista_de_asambleas_de_la_Comunidad_de_Madrid.
7. Castells, *Networks of Outrage and Hope.*
8. "Democracia real ya" was both a common slogan during the Spanish anti-austerity protests and name of one of the groups participating in 15M. The Portuguese group Verdadeira Democracia Já, who borrowed the phrase from the Spanish movement, were the primary organizers of the occupation of Rossio Square.
9. For a detailed review of the global municipalist movement of the 2010s, including a discussion of the Ahora Madrid and Cidadãos por Lisboa coalitions, see Barcelona en Comú, Bookchin, and Colau, *Fearless Cities.*
10. Berlant, *Cruel Optimism*, 9.

CHAPTER 4

1. Son de cal y salmuera. Viejas ya desde siempre.
   Armadura oxidada con relleno de escombros.
   Tienen duros los ojos como fría cellisca.

Los cabellos marchitos como hierba pisada.
Y un vinagre maligno les recorre las venas.

Van temprano a la compra. Huronean los puestos.
Casi escarban. Eligen los tomates chafados.
Las naranjas mohosas. Maceradas verduras
que ya huelen a estiércol. Compran sangre cocida
en cilindros oscuros como quesos de lodo
y esos bofes que muestran, sonrosados y tímidos,
una obscena apariencia.

Al pagar, un suspiro les separa los labios
explorando morosas en el vientre mugriento
de un enorme y raído monedero sin asas
con un miedo feroz a topar de improviso
en su fondo la última cochambrosa moneda.

Ángela Figuera Aymerich, "Mujeres Del Mercado," *Guaraguao* 23, no. 61 (2019): 137–38. Translation by Jess Combs. Further study of this piece, along with other selections of Figuera Aymerich's work, can be found in Jill Robbins, "La mujer en el umbral: La simbología de la madre en la poesía de Ángela Figuera," *Anales de la literatura española contemporánea* 25, no. 2 (2000): 557–85.

2. Sharon Zukin, *Landscapes of Power: From Detroit to Disney World* (University of California Press, 2000).
3. Vincenzo Maiello defines *mercados de abastos* according to the parameters of the World Union of Wholesale Markets, "Recogemos la definición elaborada por el 'Grupo de trabajo de mercados minoristas' de la WUWM (2006): 'se entiende por mercados minoristas a aquellas instalaciones, normalmente edificios cubiertos, que reúnen una variedad de establecimientos comerciales y empresarios minoristas que ofrecen una amplia oferta comercial de productos alimentarios de consumo diario, complementada por otros productos no alimentarios, todo ello bajo una unidad de gestión.' Por tanto, no se incluye a los mercados mayoristas alimentarios, ni a otros mercados minoristas no alimentarios, ambulantes o al aire libre." See "El mercado de los mercados: Análisis de los procesos de transformación de los mercados municipales de abastos de Madrid" (Grupo de trabajo mercados y espacios públicos ASF-Madrid, 2014).
4. It serves to note, briefly, the origins of the *mercados de abastos* in contemporary Madrid. The city's modern network of municipal markets dates to two development plans from the early twentieth century: the Plan General de Mercados

(1931), which was designed under the authority of the Second Republic, and the Plan Especial de Mercados (1939–1943), enacted during the early years of the Franco regime. For more details regarding these plans see Alejandro Rodríguez Sebastián, "Los nuevos mercados municipales de Madrid," *Working Paper Series Contested Cities*, March 25, 2014, http://contested-cities.net/working-papers/2014/los-nuevos-mercados-municipales-de-madrid/ and Paula Ramos López, "Evolución tipológica del mercado de abastos en Madrid" (Universidad Politécnica de Madrid, 2020).

5. The journal *Urbanismo*, published by the Colegio Oficial de Arquitectos de Madrid between 1987 and 1998, has several articles detailing the city's suburban growth during this period. See Colegio Oficial de Arquitectos de Madrid (COAM), "Revista Urbanismo COAM," accessed June 22, 2023, https://www.coam.org/es/fundacion/biblioteca/revista-urbanismo-coam. In addition, there are a broad number of articles discussing shifting commercial models and their corresponding impact on the built environment during the late twentieth and early twenty-first centuries in Spain. See, for example, Ramón López de Lucio et al., "Centros urbanos frente a nuevas centralidades comerciales. Un análisis del sur metropolitano de Madrid," *Cuadernos de Investigación Urbanística*, no. 14 (September 1, 1996); Eulalia Ruiz Palomeque, Enrique Rivera Pozo, and Maria Luisa de Lázaro y Torres, "Nuevas formas de comercio y consumo en Madrid: las grandes superficies," *Estudios Geográficos* 61, no. 238 (March 1, 2000): 125–44.
6. The first Dia supermarket was opened in Madrid in 1979 in the Saconia development near Antonio Machado. In 1989, the company debuted their franchising scheme, which expanded their presence throughout the city. "Nuestra Historia," *Día*, accessed June 5, 2023, https://diacorporate.com/nuestra-historia/. The region's first Carrefour, an *hipermercado*, opened in Majadahonda in 1977. As of 2017 there were 24 *hipermercados*, 29 *supermercados* and 128 express markets in the province of Madrid. "Carrefour celebra 40 años en Madrid - detalle nota de prensa - Carrefour España," accessed June 5, 2023, https://www.carrefour.es/grupo-carrefour/sala-de-prensa/noticias2015.aspx?tcm=tcm:5-44830.
7. Some reports discussing these challenges include Josep Puxeu Rocamora, "Remodelación de mercados tradicionales. Modernización comercial y rehabilitación urbana," *Distribución y consumo*, no. 11 (1993): 32–35; Ángel Juste, "Mercados minoristas tradicionales. La remodelación necesaria," *Distribución y consumo*, no. 11 (1993): 10–26.
8. "Los mercados municipales han constituido, y siguen constituyendo, una de las grandes bases integradoras de las ciudades. Pirenne escribía que las ciudades son hijas del comercio y, dentro del comercio, hay que destacar el importante

papel generador de los mercados de abastos identificados en ocasiones como aglutinadores tradicionales de la vida en la ciudad." Javier Casares Ripol and Alfonso Rebollo Arévalo, "Mercados minoristas tradicionales: Situación actual y alternativas de actuación," *Distribución y consumo*, no. 7, no. 32 (1997): 75–114.

9. Juan Ignacio Robles, "Comercio urbano en espacios metropolitanos: Mercados, vidas y barrios," *Distribución y consumo*, no. 22 (2008): 19–31.
10. "El mercado es un espacio de encuentro entre vecinos, que intercambian información, favores y bienes, reforzando las relaciones sociales mutuas. Los mercados son ámbitos de sociabilidad donde la larga historia de venta y compra entre clientes y comerciantes, a veces, transmitida de generación en generación (de padres/madres a hijos/hijas) conforma unas fuertes relaciones de reciprocidad entre comerciantes y clientes basadas en el conocimiento y en la confianza mutuos," "Comercio urbano," 20.
11. Zukin, *Naked City*, 6.
12. Ayuntamiento de Madrid, "Plan de innovación y transformación de los mercados de Madrid: 2003–2011: Ocho años impulsando el comercio," 2003, http://www.madrid.es/Unidades.
13. For a discussion of the parameters of the *Plan de Innovación*, and the later *Plan Estratégico de Modernización de los Mercados de Madrid (2012–2015)* and the *Ordenanza de Mercados Municipales ANM 2010/62* see Rodríguez Sebastián, "Los nuevos mercados municipales de Madrid."
14. Cited in "El nuevo-viejo San Antón," *El País*, July 18, 2007, sec. Actualidad, https://elpais.com/elpais/2007/07/18/actualidad/1184746627_850215.html.
15. See Juan Ignacio Robles, "Mercado de San Antón. Madrid," *Distribución y consumo* 81, no. 5 (2013): 77–82. Oriol Güell reports on the discord over this decision in "El 'súper' se come el mercado de Chueca," *El País*, July 27, 2006, sec. Madrid, https://elpais.com/diario/2006/07/28/madrid/1154085855_850215.html. The San Antón renovations were reported to have cost approximately 20.5 million euros, with around 6.5 euros covered by subsidies from the Ayuntamiento and Comunidad de Madrid. See Maiello, "El mercado de los mercados: Análisis de los procesos de transformación de los mercados municipales de abastos de Madrid," 11; Rodríguez Sebastián, "Los nuevos mercados municipales de Madrid," 7.
16. Robles, "Mercado de San Antón. Madrid," 79.
17. Rodríguez Sebastián discusses how pricing structures varied between remodeled markets in "Los nuevos mercados municipales de Madrid."
18. See, for example, critiques of the market cited in Paula Delgado Labrandero, "Renace el céntrico Mercado de San Antón," El Mundo, May 17,

2011, https://www.elmundo.es/elmundo/2011/05/17/madrid/1305633400.html, accessed June 27, 2023.

19. Juan Ignacio Robles, includes a detailed timeline of these renovations in "El Mercado de San Miguel. Madrid," *Distribución y consumo* 21, no. 11 (2011): 103–6.
20. "About Us," Mercado de San Miguel, n.d., https://mercadodesanmiguel.es/en/#about-us.
21. "About Us," Mercado de San Miguel.
22. According to a 2013 article published by Europa Press, the Mercado de San Miguel was receiving over 85,000 weekly visitors, of which 40 percent hailed from Madrid, 20 percent from other regions of Spain, and 40 percent from abroad. *Europa Press*, "El Mercado de San Miguel recibe unos 85.000 visitantes semanales, de los que un 40% son madrileños," April 14, 2013, https://www.europapress.es/madrid/noticia-mercado-san-miguel-recibe-85000-visitantes-semanales-40-son-madrilenos-20130414135018.html.
23. El verdadero momento en el que me decidí a realizar esta investigación tuvo lugar una noche paseando por Madrid con amigos, parados frente a los ventanales del mercado de San Miguel, observando a la gente que en su interior degustaba excelentes vinos y consumía tapas diseñadas con el gusto más exquisito. Fue entonces cuando llegamos a una concisa pero profunda conclusión: "esto ya no es un mercado." Rodríguez Sebastián, "Los nuevos mercados municipales de Madrid."
24. Svetlana Boym, "Nostalgia," Atlas of Transformation, © 2011, http://monument-totransformation.org/atlas-of-transformation/html/n/nostalgia/nostalgia-svetlana-boym.html.
25. Svetlana Boym, *The Future of Nostalgia* (Basic Books, 2001), 41.
26. More than twenty of Madrid's network of municipal markets were constructed in the twentieth century during the postwar era, under the guise of the Franco regime's urban expansion plans. See Ramos López, "Evolución tipológica del mercado de abastos en Madrid."
27. Alberto Riesco-Sanz discusses migrant entrepreneurship and commerce in Lavapiés from the late 90s to the 2010s in "Empresarialidad inmigrante: inmigración y comercio en Embajadores/Lavapiés," published in *Barrios multiculturales: Relaciones interétnicas en los barrios de San Francisco (Bilbao) y Embajadores/Lavapiés (Madrid)*, by Alfonso Pérez Agote, Benjamín Tejerina, and Margarita Barañano (Editorial Trotta, 2010), 260–79.
28. "Historia," *Mercado Municipal de San Fernando*, n.d., https://mercadodesanfernando.es/historia.

29. Cristina Expósito, "Lavapiés estrena centro de salud sobre el Mercado de San Fernando," *Madridiario*, accessed June 28, 2023, https://www.madridiario.es/noticia/5791/centro/lavapies-estrena-centro-de-salud-sobre-el-mercado-de-san-fernando.html.
30. Marta Fernández Maeso, "Renovar un mercado de barrio, versión Lavapiés," *El País*, March 30, 2012, sec. Madrid, https://elpais.com/ccaa/2012/03/29/madrid/1333045590_721372.html.
31. Fernández Maeso, "Renovar un mercado de barrio, versión Lavapiés."
32. "Hubo un encuentro de dos días para ver qué podíamos hacer entre muchos colectivos que teníamos algunas ideas comunes y al lado estaba el mercado que estaba al punto de cerrar ...Lo miramos entre varios grupos y decidimos entrar varios grupos a la vez para levantar el mercado." Asunción, personal interview, 2015.
33. CSOA *El Laboratorio* was first established in 1997 as a squatted collective at number 68 of Calle Embajadores. For a deeper dive into the social and spatial significance of the Tabacalera see, for example, Feinberg, "From Cigarreras to Indignados: Spectacles of Scale in the CSA La Tabacalera of Lavapiés, Madrid," *International Journal of Iberian Studies* 26, no. 1/2 (November 2013): 21–39; Margarita Rodríguez Ibáñez, "La Cultura Localizada como respuesta social a la Red: El caso de la Fábrica de la Tabacalera en Madrid," *E-RPH*, no. 14 (October 1, 2015).
34. Feinberg and Larson, "Cultivating the Square," 123.
35. Feinberg and Larson study these two sites in detail in "Cultivating the Square." In doing so, they claim, "in the refuse of an urban landscape transformed by economic crisis, the repurposing of the urban is one way that citizens can cultivate the 'latent gardens' around them, thereby asserting their right to the city once again," 123.
36. "El objetivo nuestro es hacer un mercado del barrio. Para todo el mundo. Para que todo el mundo tenga acceso. De hecho, es uno de los principios que acordamos cuando entramos en el mercado de que los precios tenían que ser asequibles para la mayoría de la gente. Esa es una de las diferencias que hay con el Mercado de San Miguel, que tienen muy buenos productos, pero son muy caros. Entonces está enfocado a una gente muy determinada, el turismo y a gente con dinero, la gente que puede gastárselo." Asunción, Personal interview, 2015.
37. Due to the grassroots nature of the movement, the push to repopulate and rethink the market was not tied to a single group or cause (much like 15-M itself). Fernández Maeso's article captures several catalyzing factors for its redevelopment in the following description, "Parte de los nuevos comerciantes de San Fernando se conocían previamente. Pero cada uno llegó por una

cosa. Por un amigo. Por las jornadas de la Plataforma en Defensa de los Mercados de Abastos celebradas hace unos meses en La Tabacalera, en las que se abría la posibilidad de montar este tipo de negocio. Por ganas, por necesidad de montar un negocio. Por la rebaja del precio de los alquileres" Fernández Maeso, "Renovar un mercado de barrio, versión Lavapiés."

38. "La Asociación de Comerciantes del Mercado de San Fernando, integrada por la totalidad de sus comerciantes, es la entidad concesionaria de este Mercado Municipal. El órgano máximo de la asociación es la Asamblea, que se celebra como mínimo una vez al año. El órgano representativo es la Junta Directiva conformada por un Presidente o una Presidenta, un Vicepresidente o una Vicepresidenta, un Secretario o una Secretaria, un Tesorero o una Tesorera y por Vocales. La Junta Directiva se renueva cada 3 años." "Asociación de comerciantes - Mercado de San Fernando," Mercado de San Fernando, May 26, 2017, https://web.archive.org/web/20170526213126/http://www.mercadodesanfernando.es:80/asociacion-de-comerciantes/.

39. "Tradición y *alternativismo* en un mismo espacio y con igual objetivo: dar alas al comercio tradicional."

40. "no está orquestado para turistas por el Ayuntamiento, ni es la última invención ecopija." "El Mercado de San Fernando," *La playa de Madrid*, June 23, 2012, http://www.laplayademadrid.es/archives/4896.

41. "Y luego por otro lado también estamos conviviendo con muchos, por ejemplo, banglas, que vienen de Bangladesh que vienen a vivir aquí y todos se ponen una tienda de algo para vender. Entonces venden muy barato, los horarios son súper largos, es decir que no tienen . . . aquí siempre ha habido un horario de cerrar a las ocho de la noche pero bueno . . . el horario fue una causa de la Comunidad de Madrid, nos está gobernando durante mucho tiempo, son liberales, ultraliberales, y legalizaron todo el horario en Madrid entonces la gente puede abrir 24 horas. Entonces la gente, por ejemplo banglas o los chinos están todo el día en la tienda, no hacen vida. Solo viven de la tienda. Están desde que se levantan hasta que se acuestan. A las dos de la noche están abiertos. Entonces también a la vez hay una competencia con los mismos comerciantes autóctonos de aquí." Asunción, personal interview, 2015.

42. Donovan, "'Se ríen de la crisis': Chinese Immigration as Economic Invasion in Spanish Film and Media," *Revista de Estudios Hispánicos* 51 (2017): 373.

43. Members of the market collective were required to abide by common hours of operation including opening at nine am, closing for a break mid-day on Mondays, and as early as five pm on Saturdays. This posed particular challenges for posts that offered products that shoppers could obtain outside of the market in stores that were not bound by these limited hours of operation.

44. Mercado de San Fernando, "Los puestos," June 15, 2015, https://web.archive.org/web/20150615002616/http://www.mercadodesanfernando.es/category/los-puestos/.
45. "no están libres de violencias sexistas, homófobas, racistas, que son reproducciones de las que se dan fuera de estos microcosmos, en la ciudad, en los medios, las redes sociales, en la sociedad en general." Gracia Trujillo, "La protesta dentro de la protesta. Activismos queer/cuir y feministas en el 15M," *Encrucijadas: Revista crítica de ciencias sociales* 12 (2016): 15.
46. "preocupación constante por el otro, el que no está ya aquí, entre nosotros." Amador Fernández-Savater, "El nacimiento de un nuevo poder social," *Hispanic Review* 80, no. 4 (2012): 677.
47. Berlant, *Cruel Optimism*, 194.
48. Álex, personal interview, 2015.
49. Zukin, *Naked City*, 21–22.
50. "Manifestación por los derechos del turista," Lavapiés ¿dónde vas?, n.d., https://lavapiesdondevas.wordpress.com/miercoles/manifestacion-internacional-por-los-derechos-del-turista.
51. "7. Que los castizos nos hagan francachelas," "14. Cierre de bares con camareros feos que lleven uniforme, camisas blancas o chalequillo."
52. "Que se eliminen los antiestéticos Mercados con productos frescos y se sustituyan por barecitos guays para tomarse el vermut."

CHAPTER 5

1. Mirzoeff, *The Right to Look*, 2.
2. He continues, "Pixels are the visible result of everything produced by a computer, from words created by a word processor to all forms of image, sound, and video. Actions are things we do with those cultural forms to make changes, small or large, from a direct political action to a performance—whether in everyday life or in a theater—a conversation or a work of art," Mirzoeff, *How to See the World* (Basic Books, 2015), 293.
3. PorFavor, like many involved in the urban art scene, keeps his identity private.
4. El futuro: Lavapiés 2029.
5. The term counter mapping is commonly attributed to sociologist Nancy Peluso, who uses the phrase in her article "Whose Woods are These? Counter-Mapping Forest Territories in Kalimantan, Indonesia." She describes it as a map-making process in which communities appropriate the state's techniques of formal mapping and make their own maps as alternatives to those used by the government. See "Whose Woods Are These? Counter-Mapping

Forest Territories in Kalimantan, Indonesia," *Antipode* 27, 4 (October 1995): 383–406.

6. One of the foremost theorizations of the networked nature of 15-M is found in Castells, *Networks of Outrage and Hope.*
7. PorFavor noted during our interview that he learned many artistic techniques in workshops held at the Tabacalera, another indication of the centrality of this venue to community-engaged urban initiatives, particularly in the wake of the 15-M *acampadas.*
8. The artist has published many photographs of his work since 2013 on his Instagram page, "@porfavorhh," Instagram, accessed July 31, 2023, https://www.instagram.com/porfavorhh/.
9. "Potenciar la creación artística en el barrio de una manera abierta y participativa y de contribuir a su disfrute de un modo cercano y cotidiano." Asociación de Comerciantes de Lavapiés, "'Convocatoria' C.A.L.L.E.," 2016, https://xn--lavapisgya.com/CALLE/wp-content/uploads/2016/04/ConvocatoriaCALLE2016-1.pdf.
10. Stephen Pritchard, "Artwashing: Social Capital and Anti-Gentrification Activism," *Colouring in Culture*, June 17, 2017, https://colouringinculture.org/uncategorized/artwashingsocialcapitalantigentrification.
11. Through spatial tactics, as defined by Michel DeCerteau, citizens confront and circumvent hegemonic control over the way that one experiences urban environments. See *The Practice of Everyday Life*, trans. Stephen Rendall (University of California Press, 1984).
12. "Leit Motiv: El futuro, Lavapiés 2029: Lavapiés es un barrio madrileño con personalidad única. En él conviven más de 50 nacionalidades distintas con generaciones nacidas en el propio barrio desde comienzos del siglo XX hasta nuestros días. Sus calles bulliciosas y coloridas emanan arte y cultura por sus cuatro costados, empezando por sus teatros y salas de conciertos, hasta las expresiones más libres y rupturistas. Todo ello mezclado con bares y comercios, algunos centenarios y castizos y otros superlativamente modernos y underground, de cercanía, alejados de cadenas o franquicias, sino genuinos y auténticos que colaboran en generar la peculiar atmósfera de Lavapiés. Desde C.A.L.L.E. 2016 queremos pensar, reflexionar y crear acerca del FUTURO, desde un carácter abierto hasta lo más concreto, teniendo en esta edición el leit motiv Lavapiés 2029," "Convocatoria," *C.A.L.L.E.*, 2016.
13. "Centro comercial multiétnico al aire libre, una especie de parque temático [dónde] la gente va a observar cómo era Lavapiés antes." PorFavor, personal interview, 2017.
14. Several geographers and historians critically examine maps as cultural productions layered with power dynamics. Stephen Hanna and Vincent Del Casino

establish a framework for reading maps as representational practices, pushing against the binaries in geocriticism that privilege one set of knowledge production over another. "Beyond The 'Binaries': A Methodological Intervention for Interrogating Maps as Representational Practices," *ACME: An International E-Journal for Critical Geographies* 4, no. 1 (2005): 34–56.

15. As Mark Gottdiener writes "There is no consumption of space without a corresponding and prior production of space." "Consumption of Space and Spaces of Consumption," *Architectural Design* 68 (1998): 12.
16. Mitchell, *The Right to the City*, 3.
17. "No intente ayudar a escapar del parque a los indígenas bajo ningún concepto."
18. During our conversation, PorFavor noted that he had decided on a location for each reservation by mapping out his personal observations of socio-spatial relationships within in Lavapiés. While this way of producing the map was also form of organizing perceptions of the Other, the artist did so in order to parody these didactic texts. While this raises a provocative tension that should be acknowledged, further analysis is beyond the scope of this close reading.
19. "Asómbrese con las costumbres y ritmos del continente más expoliado por el mundo civilizado."
20. Pilar Álvarez, "Metro ingresará tres millones por el patrocinio publicitario de la línea 2," *El País*, April 23, 2013, sec. Madrid, https://elpais.com/ccaa/2013/04/23/madrid/1366711053_623450.html.
21. "Ley Orgánica 5/2002, de 27 de junio, sobre Drogodependencias y otros Trastornos Adictivos," n.d., https://www.boe.es/eli/es-md/l/2002/06/27/57A4.p0323335?cdestado=P&nmnorma=1779&opcion=VerHtml#no-back-button.; "Ley Orgánica 4/2015, de 30 de marzo, de protección de la seguridad ciudadana," n.d., https://boe.es/buscar/pdf/2015/BOE-A-2015-3442-consolidado.pdf.
22. The decision was made as part of a broader safety plan by then-mayor Alberto Ruiz Gallardón, with Lavapiés as the fourth part of the city center in which such cameras were erected, following Calle de la Montera and Plaza de la Luna, both known as centers of sex work and other illicit activity. CCTV technology, in this instance, was leveraged as an invisible shield meant to quell public anxiety related to criminal activity. See Octavio Fraile, "División entre los vecinos de Lavapiés por las cámaras de vigilancia," *20minutos* December 20, 2009, https://www.20minutos.es/noticia/595015/0/division/lavapies/camaras.
23. Mirzoeff, *The Right to Look*, 4.
24. "Iba a montar como un 'stand'; iba a hacer unos folletitos trípticos de estos de información un poco en el sentido del cartel, explicando un poco los itinerarios. Y mi idea era ponerme allí un poco como puesto de información a toda la gente que pasara y les dando mi planito de Lavapiés gentrificado y estar allí

con el cartel puesto y vamos, si hubiera tirado para adelante hubiera tenido también otro tipo de desarrollo. Pero sobre todo era eso, estar por allí repartiendo folletos un poco, denunciando." PorFavor, personal interview, 2017.

25. For more on the history of La Quimera see 15Mpedia, "CSROA La Quimera," *15Mpedia*, accessed July 10, 2023, //15mpedia.org/wiki/CSROA_La_Quimera.
26. José Smith Vargas, "Bouldrilhar na Mouraria," 2012, https://www.behance.net/josesmithvargas.
27. In *Simulacra and Simulation*, Baudrillard writes "Today abstraction is no longer that of the map, the double, the mirror, or the concept. Simulation is no longer that of a territory, a referential being, or a substance. It is the generation by models of a real without origin or reality: a hyperreal. The territory no longer precedes the map, nor does it survive it," 1.
28. "It is the generation by models of a real without origin or reality: a hyperreal." Baudrillard, *Simulacra and Simulation*, 1.
29. Câmara Municipal de Lisboa. "Mouraria - Berço do Fado," *Informações e Serviços*, accessed July 12, 2023, https://informacoeseservicos.lisboa.pt/contactos/diretorio-da-cidade/mouraria-berco-do-fado.
30. Sánchez Fuarros, "Ai Mouraria!" 82. Emphasis added.
31. Baudrillard, "The Precession of Simulacra."
32. José Smith Vargas, "Renovar a Mouraria 1496," 2018, https://josesmithvargas.com/RENOVAR-A-MOURARIA-1496.
33. Ahmed, *The Cultural Politics of Emotion*, 11.
34. "Chega-se a este vale fértil e alegre por onde andam os sarracenos até que, com a cidade a crescer, os seus ofícios e comércios começam a ser cobiçados." While the term *sarraceno* has also been employed to refer to Arab and Middle Eastern populations and their descendants, in addition to Muslims, I have translated it to Muslim due to Vargas's focus on religion.
35. "Fez bem D. Manoel em desfazer a comuna moura e abri-la à cidade."
36. "Tanta gente em Lisboa que nunca passeou por estas ruas."
37. "E purificadas estão as suas tradições."
38. Mary Douglas, *Purity and Danger: An Analysis of Concepts of Pollution and Taboo* (Routledge, 1966), 1.
39. Diana Q. Burkhart, "The Disposable Immigrant: The Aesthetics of Waste in Las Cartas de Alou," *Journal of Spanish Cultural Studies* 11, no. 2 (June 6, 2010): 155.
40. Anne McClintock, *Imperial Leather: Race, Gender, and Sexuality in the Colonial Contest* (Routledge, 1995).
41. While beyond the scope of the discussion in this chapter, there are several insightful studies that explore the relationship between religion and racial thinking in Europe during the pre-modern period. See, as examples, David

Nirenberg, "Was There Race before Modernity? The Example of 'Jewish' Blood in Late Medieval Spain," in *Was There Race before Modernity? The Example of "Jewish" Blood in Late Medieval Spain* (University of Chicago Press, 2014), 169–90; Geraldine Heng, *The Invention of Race in the European Middle Ages* (Cambridge University Press, 2018); Pamela Patton, *Blackness, Whiteness, and the Idea of Race in Medieval European Art* (Fordham University Press, 2019), 154–65.

42. "Se calhar não tens, simplesmente, jeito para o negócio."
43. "De modo algum! Aliás, os problemas desta cidade estão mesmo quase a terminar."

CONCLUSION

1. "Salut aísla a unas 25 personas por el primer caso de coronavirus en Catalunya," *La Vanguardia*, February 25, 2020, https://www.lavanguardia.com/vida/20200225/473782485232/coronavirus-primer-caso-cataluna.html. While the first on the peninsula, this was the second case in Spanish territory. A confirmed case of COVID was reported days earlier on January 31 in the Canary Islands. See Sandra Pulido, "España confirma su primer caso de coronavirus," *Gaceta Médica*, January 31, 2020, https://gacetamedica.com/investigacion/espana-confirma-su-primer-caso-de-coronavirus.
2. Distanciamiento social, @DosJotas2js, Instagram, May 26, 2020.
3. Adrianna Freedman, "This Video of a Trainer Leading a Quarantine Workout Class Will Give You All the Feels," Men's Health, March 17, 2020, https://www.menshealth.com/entertainment/a31676138/trainer-spain-leads-quarantined-apartment-workout-coronavirus.
4. Luis de Vega, "Los 42 km del maratón de Madrid corridos en una terraza de siete metros de Hortaleza," *El País*, April 26, 2020, https://elpais.com/espana/madrid/2020-04-26/los42-km-del-maraton-de-madrid-corridos-en-una-terraza-de-siete-metros-de-hortaleza.html.
5. "Esa es la verdadera pandemia, permanente y criminal."
6. "Poner separadas cosas que estaban juntas o ponerlas más distanciadas de lo que estaban=distanciamiento social" "Todo sigue con la misma distancia incluso más."
7. Berlant, *Cruel Optimism*, 8.
8. Berlant, *Cruel Optimism*, 7.
9. Marek Smid et al., "Ranking European Capitals by Exposure to Heat Waves and Cold Waves," *Urban Climate* 27 (March 1, 2019): 388–402. See also Susana Barbosa and Manuel G. Scotto, "Extreme Heat Events in the Iberia Peninsula

from Extreme Value Mixture Modeling of ERA5-Land Air Temperature," *Weather and Climate Extremes* 36 (June 1, 2022): 100448.

10. Luis I. Prádanos, *Postgrowth Imaginaries: New Ecologies and Counterhegemonic Culture in Post-2008 Spain* (Liverpool University Press, 2018), 92.

11. Both Vox and Chega take a hardline nationalist and conservative approach to issues such as immigration, abortion, LGBTQ+ rights, and religious freedom, and advocate for the principles of a free-market economy. A number of scholarly interventions since the late 2010s discuss the rise of the radical right on the Iberian Peninsula including Carles Ferreira, "Vox como representante de la derecha radical en España: un estudio sobre su ideología," *Revista española de ciencia política*, no. 51 (November 2019): 73–98. Mariana S. Mendes, "'Enough' of What? An Analysis of Chega's Populist Radical Right Agenda," *South European Society & Politics* 26, no. 3 (September 2021): 329–53; Mariana S. Mendes and James Dennison, "Explaining the Emergence of the Radical Right in Spain and Portugal: Salience, Stigma and Supply," *West European Politics* 44, no. 4 (January 1, 2021): 752–75; Helder Prior, "Populismo de Direita radical em Portugal," *Media&Jornalismo* 22, no. 40 (May 1, 2022): 161–77; Arantxa Capdevila, Carlota M. Moragas-Fernández, and Josep M. Grau-Masot, "Emergencia del populismo en España: Marcos metafóricos de Vox y de su comunidad online durante las elecciones generales de 2019," *El profesional de la información* 31, no. 3 (June 5, 2022): 1–20.

BIBLIOGRAPHY

Adamiak, Czeslaw. "Mapping Airbnb Supply in European Cities." *Annals of Tourism Research* 71 (2018): 67–71.

"A fábrica das artes." *Time Out Lisboa*. May 27, 2009. https://web.archive.org/web/20130810021742/https://lxfactory.com/ficheiros/noticias/TimeOUT27Maio.pdf.

Ahmed, Sara. *The Promise of Happiness*. Duke University Press, 2010.

Ahmed, Sara. *The Cultural Politics of Emotion*, Edinburgh University Press, 2014.

Aixelà-Cabré, Yolanda. "Entre las dictaduras y el petróleo: Las migraciones trasnacionales de Guinea Ecuatorial." *Revista Andaluza de Antropología*, 3, Jan. 2012, pp. 89–103.

Almeida García, Fernando. "La política turística en España y Portugal." *Cuadernos de Turismo*, no. 30 (2012): 9–34.

Álvarez, Pilar. "Metro ingresará tres millones por el patrocinio publicitario de la línea 2," *El País*, April 23, 2013, sec. Madrid, https://elpais.com/ccaa/2013/04/23/madrid/1366711053_623450.html.

Amanece que no es poco. Directed by José Luis Cuerda, 1989.

Amore, Alberto, Cecilia de Bernardi, and Pavlos Arvanitis. "The Impacts of Airbnb in Athens, Lisbon and Milan: A Rent Gap Theory Perspective." *Current Issues in Tourism* 25, no. 20 (October 15, 2022): 3329–42.

Andreia. "Lisbon - Rose Apartment," 1881. https://www.airbnb.com/rooms/16228038?check_in=2020-10-15&check_out=2020-10-22&source_impression_id=p3_1599750741_f%2FGoG8VSucoj2OJ3.

Anzaldúa, Gloria. *Borderlands / La Frontera: The New Mestiza*, 4th ed. Aunt Lute Books, 2012.

Arrese, José Luis de. "No queremos una España de proletarios, sino de propietarios." ABC, May 2, 1959, 41.

Asociación de Comerciantes de Lavapiés. "'Convocatoria' C.A.L.L.E," 2016. https://xn--lavapis-gya.com/CALLE/wp-content/uploads/2016/04/ConvocatoriaCALLE2016-1.pdf.

Asociación de Comerciantes de Lavapiés. "Guía Tapapiés," 2019.

Asociación Legado Expo Sevilla. "¿Qué fue Expo'92?" Accessed July 30, 2023. https://legadoexposevilla.org/reportajes/que-fue-expo92/.

Associação Renovar a Mouraria. "Objectivos," 2009. http://web.archive.org/web/20090615133942/http://www.renovaramouraria.pt/a-associacao/objectivos/.

Associação Renovar a Mouraria, and Nuno Saraiva. *Visita a Mouraria*. 2015.

Atkinson, Rowland, and Gary Bridge, eds. *Gentrification in a Global Context: The New Urban Colonialism*. Housing and Society Series. Routledge, 2005.

Augé, Marc. *Non-Places: An Introduction to Supermodernity*. Translated by John Howe. Verso, 1995.

Aymerich, Ángela Figuera. "Mujeres Del Mercado." *Guaraguao* 23, no. 61 (2019): 137–38.

Ayuntamiento de Madrid. "Plan de innovación y transformación de los mercados de Madrid: 2003-2011: ocho años impulsando el comercio," 2003. http://www.madrid.es/Unidades-.

Back, Les, and Vibeke Quaade. "Dream Utopias, Nightmare Realities: Imaging Race and Culture within the World of Benetton Advertising." *Third Text* 7, no. 22 (1993): 65–80.

Baganha, Maria Ioannis, José Carlos Marques, and Pedro Góis. "Imigrantes em Portugal: uma síntese histórica." *Ler História*, no. 56 (May 1, 2009): 123–33.

Bajorek, Jennifer. *Unfixed: Photography and Decolonial Imagination in West Africa*. Duke University Press, 2020.

Ballesteros, Isolina. *Immigration Cinema in the New Europe*. Intellect Books, 2015.

Barbosa, Susana, and Manuel G. Scotto. "Extreme Heat Events in the Iberia Peninsula from Extreme Value Mixture Modeling of ERA5-Land Air Temperature." *Weather and Climate Extremes* 36 (June 1, 2022): 100448.

Barcala, Carlota. "Ejecutado el desahucio de cuatro familias en Argumosa con seis detenidos." *Diario ABC*, February 22, 2019. https://www.abc.es/espana/madrid/abci-tension-y-fuerte-presencia-policial-argumosa-antes-ejecuten-cuatro-desahucios-201902220959_noticia.html.

Barcelona en Comú, Debbie Bookchin, and Ada Colau. *Fearless Cities: A Guide to the Global Municipalist Movement*. New Internationalist, 2019.

Barthes, Roland. *Camera Lucida: Reflections on Photography*. Translated by Richard Howard. Macmillan, 1981.

Barthes, Roland. *Image-Music-Text*. Translated by Stephen Heath. Macmillan, 1977.

Baudrillard, Jean. *Simulacra and Simulation*. Translated by Sheila Glaser. University of Michigan Press, 1995.

Baudrillard, Jean. "Two Essays." Translated by Arthur B. Evans. *Science Fiction Studies* 18, no. 3 (November 1991). https://www.depauw.edu/sfs/backissues/55/baudrillard55art.htm.

Baumgarten, Britta. "Geração à Rasca and beyond: Mobilizations in Portugal after 12 March 2011." *Current Sociology* 61, no. 4 (July 1, 2013): 457–73.

Benjamin, Walter. "The Work of Art in the Age of Mechanical Reproduction." In *The Norton Anthology of Theory and Criticism*, edited by Vincent Leitch, translated by Harry Zohn, 1166–86. W.W. Norton & Company, 2001.

Berlant, Lauren. *Cruel Optimism*. Duke University Press, 2011.

Bermúdez, Silvia. *Rocking the Boat: Migration and Race in Contemporary Spanish Music*. University of Toronto Press, 2018.

Boym, Svetlana. *The Future of Nostalgia*. Basic Books, 2001.

Boym, Svetlana. "Nostalgia." Atlas of Transformation, © 2011. http://monumenttotransformation.org/atlas-of-transformation/html/n/nostalgia/nostalgia-svetlana-boym.html.

Brito Guiterres, António. "Interações reflexivas sobre o novo plano MARTIM MONIZ." Buala, 2012. https://www.buala.org/pt/cidade/interacoes-reflexivas-sobre-o-novo-plano-martim-moniz.

Burkhart, Diana Q. "The Disposable Immigrant: The Aesthetics of Waste in Las Cartas de Alou." *Journal of Spanish Cultural Studies* 11, no. 2 (June 6, 2010): 153–65.

Buttimer, Anne, and David Seamon, eds. *The Human Experience of Space and Place*. Routledge Revivals. Routledge, 2015.

Cabral, Jõao, and Berta Rato. "Urban Development for Competitiveness and Cohesion: The Expo' 98 Urban Project in Lisbon." In *The Globalized City: Economic Restructuring and Social Polarization in European Cities*, edited by Arantxa Rodriguez, Frank Moulaert, and Erik Swyngedouw, 217. Oxford University Press, 2002.

Calleja, Eduardo González, and Fredesvinta Limón Nevado. *La hispanidad como instrumento de combate: Raza e imperio en la prensa franquista durante la Guerra Civil española*. Madrid: Consejo Superior de Investigaciones Cientificas, 1988.

Câmara Municipal de Lisboa. "Mouraria - Berço do Fado," *Informações e Serviços*, accessed July 12, 2023, https://informacoeseservicos.lisboa.pt/contactos/diretorio-da-cidade/mouraria-berco-do-fado.

Câmara Municipal de Lisboa: "aiMouraria - Programa QREN Mouraria: Plano de Intervenção." Accessed July 30, 2023. https://web.archive.org/

web/20120703015642/http://www.aimouraria.cm-lisboa.pt/plano-de-intervencao.html.

Campt, Tina. *Image Matters: Archive, Photography, and the African Diaspora in Europe*. Duke University Press, 2012.

Cañedo Rodríguez, Montserrat. "Discursos vecinales sobre la inseguridad ciudadana y políticas de rehabilitación urbanística: el caso de los 'antiguos vecinos' y la ARI-Lavapiés (Madrid) desde una perspectiva antropológica." *Scripta Nova: Revista electrónica de geografía y ciencias sociales*, 2011.

Capdevila, Arantxa, Carlota M. Moragas-Fernández, and Josep M. Grau-Masot. "Emergencia del populismo en España: marcos metafóricos de Vox y de su comunidad online durante las elecciones generales de 2019." *El profesional de la información* 31, no. 3 (June 5, 2022): 1–20.

Carmo, Renato Miguel do, Rita Cachado, and Daniela Ferreira. "Desigualdades em tempos de crise: vulnerabilidades habitacionais e socioeconómicas na área metropolitana de Lisboa." *Revista portuguesa de estudos regionais* 40 (2015): 5–22.

"Carrefour celebra 40 años en Madrid - detalle nota de prensa - Carrefour España." Accessed June 5, 2023. https://www.carrefour.es/grupo-carrefour/sala-de-prensa/noticias2015.aspx?tcm=tcm:5-44830.

Carrera, Magali Marie. *Imagining Identity in New Spain: Race, Lineage, and the Colonial Body in Portraiture and Casta Paintings*. Electronic resource. University of Texas Press, 2003.

Carrière, Jean-Paul, and Christopher Demazière. "Urban Planning and Flagship Development Projects: Lessons from EXPO 98, Lisbon." *Planning, Practice and Research* 17, no. 1 (2002): 70–71.

Casa Árabe. "Quiénes somos," n.d. https://www.casaarabe.es/p/quienes-somos.

Casares Ripol, Javier, and Alfonso Rebollo Arévalo. "Mercados minoristas tradicionales: Situación actual y alternativas de actuación." *Distribución y consumo* 7, no. 32 (1997): 75–114.

Castells, Manuel. *Networks of Outrage and Hope: Social Movements in the Internet Age*. John Wiley & Sons, 2015.

Castro Caldas, José. "O impacto das medidas 'anti-crise' e a situação social e de emprego." Comité Económico e Social Europeu, 2013.

Cea D'Ancona, Maria Ángeles, and Miguel S. Valles Martínez. *Evolución del racismo y la xenofobia en España: Informe 2009*. Ministerio de Trabajo e Inmigración, 2009.

César das Neves, Jõao. *As 10 Questões da Crise*. Dom Quixote, 2011.

Chang, Julia H. *Blood Novels: Gender, Caste, and Race in Spanish Realism.* University of Toronto Press, 2022.

Charnon-Deutsch, Lou. *The Spanish Gypsy.* Pennsylvania State University Press, 2004.

Cheng, Anne Anlin. *Ornamentalism.* Oxford University Press, 2019.

Clemente, Sansão Pereira Branco. "EPUL—Empresa Pública de Urbanização de Lisboa: Da reabilitação à regeneração urbana." Master's Thesis, Universidade Lusíada de Lisboa, 2013, 72.

Cócola-Gant, Agustín. "Holiday Rentals: The New Gentrification Battlefront." *Sociological Research Online* 21 (2016): 1–9.

Colegio Oficial de Arquitectos de Madrid (COAM). "Revista Urbanismo COAM." Accessed June 22, 2023. https://www.coam.org/es/fundacion/biblioteca/revista-urbanismo-coam.

Coleman, Jeffrey K. *The Necropolitical Theater: Race and Immigration on the Contemporary Spanish Stage.* Northwestern University Press, 2020.

Colmenarejo, Juan Pablo. "Crónica de la Crisis del Euro en España ¿Qué podemos aprender?" *Actualidad Económica* 30, no. 102 (2020): 35–49.

Colvin, Michael. "Gabriel de Oliveira's 'Há Festa Na Mouraria' and the 'Fado Novo's' Criticism of the Estado Novo's Demolition of the Baixa Mouraria." *Portuguese Studies* 20 (2004): 134–51.

Compitello Malcolm. "From Planning to Design: The Culture of Flexible Accumulation in Post-Cambio Madrid." *Arizona Journal of Hispanic Cultural Studies* 3, no. 1 (1999): 199–219.

Compitello Malcolm. "Designing Madrid, 1985–1997." *Cities* 20, no. 6 (2003): 403–11.

Compitello Malcolm. "A Good Plan Gone Bad, From Operation Atocha to the Gentrification of Lavapiés." *The International Journal of the Constructed Environment* 2, no. 2 (2012): 75–93.

Comunidad de Madrid. "Fiesta de las Mayas de la Comunidad de Madrid," April 28, 2023. https://www.comunidad.madrid/cultura/patrimonio-cultural/fiesta-mayas-comunidad-madrid.

Conrado Roza, José. *The Bridal Masquerade.* 1788.

Corkill, David, and José Carlos Pina Almeida. "Commemoration and Propaganda in Salazar's Portugal: The 'Mundo Português' Exposition of 1940." *Journal of Contemporary History* 44, no. 3 (July 2009): 381–99.

Coronado, Jorge. *Portraits in the Andes: Photography and Agency, 1900–1950.* University of Pittsburgh Press, 2018.

"CSROA La Quimera." *15Mpedia*. Accessed July 10, 2023. //15mpedia.org/wiki/CSROA_La_Quimera.

Crais, Clifton C., and Pamela Scully. *Sara Baartman and the Hottentot Venus: A Ghost Story and a Biography*. Princeton University Press, 2009.

Crenshaw, Kimberlé. "Demarginalizing the Intersection of Race and Sex: A Black Feminist Critique of Antidiscrimination Doctrine, Feminist Theory, and Antiracist Politics." *University of Chicago Legal Forum* 1989, no. Article 8 (1989).

Crenshaw, Kimberlé. "Mapping the Margins: Intersectionality, Identity Politics, and Violence against Women of Color." *Stanford Law Review* 43, no. 6 (July 1991): 1241.

Dainotto, Roberto M. *Europe (in Theory)*. Duke University Press, 2006.

Diário de Notícias. "Alcindo Monteiro morreu há 25 anos. Uma vítima do racismo." June 10, 2020. Accessed July 26, 2023.

DeCerteau, Michel. *The Practice of Everyday Life*. Translated by Stephen Rendall. University of California Press, 1984.

Delaunay, Morgane. "Portugal e o regresso dos colonos de Angola e Moçambique." *Cidades: Comunidades e territórios*, no. 44 (June 15, 2022). https://journals.openedition.org/cidades/5728.

Deleuze, Giles, and Felix Guattari. *New Mappings in Politics, Philosophy, and Culture*. Edited by Eleanor Kaufman and Kevin Jon Heller. University of Minnesota Press, 1987.

Delgado Labrandero, Paula. "Renace el céntrico Mercado de San Antón" *El Mundo*, May 17, 2011. https://www.elmundo.es/elmundo/2011/05/17/madrid/1305633400.html.

Delgado Ruíz, Manuel. *La ciudad mentirosa: Fraude y miseria del "modelo Barcelona."* Catarata, 2009.

Delgado Ruíz, Manuel. "La ciudad levantada. La barricada y otras transformaciones radicales del espacio urbano." *Arquitectonics: Mind, Land and Society*, Hacia un urbanismo alternativo, no. 19–20 (2010): 137–53.

Día. "Nuestra Historia." Accessed June 5, 2023. https://diacorporate.com/nuestra-historia/.

Diario ABC. "El origen popular del traje de chulapo, una indumentaria con gran recorrido histórico," May 14, 2014. https://www.abc.es/madrid/gente-estilo/20140514/abci-origen-significado-indumentaria-chulapa-201405091055.html.

Dias Coelho, Beatriz, and Rita Pereira Carvalho. "Vida a polémicas do Martim Moniz." *Jornal i*, n.d. https://ionline.sapo.pt/especiais/vida-e-polemicas-do-martim-moniz.

Dias Felner, Ricardo. "Cerco ao Martim Moniz." *Público*, June 19, 1999. https://www.publico.pt/1999/06/19/jornal/cerco-ao-martim-moniz-135077.

Díaz Orueta, Fernando. "Madrid: Urban Regeneration Projects and Social Mobilization." *Cities* 24, no. 3 (2007).

Domingo de Carnaval. Directed by Edgar Neville, 1945.

Domínguez, Quaglieri, Alan, and Antonio Paolo Russo. "Paisajes urbanos en la época post-turística. Propuesta de un marco analítico." *Scripta nova* 14, no. 323 (May 2010). http://www.ub.edu/geocrit/sn/sn-323.htm.

Donovan, Mary Kate. "'Se ríen de la crisis': Chinese Immigration as Economic Invasion in Spanish Film and Media." *Revista de estudios hispánicos* 51 (2017): 369–93.

Donovan, Mary Kate. "Memory and Migrant Solidarity in Icíar Bollaín's *En tierra extraña.*" *Journal of Spanish Cultural Studies* 21, no. 4 (October 1, 2020): 547–64.

Douglas, Mary. *Purity and Danger: An Analysis of Concepts of Pollution and Taboo.* Routledge, 1966.

Du Bois, W. E. B. *Black Reconstruction in America: Toward a History of the Part Which Black Folk Played in the Attempt to Reconstruct Democracy in America, 1860–1880.* Transaction Publishers, 2013.

Earle, Rebecca. "The Pleasures of Taxonomy: Casta Paintings, Classification, and Colonialism." *The William and Mary Quarterly* 73, no. 3 (2016): 428.

Eco, Umberto. *Travels in Hyperreality.* Mariner Books, 1990.

"ECRI Report on Portugal." Strasbourg: Council of Europe, 2013. https://www.refworld.org/docid/51dd50db4.html.

El País. "El nuevo-viejo San Antón." July 18, 2007, sec. Actualidad. https://elpais.com/elpais/2007/07/18/actualidad/1184746627_850215.html.

"Embajadores and Euljiro Are on the List of Time Out's Coolest Neighbourhoods Right Now – Hackney and Williamsburg Are Not." Accessed September 26, 2024. https://www.timeout.com/about/latest-news/embajadores-and-euljiro-are-on-the-list-of-time-outs-coolest-neighbourhoods-right-now-hackney-and-williamsburg-are-not-092018.

En tierra extraña. Directed by Icíar Bollaín, 2014.

Encinas Ferrer, Carlos, and Juan Tugores Ques, eds. *La crisis del euro y su impacto en la economía y la sociedad.* Economía UB 02. Universitat de Barcelona, Publicacions i Edicions, 2015.

Estevens, Ana, Augustín Cócola-Gant, Daniel Malet Calvo, and Filipe Matos. "Arts and Culture in Lisbon's Recent Revitalization: Observing Mouraria and Intendente Square through Alternative Local Initiatives as Drivers of Marginal Gentrification." *Interventions Économiques*, no. 63 (March 1, 2020). http://journals.openedition.org/interventionseconomiques/8647.

"Estudo sobre novas dinâmicas residenciais económicas e urbanísticas no centro histórico de Lisboa," *Quaternaire Portugal*, June 2017. https://www.

jf-santamariamaior.pt/wp-content/uploads/2018/04/Enquadramento-e-diagnostico.pdf.

Europa Press. "El Mercado de San Miguel recibe unos 85.000 visitantes semanales, de los que un 40% son madrileños." Europa Press, April 14, 2013. https://www.europapress.es/madrid/noticia-mercado-san-miguel-recibe-85000-visitantes-semanales-40-son-madrilenos-20130414135018.html.

"Exposição de fotografia 'All Around Us' de Gonçalo Gaioso," *The Gentleman*, May 18, 2013. https://thegentleman.pt/2013/05/exposicao-de-fotografia-all-around-us-de-goncalo-gaioso.

Expósito, Cristina. "Lavapiés estrena centro de salud sobre el Mercado de San Fernando." *Madridiario*. Accessed June 28, 2023. https://www.madridiario.es/noticia/5791/centro/lavapies-estrena-centro-de-salud-sobre-el-mercado-de-san-fernando.html.

Fanon, Frantz. *Black Skin, White Masks*. Translated by Richard Philcox. Grove Press, 2008.

Feinberg, Matthew. "From Cigarreras to Indignados: Spectacles of Scale in the CSA La Tabacalera of Lavapiés, Madrid." *International Journal of Iberian Studies* 26, no. 1/2 (November 2013): 21–39.

Feinberg, Matthew. *From the Theater to the Plaza: Spectacle, Protest, and Urban Space in Twenty-First-Century Madrid*. McGill-Queen's University Press, 2022.

Feinberg, Matthew, and Susan Larson. "Cultivating the Square: Trash, Recycling, and the Cultural Ecology of Post-Crisis Madrid." In *Ethics of Life: Contemporary Iberian Debates*, edited by Katarzyna Olga Beilin and William Viestenz, 113–42. Vanderbilt University Press, 2016.

Feixa, Carles, and Jordi Nofre, eds. *#GeneraciónIndignada: Topías y utopías del 15M*. Primera edición. Ensayo Milenio 55. Milenio, 2013.

Fernández Maeso, Marta. "Renovar un mercado de barrio, versión Lavapiés." *El País*, March 30, 2012, sec. Madrid. https://elpais.com/ccaa/2012/03/29/madrid/1333045590_721372.html.

Fernández Navarrete, Donato. "La crisis económica española: Una gran operación especulativa con graves consecuencias." *Estudios internacionales (Santiago)* 48, no. 183 (January 2016): 119–51.

Fernández-Savater, Amador. "El nacimiento de un nuevo poder social." *Hispanic Review* 80, no. 4 (2012): 677.

Ferreira, Carles. "Vox como representante de la derecha radical en España: Un estudio sobre su ideología" *Revista española de ciencia política*, no. 51 (November 2019): 73–98.

Fikes, Kesha. *Managing African Portugal: The Citizen-Migrant Distinction*. Duke University Press, 2009.

Fleetwood, Nicole R. *Troubling Vision: Performance, Visuality, and Blackness.* University of Chicago Press, 2011.

Flesler, Daniela. *The Return of the Moor: Spanish Responses to Contemporary Moroccan Immigration.* Purdue University Press, 2008.

Flores de otro mundo. Directed by Icíar Bollaín, 1999.

Fraile, Octavio. "División entre los vecinos de Lavapiés por las cámaras de vigilancia." *20minutos*, December 20, 2009. https://www.20minutos.es/noticia/595015/0/division/lavapies/camaras.

Fra-Molinero, Baltasar. "The Suspect Whiteness of Spain." In *At Home and Abroad: Historicizing Twentieth-Century Whiteness in Literature and Performance*, edited by LaVinia Delois Jennings, 147–69. University of Tennessee Press, 2009.

Fraser, Benjamin. *Henri Lefebvre and the Spanish Urban Experience: Reading the Mobile City.* Bucknell University Press, with Rowman & Littlefield, 2011.

Fraser, Benjamin. *Toward an Urban Cultural Studies.* Palgrave Macmillan, 2015.

Freedman, Adrianna. "This Video of a Trainer Leading a Quarantine Workout Class Will Give You All the Feels." *Men's Health*, March 17, 2020. https://www.menshealth.com/entertainment/a31676138/trainer-spain-leads-quarantined-apartment-workout-coronavirus.

Freyre, Gilberto. *Casa-grande & Senzala.* 43 ed. Record, 2001.

Freyre, Gilberto. *O mundo que o português criou: aspectos das relações sociais e de cultura do Brasil com Portugal e as colônias portuguesas.* É Realizações Editora, 2010.

Furtado, Elsa, and Tânia Fernandes. "Mercado de Fusão do Martim Moniz recebe a exposição de Gonçalo Gaioso All Around Us." *CH - Magazine de Cultura, Lazer e Viagens*, May 17, 2013. https://chmagazine.pt/mercado-de-fusao-do-martim-moniz-recebe-a-exposicao-de-goncalo-gaioso-all-around-us/.

Fusco, Coco. "Racial Time, Racial Marks, Racial Metaphors." In *Only Skin Deep: Changing Visions of the American Self*, edited by Coco Fusco and Brian Wallis, 13–50. International Center of Photography in association with Harry N. Abrams, Inc, 2003.

Garcia-Ayllon, Salvador. "Urban Transformations as an Indicator of Unsustainability in the P2P Mass Tourism Phenomenon: The Airbnb Case in Spain through Three Case Studies." *Sustainability* 10 (2018): 1–21.

Gaspar, Sofia, and Fernando Ampudia de Haro. "Buying Citizenship? Chinese Golden Visa Migrants in Portugal." *International Migration* 58, no. 3 (June 1, 2020): 58–72.

getLISBON. "Fado in the Urban Art of Lisbon," June 2, 2021. https://getlisbon.com/discovering/fado-in-the-urban-art-of-lisbon.

Glass, Ruth. *London: Aspects of Change*. London: MacGibbon and Kee, 1964.

Góis, Pedro, and José Carlos Marques. "Retrato de um Portugal migrante: a evolução da emigração, da imigração e do seu estudo nos últimos 40 anos." *E-Cadernos CES*, no. 29 (June 15, 2018).

Gomes, Pedro. "The Birth of Public Space Privatization: How Entrepreneurialism, Convivial Urbanism and Stakeholder Interactions Made the Martim Moniz Square, in Lisbon, 'Privatization-Ready.'" *European Urban and Regional Studies* 27, no. 1 (2020): 86–100.

Gómez, Virginia. "La Policía detiene a seis personas en el desalojo de cuatro vecinas de Argumosa tras un año sin pagar." *El Mundo*, February 22, 2019, sec. Madrid. https://www.elmundo.es/madrid/2019/02/22/5c6fcodbfdddffoo628b4619.html.

Gonçalo Gaioso Photography. "About Gaioso." Accessed May 10, 2023. https://cargocollective.com/gaioso/about-gaioso.

Goode, Joshua. *Impurity of Blood: Defining Race in Spain, 1870–1930*. Louisiana State University Press, 2009.

Gottdiener, Mark. "Consumption of Space and Spaces of Consumption." *Architectural Design* 68 (1998): 12–15.

Govers, Robert, and Frank Go. *Place Branding: Glocal, Virtual and Physical Identities, Constructed, Imagined and Experienced*. Palgrave Macmillan, 2009.

Gray, Lila Ellen. *Fado Resounding: Affective Politics and Urban Life*. Duke University Press, 2014.

Grillo, Ralph. "Cultural Essentialism and Cultural Anxiety." *Anthropological Theory* 3 (2003): 157–73.

Güell, Oriol. "El 'súper' se come el mercado de Chueca." *El País*, July 27, 2006, sec. Madrid. https://elpais.com/diario/2006/07/28/madrid/1154085855_850215.html.

Guilherme, Carmen and Daniela Soares Ferreira. "Junta de Freguesia de Santa Maria Maior anuncia número de alerta para denunciar alojamento local ilegal." *Jornal SOL*. Accessed March 30, 2023. https://sol.sapo.pt/artigo/652675/junta-de-freguesia-de-santa-maria-maior-anuncia-n-mero-de-alerta-para-denunciar-alojamento-local-ilegal.

Hanna, Stephen, and Vincent Del Casino. "Beyond The 'Binaries': A Methodological Intervention for Interrogating Maps as Representational Practices." *ACME: An International E-Journal for Critical Geographies* 4, no. 1 (2005): 34–56.

Hannigan, John. *Fantasy City: Pleasure and Profit in the Postmodern Metropolis*. Routledge, 1998.

Harvey, David. "From Managerialism to Entrepreneurialism: The Transformation in Urban Governance in Late Capitalism." *Geografiska Annaler: Series B, Human Geography* 71, no. 1 (April 1989): 3–17.

Harvey, David. "The Art of Rent: Globalisation, Monopoly and the Commodification of Culture." *Socialist Register* 38 (2002): 93–110.

Harvey, David. *The New Imperialism*. Oxford University Press, 2003.

Harvey, David. *Social Justice and the City*. 2nd ed. University of Georgia Press, 2009.

Harvey, David. *Rebel Cities: From the Right to the City to the Urban Revolution*. Verso, 2012.

Hawthorne, Camilla. "Black Matters Are Spatial Matters: Black Geographies for the Twenty-first Century." *Geography Compass* 13, no. 11 (November 2019).

Heng, Geraldine. *The Invention of Race in the European Middle Ages*. Cambridge University Press, 2018.

Hering Torres, Max S. "La limpieza de sangre. Problemas de interpretación: acercamientos históricos y metodológicos." *Historia Crítica* 45 (2011): 32–55.

Hill Collins, Patricia. *Intersectionality as Critical Social Theory*. Duke University Press, 2019.

Hirsch, Marianne. *Family Frames: Photography, Narrative, and Postmemory*. Harvard University Press, 1997.

"Historia." *Mercado Municipal de San Fernando*, n.d. https://mercadodesanfernando.es/historia.

Hobson, Janell. *Venus in the Dark: Blackness and Beauty in Popular Culture*. Routledge, 2018.

Holleran, Max. "Buying Up the Semi-Periphery: Spain's Economy of 'Golden Visas.'" *Ethnos: Journal of Anthropology* 86, no. 4 (October 2021): 730–49.

Holmes, Rachel. *African Queen: The Real Life of the Hottentot Venus*. Random House, 2006.

Holmes, Rachel. *The Hottentot Venus: The Life and Death of Saartjie Baartman: Born 1789–Buried 2002*. London: Bloomsbury, 2008.

hooks, bell. "Selling Hot Pussy." In *Black Looks: Race and Representation*, 61–77. South End Press, 1992.

"Hombre atracado y apuñalado, presuntamente, por un súbdito marroquí." *El País*, July 22, 1981, sec. Madrid. https://elpais.com/diario/1981/07/22/madrid/364649061_850215.html.

Iannone, Catalina. "Invented Difference: On Inter-Culturality in Mouraria's Mercado de Fusão." *Journal of Lusophone Studies*, September 2017, 101–21.

Imagineers. *Walt Disney Imagineering: A Behind the Dreams Look at Making the Magic Real*. Hyperion, 1996.

"Imigração preocupa o bairro da Mouraria," *Jornal de Notícias*. April 11, 1999.

"Informe Raxen: Racismo, Xenofobia, Antisemitismo, Islamofobia, Neofascismo, Homofobia y otras manifestaciones relacionadas de Intolerancia a través de los hechos." Movimiento contra la Intolerancia, 2010. http://www.movimientocontralaintolerancia.com/html/raxen/raxen.asp.

Instagram. "@porfavorhh." Accessed July 31, 2023. https://www.instagram.com/porfavorhh/.

Instagram. "Time Out Travel on Instagram," September 19, 2018. https://www.instagram.com/p/Bn5uF--j6Me/.

Janer, Zilkia. "(IN)EDIBLE NATURE: New World Food and Coloniality." *Cultural Studies* 21, no. 2–3 (March 2007): 385–405.

Jefatura de Estadio. "Ley 51/1982, de 13 de julio, de modificación de los artículos 17 al 26 de Código Civil." BOE, July 1982. https://www.boe.es/eli/es/l/1982/07/13/51.

John, Matt St. "Remembering Spain's First Official Hate Crime." *El País English*, June 23, 2017. https://english.elpais.com/elpais/2017/06/23/trans_iberian/1498204402_391675.html.

José. "Buardilla Con Encanto En Lavapiés." Accessed September 15, 2020. https://www.airbnb.com/rooms/11731488/location?location=Madrid%2C%20Spain&check_in=2020-09-15&check_out=2020-09-26&source_impression_id=p3_1598366518_sgIQWmPvaRRZij8y.

"José Filipe, o nome por trás da nova cena cultural de Lisboa." In *Lux/Good: Tudo sobre turismo na nova cena de Lisboa*, 2012. http://luxgood.blogspot.com/2012/09/jose-filipe-o-nome-por-tras-da-nova.html.

Juliá, Santos, David R. Ringrose, and Cristina Segura. *Madrid: Historia de una capital*. Alianza Editorial: Fundación Caja de Madrid, 1994.

Juste, Ángel. "Mercados minoristas tradicionales. La remodelación necesaria." *Distribución y consumo*, no. 11 (1993): 10–26.

Justino, David. "Emigration from Portugal: Old Wine in New Bottles?" Migration Policy Institute, February 2016. http://www.migrationpolicy.org/research/emigration-portugal-old-wine-new-bottles.

Kalter, Christoph. *Postcolonial People: The Return from Africa and the Remaking of Portugal*. Cambridge University Press, 2022.

Katzew, Ilona. *Casta Painting: Images of Race in Eighteenth-Century Mexico*. Yale University Press, 2004.

Keil Amaral, Francisco. *Lisboa: uma cidade em transformação*. Publicações Europa-América, 1969.

Kim, Yeon-Soo. *The Family Album: Histories, Subjectivities, and Immigration in Contemporary Spanish Culture*. Bucknell University Press, 2005.

Kirshenblatt-Gimblett, Barbara. *Destination Culture: Tourism, Museums, and Heritage*. University of California Press, 1998.

Labanyi, Jo. "Miscegenation, Nation Formation and Cross-Racial Identifications in the Early Francoist Folkloric Film Musical," in *Hybridity and Its Discontents: Politics, Science, Culture*, edited by Avtar Brah and Annie Coombes, 56–71. Taylor and Francis, 2000.

La playa de Madrid. "El Mercado de San Fernando." Accessed July 31, 2023. http://www.laplayademadrid.es/archives/4896.

La Vanguardia. "Más de 11 de años de prisión por el crimen que desencadenó los incidentes racistas en El Ejido." October 21, 2003, sec. Sociedad. https://www.lavanguardia.com/vida/20031021/51262782855/mas-de-11-de-anos-de-prision-por-el-crimen-que-desencadeno-los-incidentes-racistas-en-el-ejido.html.

La Vanguardia. "El mantero Mame Mbaye no murió por la persecución policial en Lavapiés." April 22, 2019. https://www.lavanguardia.com/local/madrid/20190422/461782142437/mantero-mbaye-lavapies-no-murio-persecucion-policial.html.

Larson, Susan. "Shifting Modern Identities in Madrid's Recent Urban Planning, Architecture and Narrative." *Cities* 20, no. 6 (2003): 395–402.

Laska, Shirley Bradway, and Daphne Spain, eds. *Back to the City: Issues in Neighborhood Renovation*. Pergamon Policy Studies on Urban Affairs. Pergamon Press, 1980.

Lavapiés ¿dónde vas? "Manifestación por los derechos del turista." n.d. https://lavapiesdondevas.wordpress.com/miercoles/manifestacion-internacional-por-los-derechos-del-turista.

Lee, Dayne. "How Airbnb Short-Term Rentals Exacerbate Los Angeles' Affordable Housing Crisis: Analysis and Policy Recommendations." *Harvard Law and Policy Review* 10, no. 1 (2016): 229–53.

Lees, Loretta, Hyun Bang Shin, and Ernesto López-Morales. *Global Gentrifications: Uneven Development and Displacement*. Policy Press, 2015.

Lefebvre, Henri. *The Production of Space*. Translated by Donald Nicholson-Smith. Blackwell Publishing, 1991.

Lestegás, Iago. "Lisbon After the Crisis: From Credit-Fuelled Suburbanization to Tourist-Driven Gentrification." *International Journal of Urban and Regional Research* 43, no. 4 (July 1, 2019): 705–23.

Leston Bandeira, Mário. "Dinâmicas demográficas e envelhecimento da população portuguesa." *Fundação Francisco Manuel dos Santos*, March 4, 2015. https://www.ffms.pt/pt-pt/estudos/dinamicas-demograficas-envelhecimento-da-populacao-portuguesa.

Ley, Marta. "Así se vacía un barrio por culpa de la gentrificación: el caso de Lavapiés." *El Mundo*, June 8, 2017. https://www.elmundo.es/grafico/madrid/2017/08/06/596cdf3ee2704e07148b45eb.html.

"Ley Orgánica 4/2015, de 30 de marzo, de protección de la seguridad ciudadana," n.d. https://www.boe.es/eli/es/lo/2015/03/30/4.

"Ley Orgánica 5/2002, de 27 de junio, sobre drogodependencias y otros trastornos adictivos," n.d. https://www.boe.es/eli/es-md/l/2002/06/27/5

"Lista de asambleas de la Comunidad de Madrid." *15Mpedia*. Accessed May 31, 2023. //15mpedia.org/wiki/Lista_de_asambleas_de_la_Comunidad_de_Madrid.

"Lisbon's Hippest Neighborhood: A Pocket Guide to Mouraria." *Suitcase: The Culture of Travel*, 2018. https://suitcasemag.com/articles/lisbons-hippest-neighbourhood-mouraria.

López de Lera, Diego. "La inmigración en España a fines del siglo XX. Los que vienen a trabajar y los que vienen a descansar," *Reis*, no. 71/72 (1995): 225–45.

lookmagpt. "À conversa com José Filipe Rebelo Pinto." *LOOKmag* (blog), September 13, 2016. https://lookmag.pt/blog/conversa-jose-filipe-rebelo-pinto.

López de Lucio, Ramón, Francisco Javier González, Emilio Parrilla Gorbea, Javier Ruiz Sánchez, and Teresa Ruiz Sánchez. "Centros urbanos frente a nuevas centralidades comerciales. Un análisis del sur metropolitano de Madrid." *Cuadernos de investigación urbanística*, no. 14 (September 1, 1996).

López López, Ángel. "Historia de Lavapiés. El latido de Madrid que resiste a lo largo del tiempo." *El salto diario*, August 8, 2019. https://www.elsaltodiario.com/laplaza/historia-origen-barrio-lavapies-madrid.

Loureiro, Ángel. "Spanish Nationalism and the Ghost of Empire." *Journal of Spanish Cultural Studies* 4, no. 1 (2003): 65–76.

Lukas, Scott A. "The Themed Space: Locating Culture, Nation, and Self." In *The Themed Space: Locating Culture, Nation, and Self*. Edited by Scott Lukas, 75–95. Lexington Books, 2007.

Lusa. "Número de Licenciados a Emigrar Aumentou 49,5% Entre 2009 e 2011." *Público*, March 1, 2012, https://www.publico.pt/2012/03/01/economia/noticia/numero-de-licenciados-a-emigrar-aumentou-495-entre-2009-e-2011-1535996.

Lusa. "Cordão humano pede suspensão imediata de obras no Martim Moniz." *Diário de Notícias*, February 2, 2019. https://www.dn.pt/pais/cordao-humano-pede-suspensao-imediata-de-obras-no-martim-moniz-10527989.html.

Maeztu, Ramiro de. *Defensa de la hispanidad*. ePubLibre, 1934. http://archive.org/details/de-maeztu-ramiro.-defensa-de-la-hispanidad-1934-2014.

Maiello, Vincenzo. "El mercado de los mercados: Análisis de los procesos de transformación de los mercados municipales de abastos de Madrid." Grupo de trabajo mercados y espacios públicos ASF-Madrid, 2014.

Malheiros, Jorge, and Alina Esteves. "Diagnóstico da população imigrante em Portugal: Desafios e potencialidades." Lisbon: Alto Comissariado para a Imigração e Diálogo Intercultural, 2013.

Marcilhacy, David. "La Hispanidad bajo el franquismo : El americanismo al servicio de un proyecto nacionalista." In *Imaginarios y representaciones de España durante el franquismo*, edited by Stéphane Michonneau and Xosé M. Núñez-Seixas, 73–102. Casa de Velázquez, 2014.

Marco. "Charming and Traditional Lisbon Apartment," n.d. https://www.airbnb.com/rooms/19671102?check_in=2020-10-15&check_out=2020-10-22&source_impression_id=p3_1599749435_NVfmCxneyPW%2BZgKT.

"Martim Moniz com 'nova vida.'" *Jornal Expresso*, June 8, 2012. www.cmjornal.pt/cultura/detalhe/martim-moniz-com-nova-vida.

Martín-Cabrera, Luis. "Postcolonial Memories and Racial Violence in *Flores de otro mundo*." *Journal of Spanish Cultural Studies* 3, no. 1 (January 1, 2002): 43–56.

Martin-Márquez, Susan. *Disorientations: Spanish Colonialism in Africa and the Performance of Identity*. Yale University Press, 2008.

Massey, Doreen. *Space, Place, and Gender*. University of Minnesota Press, 1994.

Matias, Ana. "Imagens e estereótipos da sociedade portuguesa sobre a comunidade chinesa. Interacção multissecular via Macau," 2007. https://repositorio.iscte-iul.pt/handle/10071/1270.

Matias Ferreira, Vítor, and Francesco Indovina. *A Cidade da Expo'98*. Bizancia, 1999.

Maurício, Fernando. "O meu bairro" n.d.

Mbembe, Achille. *Necropolitics*. Duke University Press, 2019.

McClintock, Anne. *Imperial Leather: Race, Gender, and Sexuality in the Colonial Contest*. Routledge, 1995.

Mendes, Luís. "Gentrification and the New Urban Social Movements in Times of Post-Capitalist Crisis and Austerity Urbanism in Portugal." *Arizona Journal of Hispanic Cultural Studies* 22 (2018): 199–215.

Mendes, Luís. "Bye Bye Lisbon: Tourism Gentrification Impacts on Lisbon´s Inner-City Housing Market." In *Advances in Hospitality, Tourism, and the Services Industry*, edited by Cláudia Ribeiro de Almeida, Alfred Quintano, Moisés Simancas, Raquel Huete, and Zélia Breda, 136–55. IGI Global, 2020.

Mendes, Mariana S. "'Enough' of What? An Analysis of Chega's Populist Radical Right Agenda." *South European Society & Politics* 26, no. 3 (September 2021): 329–53.

Mendes, Mariana S., and James Dennison. "Explaining the Emergence of the Radical Right in Spain and Portugal: Salience, Stigma and Supply." *West European Politics* 44, no. 4 (January 1, 2021): 752–75.

Menezes, Marluci. *Mouraria, retalhos de um imaginário: Significados urbanos de um bairro de Lisboa*. Celta, 2004.

Menezes, Marluci. "A praça do Martim Moniz: Etnografando lógicas socioculturais de inscrição da praça no mapa social de Lisboa." *Horizontes Antropológicos* 15, no. 32 (2009): 306.

Mercado de Fusão. "OPEN AIR CINEMA - MARTIM MONIZ." Facebook, 2013. https://www.facebook.com/events/mercado-fus%C3%A3o-martim-moniz/open-air-cinema-martim-moniz-lan%C3%A7amento-4-de-setembro/581968781841377/.

Mercado de San Fernando. "Asociación de comerciantes - Mercado de San Fernando," May 26, 2017. https://web.archive.org/web/20170526213126/http://www.mercadodesanfernando.es:80/asociacion-de-comerciantes/.

Mercado de San Fernando. "Los Puestos," June 15, 2015. https://web.archive.org/web/20150615002616/http://www.mercadodesanfernando.es/category/los-puestos/.

Mercado de San Miguel. "About Us," n.d. https://mercadodesanmiguel.es/en/#about-us.

"Migrantour Sustainable Routes," n.d. http://www.migrantour.org/en/migrantour-sustainable-routes.

Ministério da Economia e da Inovação. *Plano Estratégico Nacional do Turismo: Para o desenvolvimento do turismo em Portugal*, 2007. https://web.archive.org/web/20070307211048/http://www.dgturismo.pt/stellent/groups/publico/documents/conhecimento/id_006806.pdf.

Ministerio para la Transición Ecológica y el Reto Demográfico. "¿Qué es el Reto Demográfico?" Accessed November 28, 2022. https://www.miteco.gob.es/es/reto-demografico/temas/que-es/.

Mirzoeff, Nicholas. *The Right to Look: A Counterhistory of Visuality*. Duke University Press, 2011.

Mirzoeff, Nicholas. *How to See the World*. Basic Books, 2015.

Mitchell, Don. *The Right to the City: Social Justice and the Fight for Public Space*. Guilford Press, 2003.

Montse. "Sunny & Spacious room in Central Madrid," n.d. https://www.airbnb.com/rooms/2254525?check_in=2022-01-07&check_out=2022-01-09&guests=1&adults=1&s=67&unique_share_id=8d0bd437-e3b4-4980-bb5c-0d7df9a46d67.

Moreno-Caballud, Luis. *Cultures of Anyone: Studies on Cultural Democratization in the Spanish Neoliberal Crisis*. Liverpool University Press, 2015.

Moskowitz, P. E. *How to Kill a City: Gentrification, Inequality, and the Fight for the Neighborhood*. Nation Books, 2017.

Mota Santos, Paula. "The Imagined Nation: The Mystery of the Endurance of the Colonial Imaginary in Postcolonial Times." In *Tourism Imaginaries:*

Anthropological Approaches, edited by Noel Salazar and Nelson Graburn, 194–219. Berghahn, 2014.

Muévome. "Origen de la fiesta de la Maya," April 11, 2011. https://web.archive.org/web/20140118045228/http://www.muevome.com/2011/04/origen-de-la-fiesta-de-la-maya.html.

Município de Lisboa. "Núcleo Histórico da Mouraria." Accessed January 25, 2024. https://www.lisboa.pt/temas/urbanismo/planeamento-urbano/planos-de-urbanizacao/detalhe/nucleo-historico-da-mouraria.

Murray, N. Michelle. *Home Away from Home: Immigrant Narratives, Domesticity, and Coloniality in Contemporary Spanish Culture*. University of North Carolina Press, 2018.

Naím, Moisés. "El Plan B: 700 millones desean emigrar." *El País*, February 21, 2010.

NCS Produção, Som e Video. "Mercado de Fusão," 2013. https://web.archive.org/web/20130611060202/http://www.ncs.pt/mercadodefusao.php.

Neely, Brooke, and Michelle Samura. "Social Geographies of Race: Connecting Race and Space." *Ethnic and Racial Studies* 34, no. 11 (November 2011): 1933–52.

Nelson, Steve. "Walt Disney's EPCOT and the World's Fair Performance Tradition." *The Drama Review: TDR* 30, no. 4 (1986): 106–46.

Nirenberg, David. *Was There Race before Modernity? The Example of "Jewish" Blood in Late Medieval Spain*. University of Chicago Press, 2014.

Nuno. "Capelão 15 - 20," n.d. https://www.airbnb.com/rooms/28556083?check_in=2022-11-18&check_out=2022-11-20&guests=1&adults=1&s=67&unique_share_id=ad95a68c-883e-4d0a-9207-a5525c2f4196.

Nye, Joseph S. "Soft Power." *Foreign Policy*, no. 80 (1990): 153–71.

Observatorio Metropolitano. *La apuesta municipalista: La democracia empieza por lo cercano*. Traficantes de Sueños, 2023. https://traficantes.net/libros/la-apuesta-municipalista.

Observatorio Metropolitano. *Paisajes devastados: Después del ciclo inmobiliario: Impactos regionales y urbanos de la crisis*. Traficantes de Sueños, 2013.

Observatorio sobre Crises e Alternativas. "A anatomia da crise: Identificar os problemas para construir as alternativas." Centro de Estudos Socias Laboratório Associado: Universidade de Coimbra, 2013.

Oldenburg, Ray. *The Great Good Place: Cafes, Coffee Shops, Bookstores, Bars, Hair Salons, and Other Hangouts at the Heart of a Community*. Da Capo Press, 1999.

Omi, Michael, and Howard Winant. *Racial Formation in the United States*, 3rd ed. Routledge, 2015.

Ossos. Directed by Pedro Costa, 1997.

Palomeque, Eulalia Ruiz, Enrique Rivera Pozo, and Maria Luisa de Lázaro y Torres. "Nuevas formas de comercio y consumo en Madrid: las grandes superficies." *Estudios Geográficos* 61, no. 238 (March 1, 2000): 125–44.

Palos-Sánchez, Pedro, and Marisol Correia. "The Collaborative Economy Based Analysis of Demand: Study of Airbnb Case in Spain and Portugal." *Journal of Theoretical and Applied Electronic Commerce Research* 13, no. 3 (September 2018): 85–98.

Parsons, Deborah. *A Cultural History of Madrid: Modernism and the Urban Spectacle*. Berg, 2003.

Patton, Pamela, ed. *Envisioning Others: Race, Color, and the Visual in Iberia and Latin America*. Brill, 2015.

Patton, Pamela. *Blackness, Whiteness, and the Idea of Race in Medieval European Art*. Fordham University Press, 2019.

Peluso, Nancy. "Whose Woods Are These? Counter-Mapping Forest Territories in Kalimantan, Indonesia." *Antipode* 27, 4 (October 1995): 383–406.

Pereira dos Santos, Jõao, Duarte Gonçalves, and Susana Peralta. "Short-Term Rental Bans and Housing Prices: Quasi-Experimental Evidence from Lisbon." Discussion Paper Series. ISEG- University of Lisbon: IZA Institute of Labor Economics, 2022.

Pérez Galdós, Benito. *Misericordia*, 19th ed. Edited by Luciano García Lorenzo. Cátedra, 2016.

Pérez López, Laura. "Exiliados argentinos en la España de la transición: La imagen de un diario español (*El País*)." In *Actas del IV Simposio de Historia Actual: Logroño, 17–19 de octubre de 2002*, 893–914. Instituto de Estudios Riojanos, 2004.

Pincha, Jõao Pedro. "Há 17 famílias num prédio da Mouraria que vão ficar sem casa." *Público*, February 22, 2017. https://www.publico.pt/2017/02/22/local/noticia/ha-17-familias-que-vao-ficar-sem-casa-num-predio-da-mouraria-1762862.

Pincha, Jõao Pedro. "Casa cheia disse 'não' aos contentores no Martim Moniz." *Público*, November 21, 2018. https://www.publico.pt/2018/11/21/local/noticia/casa-cheia-nao-contentores-martim-moniz-1851848.

Pincha, Jõao Pedro. "'Queremos um jardim,' gritou-se no Martim Moniz." *Público*, February 2, 2019. https://www.publico.pt/2019/02/02/local/noticia/queremos-jardim-gritouse-martim-moniz-1860498.

Pinho, Filipa, and Rui Pena Pires. "Espanha." Observatório da Emigração, 2013.

Poole, Deborah. *Vision, Race, and Modernity*. Princeton University Press, 1997.

Poole, Deborah. "An Excess of Description: Ethnography, Race, and Visual Technologies." *Annual Review of Anthropology* 34 (2005): 159–79.

Prádanos, Luis I. *Postgrowth Imaginaries: New Ecologies and Counterhegemonic Culture in Post-2008 Spain*. Liverpool University Press, 2018.

Presidencia del Gobierno. "Real Decreto 998/2012, de 28 de junio, por el que se crea el Alto Comisionado del Gobierno para la Marca España y se modifica el Real Decreto 1412/2000, de 21 de julio, de creación del Consejo de Política Exterior," Pub. L. No. Real Decreto 998/2012, § 1, BOE-A-2012-8672 46129 (2012). https://www.boe.es/eli/es/rd/2012/06/28/998.

Prior, Helder. "Populismo de Direita radical em Portugal." *Media&Jornalismo* 22, no. 40 (May 1, 2022): 161–77.

Pritchard, Stephen. "Artwashing: Social Capital and Anti-Gentrification Activism." *Colouring in Culture*, June 17, 2017. https://colouringinculture.org/uncategorized/artwashingsocialcapitalantigentrification.

Pulido, Sandra. "España confirma su primer caso de coronavirus." *Gaceta Médica*, January 31, 2020. https://gacetamedica.com/investigacion/espana-confirma-su-primer-caso-de-coronavirus/.

Puxeu Rocamora, Josep. "Remodelación de mercados tradicionales. Modernización comercial y rehabilitación urbana." *Distribución y consumo*, no. 11 (1993): 32–35.

Quijano, Aníbal. "Coloniality of Power and Eurocentrism in Latin America." *International Sociology* 15, no. 2 (June 1, 2000): 215–32.

Quijano, Aníbal. "Coloniality and Modernity/Rationality." *Cultural Studies* 21, no. 2–3 (2007): 168–78.

Ramiro, Pedro. *Marca España: ¿a quién beneficia?* Icaria, 2014.

Ramos López, Paula. "Evolución tipológica del mercado de abastos en Madrid." Universidad Politécnica de Madrid, 2020.

Rêgo, Cacilda, and Marcus Brasileiro, eds. *Migration in Lusophone Cinema.* Palgrave Macmillan, 2014.

Relph, Edward. *Place and Placelessness.* Pion, 1976.

Répide, Pedro de. *Las calles de Madrid*, 4th ed. Afrodisio Aguado, 1981.

Repinecz, Martin. *Volatile Whiteness.* University of Toronto Press, 2025.

Ribeiro, António Pinto. "Para acabar de vez com a lusofonia." *Lusotopie* 17, no. 2 (2018): 220–26.

Riesco-Sanz, Alberto. "Empresarialidad inmigrante: inmigración y comercio en Embajadores/Lavapiés." In *Barrios multiculturales: Relaciones interétnicas en los barrios de San Francisco (Bilbao) y Embajadores/Lavapiés (Madrid)*, edited by Alfonso Pérez Agote, Benjamín Tejerina, and Margarita Barañano, 260–79. Editorial Trotta, 2010.

Ritzer, George, and Allan Liska. "'McDisneyization' and Post-Tourism': Complementary Perspectives on Contemporary Tourism." In *Touring Cultures: Transformations of Travel and Theory*, edited by Chris Rojek and John Urry, 96–112. Routledge, 1997.

Robbins, Jill. "La mujer en el umbral. La simbología de la madre en la poesía de Ángela Figuera." *Anales de la literatura española contemporánea* 25, no. 2 (2000): 557–85.

Robbins, Jill. *Poetry and Crisis: Cultural Politics and Citizenship in the Wake of the Madrid Bombings*. University of Toronto Press, 2019.

Robles, Juan Ignacio. "Comercio urbano en espacios metropolitanos: Mercados, vidas y barrios." *Distribución y consumo* 22 (2008): 19–31.

Robles, Juan Ignacio. "El Mercado de San Miguel. Madrid." *Distribución y consumo* 21, no. 11 (2011): 103–6.

Robles, Juan Ignacio. "Mercado de San Antón. Madrid." *Distribución y consumo* 81, no. 5 (2013): 77–82.

Rodrigues, Irene de Assunção. "Flows of Fortune: The Economy of Chinese Migration to Portugal." PhD diss., Universidade de Lisboa, 2012.

Rodrigues, Leonardo, Francisco Silva, and Tiago Lopes. "Alojamento local no centro histórico da cidade de Lisboa:" *Finisterra*, May 19, 2022, 65–86.

Rodrigues, Nuno Miguel Duarte. "Intervenções, espacialidades e relações de poder: O caso da praça do Martim Moniz." Instituto Universitário de Lisboa and Universidade Nova de Lisboa, 2014.

Rodrigues, Teresa. *Nascer e morrer na Lisboa oitocentista: migrações, mortalidade e desenvolvimento*. Cosmos história 10. Edições Cosmos, 1995.

Rodrigues, Teresa. *Cinco séculos de quotidiano: a vida em Lisboa do século XV aos nossos dias*. Cosmos história 20. Edições Cosmos, 1997.

Rodríguez Ibáñez, Margarita. "La Cultura Localizada como respuesta social a la Red: El caso de la Fábrica de la Tabacalera en Madrid." *E-RPH*, no. 14 (October 1, 2015).

Rodríguez Sebastián, Alejandro. "Los nuevos mercados municipales de Madrid." *Working Paper Series Contested Cities*, March 25, 2014, 2.

Roelofsen, Maartje, and Claudio Minca. "The Superhost: Biopolitics, Home and Community in the Airbnb Dream-World of Global Hospitality." *Geoforum* 91 (2018): 170–81.

Roh, David, Betsy Huang, and Greta Niu. "Technologizing Orientalism." In *Techno-Orientalism: Imagining Asia in Speculative Fiction, History, and Media*, edited by David Roh, Betsy Huang, and Greta Niu, 1–20. Rutgers University Press, 2015.

"Rua dos Lagares." *Museo de los desplazados*. Accessed May 25, 2023. https://www.lefthandrotation.com/museodelosdesplazados/colaboraciones/habita-rua-dos-lagares/.

Ruiz, María Isabel Romero. "Black States of Desire: Josephine Baker, Identity and the Sexual Black Body." *Revista de Estudios Norteamericanos* 16 (2012): 125–39.

Russo, Paolo, and Greg Richards. *Reinventing the Local in Tourism: Producing, Consuming and Negotiating Place*. Channel View Publications, 2016.

Sadlier, Darlene J. *The Portuguese-Speaking Diaspora: Seven Centuries of Literature and the Arts*. University of Texas Press, 2016.

Said, Edward W. *Orientalism*. Vintage Books, 1979.

"Salut aísla a unas 25 personas por el primer caso de coronavirus en Catalunya." *La Vanguardia*, February 25, 2020. https://www.lavanguardia.com/vida/20200225/473782485232/coronavirus-primer-caso-cataluna.html.

Sánchez Fuarros, Iñigo. "'Ai, Mouraria!' Music, Tourism, and Urban Renewal in a Historic Lisbon Neighbourhood." *MUSICultures* 43, no. 2 (2016): 66–88.

Sambricio, Carlos. "La vivienda en Madrid, de 1939 al Plan de Vivienda Social en 1959." In *La vivienda en Madrid en la década de los cincuenta: El Plan de Urgencia Social*, 13–83. Electa, 1999.

Santaolalla, Isabel. *Los "otros": Etnicidad y "raza" en el cine español contemporáneo*. Prensas Universitarias de Zaragoza, 2005.

Sapega, Ellen. *Consensus and Debate in Salazar's Portugal: Visual and Literary Negotiations of the National Text 1933–1948*. Pennsylvania State University Press, 2008.

Sapega, Ellen. "Remembering Empire/Forgetting the Colonies: Accretions of Memory and the Limits of Commemoration in a Lisbon Neighborhood." *History and Memory* 20, no. 2 (2008): 18–38.

Saraiva, Nuno. *Cavaleiros do correio-mor*. 2015. Travessa da Mata.

Saraiva, Nuno. *Filigrana*. 2018. Largo São Carlos.

Saraiva, Nuno. *Nelson Mandela Centenário—E nunca esquecer onde Portugal esteve em 1987 e 1989*. 2018. Rua Dr Jõao Soares.

Saraiva, Nuno. *Porta 21*. 2020. Rua de São Cristóvão.

Schneider, Leann G. "Capturing Otherness on Canvas: 16th–18th Century European Representation of Amerindians and Africans." MA thesis, Kent State University, 2015.

SEGITTUR. "Planes Nacionales de Turismo" Accessed March 29, 2023. https://www.segittur.es/sala-de-prensa/planes-nacionales-de-turismo/.

Sharpe, Christina. *Monstrous Intimacies: Making Post-Slavery Subjects*. Duke University Press, 2009.

Sieber, Timothy. "Composing Lusophonia: Multiculturalism and National Identity in Lisbon's 1998 Musical Scene." *Diaspora* 11, no. 2 (2002): 163–88.

Silva, Daniel. *Empire Found: Racial Identities and Coloniality in Twenty-First-Century Portuguese Popular Cultures*. Liverpool UP, 2022.

Smid, Marek, Simone Russo, Ana Cristina Costa, Carlos Granell, and Edzer Pebesma. "Ranking European Capitals by Exposure to Heat Waves and Cold Waves." *Urban Climate* 27 (March 1, 2019): 388–402.

Smith, Linda Tuhiwai. *Decolonizing Methodologies: Research and Indigenous Peoples*, 2nd ed. Zed Books, 2012.

Smith, Neil. "Gentrification and the Rent Gap." *Annals of the Association of American Geographers* 77, no. 3 (1987): 462.

Smith Vargas, José. "Bouldrilhar na Mouraria," 2012. https://www.behance.net/josesmithvargas.

Smith Vargas, José. "Renovar a Mouraria 1496," 2018. https://josesmithvargas.com/RENOVAR-A-MOURARIA-1496.

Smith Vargas, José. *Vale dos Vencidos*. Chili com Carne, 2023.

Snyder, Jonathan. *Poetics of Opposition in Contemporary Spain: Politics and the Work of Urban Culture*. Palgrave Macmillan, 2015.

Soja, Edward. *Thirdspace: Journeys to Los Angeles and Other Real-and-Imagined Places*. Wiley-Blackwell, 1996.

Solà-Morales, Ignasi de. "Terrain Vague." In *Anyplace*, edited by Cynthia Davidson, 118–23. MIT Press, 1995.

Sola Morales, Salomé. "Precários nos querem, rebeldes nos terão! Tecnopolítica e indignación, de la Geração à Rasca a Que se lixe a Troika!" *Anuario Electrónico de Estudios en Comunicación Social "Disertaciones"* 13, no. 2 (May 13, 2020).

Sorando, Daniel, and Álvaro Ardura. *First We Take Manhattan: La destrucción creativa de las ciudades*. Catarata, 2016.

SOS Racismo Madrid. "Comunicado tras la muerte de Mame Mbaye Ndiaye." March 16, 2018. https://sosracismo.eu/muerte-de-mame-mbaye-ndiaye.

Sousa, Vítor de. "Da 'Portugalidade'à Lusofonia." Universidade do Minho Instituto de Ciências Sociais, 2015.

Sousa, Vítor de. "Identidades transnacionais e transculturais: Pós-colonialidade, lusofonias e interculturalidade. O caso do Museu Virtual da Lusofonia." *Chasqui*, no. 147 (August 2021): 105–21.

Sousa Santos, Boaventura de. "Between Prospero and Caliban: Colonialism, Postcolonialism, and Inter Identity." *Luso-Brazilian Review* 39, no. 2 (2002): 9–43.

Stanek, Mikolaj, and Jean-Michel Lafleur. "Emigración de españoles en la UE: Pautas, implicaciones y retos futuros." *Anuario CIDOB de la Inmigración*, 2017. https://www.cidob.org/es/articulos/anuario_cidob_de_la_inmigracion/2017/emigracion_de_espanoles_en_la_ue_pautas_implicaciones_y_retos_futuros.

Stoler, Ann Laura. *Duress: Imperial Durabilities in Our Times*. Duke University Press, 2016.

Stors, Natalie, and Andreas Kagermeier. "The Sharing Economy and Its Role in Metropolitan Tourism." In *Tourism and Gentrification in Contemporary Metropolises: International Perspectives*, edited by Maria Gravari-Barbas and Sandra Guinand, 181–206. Routledge, 2017.

Surcos. Directed by José Antonio Nieves Conde, Atenea Films, 1951.

The Combahee River Collective. "(1977) The Combahee River Collective Statement," November 16, 2012. https://www.blackpast.org/african-american-history/combahee-river-collective-statement-1977/.

Theo Goldberg, David. "Racial Europeanization." *Ethnic and Racial Studies* 29, no. 2 (March 2006): 331–64.

"This Saturday You Will Turn All Colours: It's Bollywood Holly in Martim Moniz" *Taste of Lisboa*, 2015. https://www.tasteoflisboa.com/blog/bollywood-holly-in-martim-moniz.

Tinic, Serra A. "United Colors and Untied Meanings: Benetton and the Commodification of Social Issues." *Journal of Communication* 47, no. 3 (September 1, 1997): 3–25.

Trujillo, Gracia. "La protesta dentro de la protesta. Activismos queer/cuir y feministas en el 15M." *Encrucijadas. Revista Crítica de Ciencias Sociales* 12 (2016): 1–18.

Tuan, Yi-Fu. *Topofilia: A Study of Environmental Perception, Attitudes and Values.* Prentice Hall, 1974.

Tuan, Yi-Fu. *Space and Place: The Perspective of Experience*. University of Minnesota Press, 1977.

Tulumello, Simone, and Giovanni Allegretti. "Articulating Urban Change in Southern Europe: Gentrification, Touristification and Financialisation in Mouraria, Lisbon." *European Urban and Regional Studies* 28, no. 2 (April 2021): 111–32.

Ulldemolins, Rius, Joaquim, and Mariano Martín Zamorano. "Spain's Nation Branding Project Marca España and Its Cultural Policy: The Economic and Political Instrumentalization of a Homogeneous and Simplified Cultural Image." *International Journal of Cultural Policy* 21, no. 1 (2015): 20–40.

Ulrik. "Mouraria I, Eco-Duplex&french Balcony&smart Access," n.d. https://www.airbnb.com/rooms/449080?location=Lisbon%2C%20Portugal&check_in=2020-10-13&check_out=2020-10-15&source_impression_id=p3_1599580257_rFWkcl%2F4ODiBwDSw&guests=1&adults=1.

Urry, John, and Jonas Larsen. *The Tourist Gaze 3.0*. SAGE Publications, 2011.

Valbuena, Juan. *Nosotros, un álbum colectivo del barrio de Lavapiés*. Casa Árabe, 2009.

Valbuena, Juan. *Noray: Libro de viajes por la ancha frontera*. Phree, 2012.

Vale de Almeida, Miguel. *An Earth-Colored Sea: "Race," Culture, and the Politics of Identity in the Postcolonial Portuguese-Speaking World*. New Directions in Anthropology, v. 22. Berghahn Books, 2004.

Valera, Juan. "Cartas americanas." 1958. https://www.cervantesvirtual.com/obra-visor/cartas-americanas--0/html.

Vasconcelos, Jõao. “Custom and Costume at a Late 1950s Marian Shrine in Northwest Portugal.” *Etnográfica* 9, no. 1 (2005): 19–48.

Vega, Luis de. “Los 42 km del maratón de Madrid corridos en una terraza de siete metros de Hortaleza.” *El País*, April 26, 2020. https://elpais.com/espana/madrid/2020-04-26/los42-km-del-maraton-de-madrid-corridos-en-una-terraza-de-siete-metros-de-hortaleza.html.

“Verão na cidade é no Mercado de Fusão Martim Moniz.” *Cultura de Borla*, August 9, 2013. http://culturadeborla.blogs.sapo.pt/1407294.html.

Vilaseca, Stephen Luis. “The 15-M Movement: Formed by and Formative of Counter-Mapping and Spatial Activism.” *Journal of Spanish Cultural Studies* 15, no. 1–2 (April 3, 2014): 119–39.

Villa de Orgaz. “Las Mayas,” June 12, 2013. https://web.archive.org/web/20130612224958/http://villadeorgaz.es/orgaz-folklore-mayas.html.

Watson, Camilla. “Canto do Sol.” Camila Watson. Accessed May 25, 2023. https://www.camillawatson.com/canto-do-sol.

Williams, Raymond. *Marxism and Literature*. Oxford University Press, 1977.

Woods Peiró, Eva. *White Gypsies: Race and Stardom in Spanish Musical Films*. University of Minnesota Press, 2012.

WRITERS DELIGHT Lisbon 2015 Martim Moniz GRAFFITI, 2018. https://www.youtube.com/watch?v=b2nHITZbMt8.

Xu, Ye. “Impact of Cultural Proximity on Destination Image and Tourists’ Perceptions: The Case of the Portuguese Cultural Festival Lusofonia in Macao.” *Journal of Vacation Marketing* 30, no. 1 (January 1, 2024): 45–57.

Yúdice, George. *The Expediency of Culture: Uses of Culture in the Global Era*. Duke University Press, 2003.

Zona J. Directed by Leonel Vieira, 1998.

Zukin, Sharon. *Landscapes of Power: From Detroit to Disney World*. University of California Press, 2000.

Zukin, Sharon. *Naked City: The Death and Life of Authentic Urban Places*. Oxford University Press, 2010.

INDEX

Page numbers in *italic* refer to figures.

www.ingramcontent.com/pod-product-compliance
Lightning Source LLC
LaVergne TN
LVHW091125080826
845145LV00008B/2053